OpenProj:™

THE OPEN SOURCE SOLUTION FOR MANAGING YOUR PROJECTS

Lisa A. Bucki

Course Technology PTR

A part of Cengage Learning

COURSE TECHNOLOGY
CENGAGE Learning™

Australia, Brazil, Japan, Korea, Mexico, Singapore, Spain, United Kingdom, United States

COURSE TECHNOLOGY
CENGAGE Learning™

OpenProj: The Open Source Solution for Managing Your Projects
Lisa A. Bucki

Publisher and General Manager, Course Technology PTR:
Stacy L. Hiquet

Associate Director of Marketing:
Sarah Panella

Manager of Editorial Services:
Heather Talbot

Marketing Manager:
Jordan Casey

Acquisitions Editor:
Mitzi Koontz

Project Editor:
Jenny Davidson

Technical Reviewer:
Faithe Wempen

PTR Editorial Services Coordinator:
Erin Johnson

Interior Layout Tech:
Bill Hartman

Cover Designer:
Mike Tanamachi

Indexer:
Sharon Shock

Proofreader:
Sara Gullion

For product information and technology assistance, contact us at
Cengage Learning Customer & Sales Support, 1-800-354-9706

For permission to use material from this text or product,
submit all requests online at **cengage.com/permissions**
Further permissions questions can be emailed to
permissionrequest@cengage.com

OpenProj is a trademark of Projity.
All other trademarks are the property of their respective owners.

Library of Congress Control Number: 2008931083

ISBN-13: 978-1-59863-817-2

ISBN-10: 1-59863-817-3

Course Technology
25 Thomson Place
Boston, MA 02210
USA

Cengage Learning is a leading provider of customized learning solutions with office locations around the globe, including Singapore, the United Kingdom, Australia, Mexico, Brazil, and Japan. Locate your local office at: **international.cengage.com/region**

Cengage Learning products are represented in Canada by Nelson Education, Ltd.

For your lifelong learning solutions, visit **courseptr.com**

Visit our corporate website at **cengage.com**

Printed in Canada
1 2 3 4 5 6 7 11 10 09

In loving memory of Bojangles, Danté, and Sweet Pea

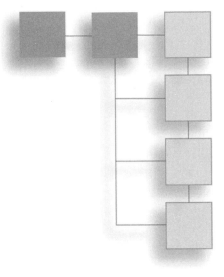

ACKNOWLEDGMENTS

Writing a book for a publisher creates a relationship where the author and publisher are sometimes taking a risk together. This is true in this case, where this book is about a brand new program that's just gaining traction in the marketplace. My thanks to Acquisitions Editor Mitzi Koontz, who made the decision to take a leap of faith with this topic.

A fine group of people contributed their talents and efforts to turn my words and illustrations into the attractive, informative book you hold now in your hands. Project Editor Jenny Davidson added her usual spit and polish to the project, keeping up a fast pace given the fact that she was assigned to the project after the book was mostly written. Way to go, Jenny! My friend and Technical Reviewer Faithe Wempen helped work the kinks out of the manuscript with her eagle eye. Thanks for the assist, Faithe. I'd also like to give a shout out to Designer Mike Tanamachi and the production team who created this great final product from the manuscript and graphics.

ABOUT THE AUTHOR

An author, trainer, and consultant, **Lisa A. Bucki** has been writing and teaching about computers and software for more than 15 years. She wrote *Managing with Microsoft Project* (multiple editions); *Learning Photoshop CS2; Dell Guide to Digital Photography: Shooting, Editing, and Printing Pictures; Teach Yourself Visually Microsoft Office PowerPoint 2007; Learning Computer Applications: Projects & Exercises* (multiple editions); *Adobe Photoshop 7 Fast & Easy;* and *Benchmark Windows Vista,* among others. Bucki has written or contributed to dozens of additional books and multimedia tutorials covering a variety of software and technology topics, including FileMaker Pro 6 for the Mac, iPhoto 2, Fireworks and Flash from Adobe, Microsoft Office applications, and digital photography. Bucki also spearheaded or developed more than 100 computer and trade titles during her association with the former Macmillan Computer Publishing (now a division of Pearson). Bucki has conducted Microsoft Project training sessions for nearly 10 years, and also runs 1x1 Media, a short-run CD and DVD duplication company.

TABLE OF CONTENTS

PART FOUR

REVIEWING AND SHARING RESULTS   **249**

PART FIVE

APPENDIXES   277

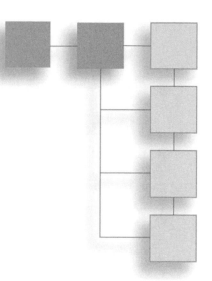

INTRODUCTION: MEETING OPENPROJ

Is This Book Right for You?

If you're looking for a book to teach you everything about the art and science of project management, put this one right down and back away slowly. This book does not endeavor to help you learn to become a professional project manager. For that, buy a project management how-to book over in the business books section.

If you've had a project thrust in your lap and have been asked to use OpenProj or want to try to use it to improve your results, buy this book now. (And please accept my thanks and appreciation for doing so!) *OpenProj: The Open Source Solution for Managing Your Projects* will teach you the essential skills for using OpenProj, providing tips and hints about how OpenProj can help you manage project progress more effectively. It also will present the type of real-world examples and techniques that apply to mainstream business people, not just technical professionals.

I've geared *OpenProj: The Open Source Solution for Managing Your Projects* to help new OpenProj users. You can count on this book to help you build a project plan, add the resources to get it done, nail down your budget, and track and share results. It will give you what you need to organize your plan and move forward, and help steer you away from the mistakes that beginners make. (And I've seen my Project students and clients make some doozies!) The end of every chapter includes Review Questions and hands-on Projects, so that you can reinforce your knowledge of key concepts and practice the skills you'll be using to build your own project plans.

With *OpenProj: The Open Source Solution for Managing Your Projects*, you *can* survive learning to use OpenProj. Properly used, the program *can* help you survive and thrive in managing your projects. When you're ready to get started, turn to Chapter 1.

OpenProj and Operating Systems

OpenProj works on different flavors of the Windows operating system, as well as other operating systems. For more information on getting and setting up OpenProj on your system, see Appendix A, "OpenProj Installation Notes."

How This Book Is Organized

Even if you're not a professional project manager, using OpenProj's tools in the proper order will enhance your productivity and success. *OpenProj: The Open Source Solution for Managing Your Project* leads you through the proven project management process that OpenProj has been designed to facilitate.

- Part One, "Your First Look at Project Management and OpenProj," gives you an overview of the project management practices that OpenProj follows and introduces the terminology and concepts you'll need to know to work effectively in the OpenProj program. You'll learn how the "home base" view of OpenProj looks, how to take advantage of guidance built in to OpenProj, and how to get help when you're stuck. The final chapter in Part One gives you a jump start, where you create, track, and report about an example project.

- Part Two, "Building a Project Plan," covers the actions you need to take to build a project plan file in OpenProj. You will learn to specify what will be done, in what order it should be done, how long it will take, who or what should be handling particular work, and what the costs add up to.

- Part Three, "Finalizing and Launching a Project," explains how your focus and use of OpenProj shifts when a project moves from the planning phase to the execution phase. You will see here how to review the project plan to make sure it's as realistic and accurate as possible, how to save initial plan information to use for later progress tracking, and how to track work to keep your project plan current.

- Part Four, "Reviewing and Sharing Results," provides you with experience in finding, viewing, printing, and otherwise sharing the valuable information in your project plan.

The book concludes with two appendixes: Appendix A provides installation information as mentioned earlier, and Appendix B provides answers to the chapter Review Questions.

How to Use This Book

If you are brand new to OpenProj and/or the project management process, I strongly recommend that you start with Chapter 1 and work through the chapters in order. In teaching other project management programs to business users, I have encountered many instances where a student thought he or she already knew how to use the program or had played around with it and thought it was obvious, only to cause themselves many hours of added work down the line because they had set up their project plans incorrectly. If you move through this book in order, you'll be able to set up a project plan correctly the first time, saving yourself later grief.

If you are in a desperate situation where you need to put together at least a basic project plan RIGHT NOW, go first to Chapter 3, "Jump Start: Create and Manage a Project." This chapter presents hands-on steps where you build and work with a basic project plan.

Along the way, you'll find special text elements that highlight key information.

When you see a *Gotta Know*, don't skip it! These boxes call your attention to information that is key, key, key!

Missteps identify common mistakes that new users make, so that you can avoid introducing problems into your project plan.

Tips provide shortcuts or hints for working more effectively.

Notes present additional technical details or steps that you may need.

Each chapter concludes with Review Questions and Projects to help you test and build on your new knowledge of OpenProj.

PART ONE

Your First Look at Project Management and OpenProj

1

THE PROJECT MANAGEMENT PROCESS AND OPENPROJ

This Chapter Teaches You How To:

- Understand how projects and project management differ from other business activities
- Follow the basic process used by professional project managers
- Become familiar with the key terms and concepts you'll need to work with OpenProj
- See how OpenProj follows the standard project management process
- Use OpenProj in the way that will be of most benefit to your success

Here you are with OpenProj installed on your system for you to use for the first time. Whether you're raring to go or facing that first startup with a few reservations, rest assured you'll find the help you need in this book. Think of this chapter as a first-day job orientation, where you'll gain insight into your work to come with OpenProj and learn more about the project management process.

Help! The Boss Wants OpenProj

Government finance and account gurus now consider "worker productivity" an important aspect of the economy to track and evaluate on a regular basis. Companies have long squeezed out more products and services by automating with robotics and computerized processes. But now, employee intelligence and production has become more of a focus, and that means businesses work harder to harvest the employee intelligence and capabilities that provide a competitive edge over other widget and gadget makers. In today's world-view, efficiencies and productivity gains come from giving experienced people the best overall tools—like OpenProj—to work smarter.

Although in the past only engineers, large commercial construction project managers, and software and Information Technology (IT) project managers used project management programs like Microsoft Office Project 2007 and OpenProj, you now can find project management software at work in a wide variety of organizations and job categories. For example, students I've taught and clients I've worked with have included:

- Educational administrators who needed to implement a new curriculum in a school system.
- Museum planners who needed to map out upcoming exhibits and schedules.
- Small construction companies who needed to provide project plans to fulfill government contract requirements.
- Health spa operators who needed to develop plans for implementing new services.
- Operators of a private park attraction who wanted a tool to plan and schedule maintenance upgrades.
- Administrative staff members responsible for working with engineers to update and publish project plans.
- Paper manufacturing company equipment operators and maintenance staff who needed to plan machine maintenance downtimes and communicate about those outages to management and others in the plant.
- Between-careers managers who wanted to add familiarity with project management software to their skill sets.

Some of the folks mentioned above identified project management software as a tool they wanted, and so they embraced the program with open minds. In other cases, the people I taught were more or less "ordered" to start using a particular project management program to document projects, no matter what levels of computer comfort or project management skills they had. Both types of students were able to learn the essentials and to build project plans, and you can, too.

Even if learning OpenProj isn't the next new job skill you'd like to have, if you stay open to learning the process as presented in this book, you'll quickly be on the path to managing your projects to better results.

What Are Projects and Project Management?

Project management is more than a résumé buzzword. Project management represents a field of study and body of information defining a growing professional discipline. The Project Management Institute (PMI) is the leading project management organization that develops the standards and models for professional project management, brought together in the *Project Management Body of Knowledge* (*PMBOK*). The group also administers conferences and project management training and certification programs. The fact that it comprises an entire field of study might be your first clue to the fact that there's more to project management than checking off items on a To Do list.

If a project manager hands you a business card with "PMP" beside her name or title, that means she is a certified Project Management Professional who has completed thousands of hours of documented on-the-job task management, many months of document project management, PMI's rigorous education curriculum, and PMI's certification exam. Achieving the PMP designation represents a significant accomplishment for dedicated project managers.

Practically speaking, however, in most organizations, a project manager is anyone who is put in charge of leading a team to manage a series of activities designed to produce specific outcomes. You might think that description applies to nearly anyone in your organization, *but* whether or not one is really acting as a project manager depends on whether the activities one is directing are actually projects.

A ***project*** is a series of activities leading to defined goals and deliverables achieved in a specified timeframe. A project has a specific starting date, and a specific ending date. A project may involve the activities of a team of people, or be a relatively complex series of activities completed by a single person. The team members may all come from one department, or they may include persons from many departments or even other companies. While a particular type of project may occur many times, ongoing activities are not considered projects. Nor are isolated To Do list items that involve a single person or activity. Table 1.1 provides a comparison list of example projects versus similar activities that are not projects.

 If you're curious about the professional field of project management and want to find books and other resources to learn more, go to www.pmi.org, the Project Management Institute's website. Other international organizations and standards also exist, such as the PRINCE2 approach widely used in the UK; to learn more about the PRINCE2 method and certifications, see http://www.prince2.org.uk and click the About PRINCE2 link. If you are entering a new job or career where project management skills and standards are a must, consult with others in the field and geographic location to learn which particular project management standards and practices apply. Wikipedia's entry about project management also lists different standards and standards organizations in the article at http://en.wikipedia.org/wiki/Project_management.

Table 1.1 Project...or Not?

Project	Not a Project
Selecting or developing and implementing a new accounting system	Managing daily Accounts Payable tasks
Designing new daily reporting system	Updating and running daily reports
Planning and holding a client seminar	Meeting with a client for an update
Planning and executing a company move to a new facility	Setting up an office for a new employee
Planning the maintenance team's work on a plumbing system upgrade	Creating the work schedule for the maintenance team
Planning and executing an equipment upgrade for a manufacturing line	Scheduling the production for a manufacturing line
Planning, writing, producing, and distributing a client newsletter	Writing a letter to a client
Planning and delivering a software upgrade to every employee's system	Repairing a software installation on a single system
Planning and building an addition to a facility	Cleaning the flooring in an office
Researching, purchasing, and deploying a new telecom system	Assigning or changing an employee's extension

What Steps Go into Managing a Project?

Whether done in a formal way or not, most organizations routinely follow what the Project Management Institute has defined as the "official" project management process, illustrated in Figure 1.1.

> **Initiating.** This phase involves defining the overall scope of the project, including objectives (goals and deliverables), what the overall project due date will be, who the stakeholders are who will be involved in or affected by the project and its outcomes, what people and equipment will be available to contribute to the project, what the budget limitations are, and what other performance measures such as quality standards must be met. During this process, you try to identify underlying assumptions that might impact project outcomes in a positive or negative way, such as whether other departments can really make the type of contribution required. Before proceeding to the next phase, all stakeholders should agree on the project's parameters.

> **Planning.** This crucial phase can make or break the project. During this phase, the project manager must detail the specific activities needed to achieve the project deliverables; define the specific people, equipment, and materials involved and the

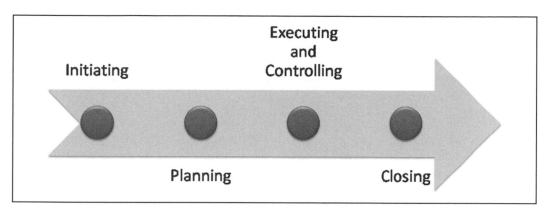

Figure 1.1 Overall phases for managing a project.

cost for each; determine which people will handle which tasks; create the detailed schedule for all aspects of the work; identify how activities relate and may impact one another; and solidify the budget. Once the project manager believes that the project plan is thorough, complete, realistic, and accurate and will result in the required goals and deliverables, she should make sure that all stakeholders buy in to and agree to the plan. At that point, the project manager should secure formal approval and signoffs as required in her organization to proceed with the project, at which point work can begin.

Having to stop a project that's been poorly planned is ultimately more costly to an organization than spending more time on planning and consensus-building. Don't make the mistake of pushing a project forward if you haven't gotten all the information that you need, may have omitted key factors, or don't have agreement that the plan makes sense and is doable. Make sure that you and your organization make the tough choices to change direction and kill or revise the plan before work and expenditures begin.

Executing. Just before work begins, the project manager should make a record of the original project plan to use as a tool for later evaluation. The project manager should set up regular communication avenues to urge team members to complete work and to gather information about actual progress in completing project activities. Tracking tools can help gauge overall project progress.

Controlling. Controlling a project primarily happens concurrent with project execution (although you can think of discipline during the initiation and planning phases as control, too). As the project manager tracks progress, she needs to identify deviations from the original plan as quickly as possible and take corrective actions, such as reassigning work, seeking more tools to complete the work, adjusting the schedule based on changes, and managing and limiting budget issues. During this phase, the project manager must respond to and manage needed changes. Execution and control also involve reporting project progress to team members and stakeholders as required.

> ***Scope creep*** happens when a project somehow morphs to encompass more than its original goals and objectives. Part of your control role as project manager is to be on the lookout for scope creep, because it obligates you to deliver more results without necessarily receiving more time, dollars, or people power. If stakeholders genuinely want to change the scope of the project, estimate the increased cost, resource, and time requirements; get the proper sign-offs on the new scope; and replan the remainder of the project as required.

Closing. While this phase may be the least formal in any company's project management routine, some type of closure typically occurs when the project is declared finished and the project team members are released from project obligations. The project manager should document lessons learned, either for herself personally or for the whole team, and provide final reports and documentation.

The professional project management discipline details numerous steps and official types of documents for planning and controlling a project. These include documents like a scope statement, project charter, statement of work, or scope change request. If your organization doesn't have any formal planning process whatsoever, you might want to explore putting some formal documents or processes in place. (A good project management book can help with this objective.)

Many organizations have other documents or systems that stand in for the types of documents called for by project management practices. For example, if a client issues a Request for Quote or Request for Proposal, that document and your response to it go a long way toward establishing the project scope, deliverables, schedule, budget, and resources needed to complete the work. The signed contract initiates the project execution, and client reporting requirements drive some aspects of control. The client's acceptance of and payment for the final work close the project's life cycle.

To increase your successful outcomes, be sure to formalize your project planning and management process in whatever fashion applies in your organization and for your team. Project management doesn't just "happen." Applying discipline, consistency, objectivity, creativity, and (when needed) flexibility throughout the process will help you drive projects forward.

Tasks, Resources, and Other Key Concepts

In developing a project plan, you will need to provide detailed answers to questions like "What work needs to be done?" and "Who or what is required to complete the work?" It is at this crucial juncture that the seeds of project failure can be planted. Many organizations and individual project managers fail to plan how and when work will be done in adequate detail. When work later begins and reveals the planning to have been incomplete and inadequate, the cost and pain to correct the situation can be tremendous. So, a successful project manager needs to bear down during the planning phase to create the best plan possible by answering the crucial questions.

"What work needs to be done?" The answer to this question is key, because you need to identify the project deliverables, and then figure out the actions required to produce those deliverables. The project manager needs to break down the overall project activities (that will produce the deliverables) into discrete actions called *tasks* (Figure 1.2). Identifying all the tasks to complete, in detail, provides the project manager with a more accurate picture of the breadth of the work involved in the project. It also can help the project manager verify that the goals and deliverables for the plan can indeed be achieved, or whether it would be appropriate to adjust the project's scope to make the project more realistic. The project manager also must arrange the tasks in the proper sequence and estimate the schedule for each task. In this way, the project manager begins to map out the overall project schedule.

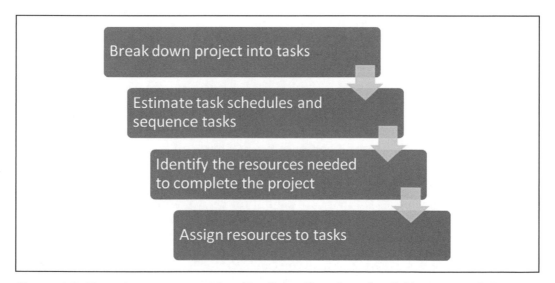

Figure 1.2 The project manager needs to identify specific tasks and available resources during project planning.

"Who or what is required to complete the work?" In answering this question, the project manager needs to list the *resources*—team members, equipment, and consumable materials—required to complete the project. This list should be comprehensive, because if the project manager fails to plan for and request all the required resources during the planning phase, needed additional resources may not be available during project execution, which would seriously damage the team's overall ability to meet project commitments.

In continuing to build the plan, the project manager must make *assignments*: deciding which specific resource(s) will complete each particular task. During this process, the project manager can begin to identify the costs associated with using each resource, thus building the budget. If a resource can't work full-time for the team or has other scheduling limitations, his tasks may need to be rescheduled, which can change the overall project schedule.

A *task* is a specific activity with a start and finish point. A *resource* is a person, item of equipment, or quantity of material used to complete a task. An *assignment* occurs when you apply a resource to a task, indicating that the resource is responsible for or will be used in completing the task.

Identifying project tasks, resources, and assignments and building a detailed schedule provides the proper roadmap for project execution, control, and closure, reducing uncertainty along the way. If you as project manager take the time and have the discipline to do the detailed planning, you give your project and team a strong base to work from in the form of clear goals and objectives.

How Does OpenProj Fit into the Process?

If building a detailed list of tasks and resources sounds like a lot of work, well, that's a painful truth. But this is where OpenProj comes in. OpenProj provides tools to facilitate the planning portion of the project management process. OpenProj helps you list tasks and can calculate the overall project schedule; OpenProj enables you to better visualize the plan and determine which tasks are more critical to project success. Because OpenProj helps you develop a more detailed and thorough plan, you can better communicate about project requirements and progress.

OpenProj provides specific views where you can build the list of project tasks and the list of project resources. You can establish how long it will take to complete each task, and easily indicate how tasks relate. Once you've done so, OpenProj calculates the project finish date for you. As you assign resources to tasks, OpenProj can recalculate the project finish date for you to reflect the impact of the assignments you make. In the final task shown in Figure 1.3, OpenProj has calculated a finish date of 6/8/10 for the project plan shown.

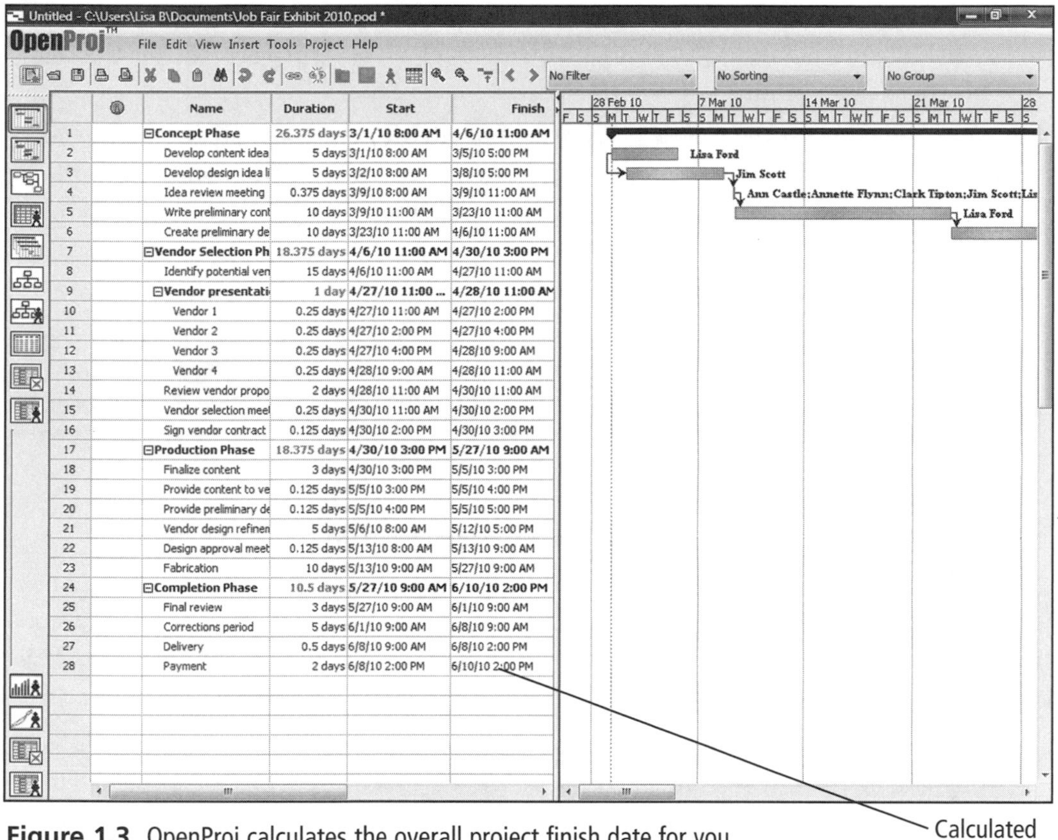

Figure 1.3 OpenProj calculates the overall project finish date for you.

Calculated finish date

While building a project plan remains a matter of putting in the required time and thought, once you've built the plan, you can take advantage of really powerful OpenProj features to review the plan to ensure it's realistic and reasonable, and then execute and control the project:

- **Views to help you identify planning problems before work begins.** OpenProj includes views where you can see whether you've assigned too much work to a resource during any time period, giving you the opportunity to correct that type of planning error before launching work on the project. You also can see which tasks are most important or critical to the overall schedule, so you can add resources to those tasks to have the greatest positive impact on the overall project completion date.

- **Tools to track work completed.** OpenProj provides you with the flexibility to update completed work on tasks one by one, in groups, or in a somewhat automatic fashion.

- **A view to enable you to compare your current plan versus your original plan.** This feature enables you to pinpoint where and how your project may have gotten off track, again so that you can take corrective action.

- **Customizable views, as well as reports, that enable you to keep team members and stakeholders up to date.** OpenProj can provide the information that various players want, so that you don't have to compile and develop different formats by hand.

You may need to create multiple versions of a project plan before the executing phase begins. Use OpenProj's views and features to do a thorough job of weeding out potential problems (and of course get input from others in the organization and team) before the work begins.

How Do I Use OpenProj to Manage for Success?

OpenProj is no substitute for your human intelligence and experience. It can't build a project plan for you, and it doesn't put project execution on "autopilot." Still, OpenProj lends tremendous value to you as project manager through some specific benefits you can realize by using it. With OpenProj, you can:

- **Build the plan in greater detail than otherwise possible.** Although it's certainly possible to create a project plan on paper or with software tools not specifically geared for project management, OpenProj gives you specific project management tools for building a detailed, comprehensive plan. With OpenProj, you can drill down and capture all the necessary planning information, setting the stage for success. Even better, OpenProj visually captures the relationship between different tasks and assignments, so you can immediately see how each task impacts others down the line.

- **Test "what-ifs" in detail.** Because OpenProj can recalculate the entire schedule based on any change you make, you can test variations on your plan before finalizing the plan and beginning execution. In this way, you can pick what you believe to be the best possible schedule.

- **Build stakeholder buy-in on the plan.** OpenProj enables you to present plan information that's both textual and graphical. OpenProj plans not only look impressive, but they provide a clear indication that you have done your homework so stakeholders can buy in with confidence.

- **Execute and communicate to the plan.** Projects can get off track when a project manager doesn't communicate adequately with the team. Stakeholders also require care and feeding in the form of solid progress reports. Take advantage of Open-

Proj's reports and views to supply information to team members and stakeholders at regular intervals as you execute the project.

- **Control and update the plan.** Track work with OpenProj to make sure that the project plan is up to date. You should set regular intervals where you'll gather task updates from resources and update the plan with that information. Then, your project plan will always have the best information available for decision-making, corrective action, or redirection. Likewise, review project budget and resource information at regular intervals to ensure the project is staying on budget and resources are pulling their weight.

- **Close and learn from the plan.** When a project concludes, the natural tendency is for lessons learned to fall by the wayside. However, with OpenProj, you always can return to the final files from earlier projects to evaluate how long particular tasks took, how well particular resources performed, and how outcomes were affected by planning errors. Your lessons learned have been captured in the OpenProj file, so you always can revisit them when planning your next project.

Chapter Review

With any luck, the overview of the project management process, your role as project manager, and OpenProj's role in the project management process presented in this chapter have made you eager to move on and learn more. This chapter explained the overall steps or phases in managing a project and why successful project managers emphasize project initiation and planning. After learning how tasks, resources, and assignments form the building blocks of any project plan, you explored how OpenProj provides the tools to help you put those building blocks together. Finally, the chapter passed on some advice about using OpenProj to manage your way to project success. Challenge yourself now with the Review Questions and Projects before moving on to the next chapter.

Review Questions

Write your answers to the following questions on a sheet of paper:

1. What's the difference between a To Do list and a project plan?
2. What are the overall steps in managing a project?
3. What is a task?
4. What is a resource?
5. What is an assignment?
6. Name one phase or part of the project management process that OpenProj can help with.

Projects

 To see example solution files created by completing the projects in this chapter, go to www.courseptr.com, click the **Downloads** link in the navigation bar at the top, type **Open-Proj** or this book's ISBN-10 number (1-59863-817-3) in the search text box, and then click **Search Downloads**.

Project 1

1. Take a sheet of paper and divide it into two columns.
2. In the left column, write down the five overall phases or stages of project management.
3. In the right column, write down at least two specific activities that might be part of that phase.

Project 2

1. Think of a project you've handled on the job recently.
2. Draw each task for the project as a box on a sheet of paper, and write the name of the task in the box.
3. Draw lines between the task boxes to show which tasks followed from previous tasks.

Project 3

1. Think of another project you've handled recently on the job or personally.
2. List the tasks performed to complete the project.
3. List the resources needed to complete the project.
4. To the right of each task, draw an arrow and then write the name(s) of the resource(s) from your resource list who handled the task.

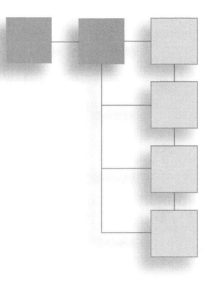

CHAPTER 2

LEARNING OPENPROJ BASICS

This Chapter Teaches You How To:

- Start and exit OpenProj
- Move around in the default view
- Display another view
- Use the Help system
- Be aware of other online resources

In terms of some of its tools, OpenProj works just like a lot of other programs. Yet OpenProj also has some unique features and aspects that sometimes confuse new users a bit. This chapter will help you get comfortable with basic features and operations in OpenProj so that you can work with confidence as you build your project plan. The chapter shows you how to start and close the OpenProj program. You will learn about the parts of the default view in OpenProj, as well as how to find information and display one of the numerous other views. The chapter teaches you how to use assistance tools like Help, and shares links to some other online resources that might be useful.

Starting Up and Shutting Down

Starting a program loads it into your computer's memory so that it's ready for you to use. When you start OpenProj, it presents the option of opening a blank file or an existing file.

Because many users will be using OpenProj on the Windows XP or Windows Vista operating system, the full startup steps for those operating systems are here:

1. Click the **Start** button on the taskbar in the lower-left corner of the screen, or press the Window key on the keyboard.
2. Click **All Programs**.
3. Click the **OpenProj** folder.
4. Click **OpenProj** in the folder.

The Windows Vista Start menu provides another fast way to open the program:

1. Click the **Start** button on the taskbar. If you see OpenProj in the left column of the Start menu, jump to Step 3.
2. Type **OpenProj**. The text you type automatically appears in the Search text box, and the left column of the Start menu lists matching programs and files, as shown in Figure 2.1.
3. Click **OpenProj** at the top of the left column on the menu.

 The default install process adds a shortcut icon for starting OpenProj to the Windows desktop. You can double-click the shortcut icon to start OpenProj.

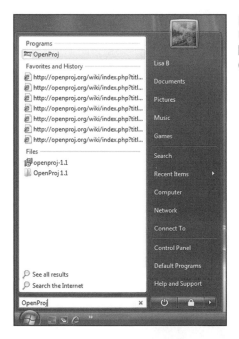

Figure 2.1
Use the Search text box to find and start OpenProj.

If you're using OpenProj on Linux or Mac OS, the startup method you use will depend on your desktop environment and how you've personalized your system. Generally speaking, use the same method to start OpenProj that you use to start other programs on your system.

No matter which method you used to start OpenProj, you may see a Try Project-ON-Demand message box or another message box about supporting OpenProj's publisher. You can click **Close** at that message box. In the Tip of the Day dialog box that may then appear, you can click **Next** to view additional tips, or **Close** to close the dialog box.

The Welcome to OpenProj dialog box (Figure 2.2) then appears, giving you the option of creating or opening a file. If you leave the **Create Project** option selected and click **OK**, OpenProj will prompt you to enter information so it can create a new, blank file. If you instead click **Open Project** and then click **OK**, the Open dialog box appears so that you can browse to and open an existing file. Creating and working with files is covered in more detail at the beginning of Chapter 4.

Figure 2.2
After you start Open-Proj, you can create or open a file.

When you've finished your work in OpenProj, you will want to close or exit the program. Closing the program closes any open files that you were working on to ensure that your work is properly secure. You can exit the OpenProj program in one of three ways on the Windows platform:

- Click **File** on the menu bar and then click **Exit**.
- Click the **Close (X)** button in the upper-right corner of the program window.
- Press **Alt+F4**.

If you've made changes to any open OpenProj file that you haven't yet saved, OpenProj prompts you to save. Be sure to click **Yes** each time OpenProj displays the message to ensure you save your changes to all of the files that you had open. (Chapter 4 provides more information about working with files in OpenProj.)

Navigating the Gantt (Default) View

OpenProj offers a fairly traditional program appearance, with a menu bar and toolbar structure, as well as buttons that give you easy access to available views. So, if you're comfortable working in other programs, you'll have a head start in learning to work in OpenProj.

Figure 2.3 shows you the OpenProj program window with its default view, called the Gantt view, displayed. The key features of the OpenProj program include the following:

- **Title bar.** The title bar across the top of the window displays the name of the program as well as the name of the current project plan file.
- **Close (X) button.** Clicking this button at the far right end of the title bar closes the OpenProj program. You can use the Minimize and Restore/Maximize buttons beside it to manipulate the size of the program window.

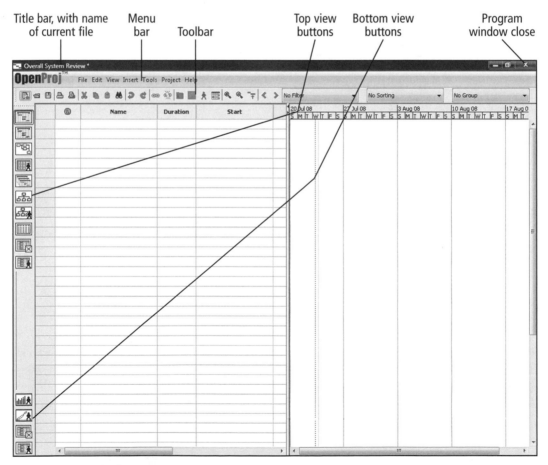

Figure 2.3 The default OpenProj view is called the Gantt view.

- **Menu bar.** This bar—just below the title bar—lists menus, or groups of commands, for working in OpenProj. Click a menu to display its commands and then click a command in the list. Clicking a command might display a submenu from which you choose additional commands or a dialog box in which you specify additional choices for executing the command.

If you see a command in this book that reads along the lines of "Choose Project, Project Information," that means to click the **Project** menu, and then click the **Project Information** command.

- **Toolbar.** OpenProj offers a single toolbar on the row below the menu bar. The toolbar offers buttons and choices that enable you to execute changes directly rather than having to choose a menu command. Click a toolbar button to run its command. To see what a toolbar button does, move the mouse pointer over it; a yellow ScreenTip with the tool's name appears. The right end of the toolbar also offers drop-down lists that you can use to apply filtering, sorting, and grouping to the information onscreen. These techniques will be covered in a later chapter.

- **Top view buttons.** The area along the left side of the window lists a number of buttons representing the available views. By default, only one view appears on the screen, and you can change to another view by clicking one of the top view buttons above the blank divider area.

- **Bottom view buttons.** If you need to examine information about a task or resource in detail, you can display a second view along the bottom of the screen by clicking one of the bottom view buttons. For example, Figure 2.4 shows a project plan file with a bottom view displayed. To toggle the bottom view off, click its button at the left again.

Sheet and Graph and More

The Gantt view consists of two sides with information (see Figure 2.5), and you need to understand how each side works in order to navigate and work comfortably in OpenProj.

The left side holds a spreadsheet portion of the view that divides information into rows and columns, with each bit of information held in an individual cell. You will build your list of tasks in the spreadsheet and arrange them in a hierarchical fashion, if the project is complex. The gray header cells across the top list the field or column names, which tell you what type of information appears in that column. The information for each task will appear on a single row, and when you add a task, its task ID number (task number) will appear in the gray row header cell to the left of the task name. You can click the **select all** button where the row and column headings intersect (it's a plain gray box in the upper-left corner) to select all the cells in the sheet.

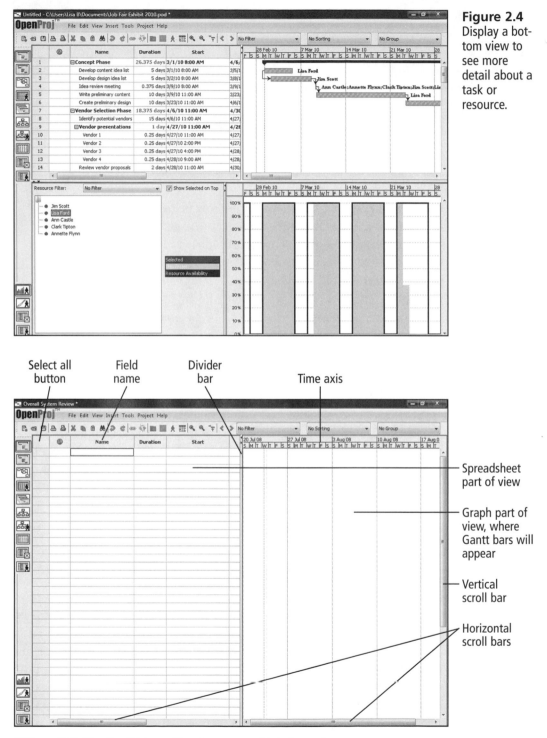

Figure 2.4
Display a bottom view to see more detail about a task or resource.

Figure 2.5 The Gantt view offers two areas with information.

A *sheet* or *spreadsheet* view holds a collection of rows and columns forming cells, and resembles an Excel spreadsheet. The *field* or column name appears at the top of each column. Each row holds the information for a single task, and a *task ID number* (task number) appears to the left of the task name.

After you start adding tasks, a Gantt bar will appear for each task in the right side of the Gantt view (see Figure 2.6). You can think of this side as the graph portion of the view. The time axis across the top of the view shows you the scheduled timeframe for each Gantt bar. This Gantt charting style has long been a preferred method of charting project schedules because it provides an easy way to see how tasks progress. By default, OpenProj includes the name of the resource(s) assigned to each task beside the task Gantt bar, making it easier to identify which resources you need to follow up with as you manage the project.

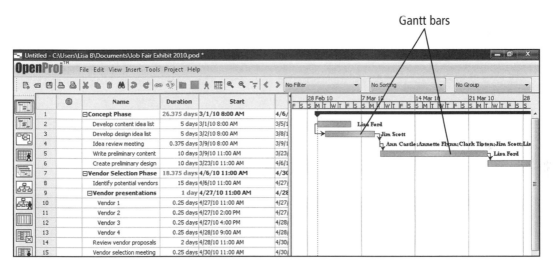

Figure 2.6 Gantt bars illustrate task schedules.

Notice in Figure 2.5 that the Gantt view includes three scroll bars: the vertical scroll bar along the right and a horizontal scroll bar at the bottom of each side of the view. You can use the vertical scroll bar to scroll the project plan down and back up. The task sheet and Gantt bar information will stay in synch (on the same row) as you scroll up and down. You can use the horizontal scroll bars to scroll each pane to the right and back to the left.

Displaying Gantt Information with Scroll To Task and Find

The first few times you engage in good planning and use OpenProj to detail all the tasks necessary in a project, you might be surprised by how long the list is. Because OpenProj gives you a central area for building the project plan, you can get a handle on projects of increasing complexity. You'll finally be able to illustrate all the work that goes into delivering the results that others in the organization want. Scrolling around through hundreds of tasks in a project plan consumes a lot of time, so OpenProj provides some navigation shortcuts.

Scrolling down and clicking a task in the spreadsheet portion of the Gantt view doesn't automatically scroll the chart portion of the view to show the selected task's Gantt bar. This becomes a bothersome issue with projects that have a long overall timeframe. For example, you might have to scroll the chart portion of the view several pages to the right to see the Gantt bar for the task selected in the sheet pane at the left.

OpenProj offers a Scroll To Task feature that enables you to snap the Gantt bar for any selected task into view in the graph portion of the Gantt view (Figure 2.7). Here's how to use Scroll To Task:

1. Scroll down the project, if needed, and then click the task name of the task to select in the sheet (left) pane.

2. Click the **Scroll to Task** button on the toolbar or choose **View, Scroll To Task.**

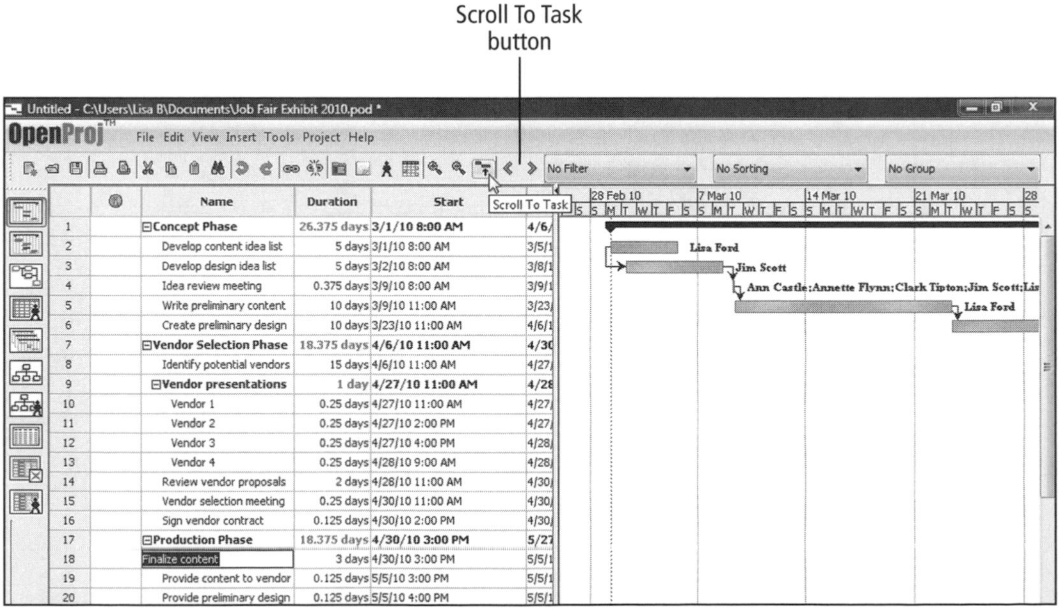

Figure 2.7 Use the Scroll to Task button to display the Gantt bar for the selected task.

Figure 2.8 shows an example of how the Scroll To Task feature works. In the top portion of the figure, you can see that Task 8 is selected in the sheet, but its Gantt bar is not fully visible in the chart. The bottom portion of the figure shows how the view looks after Scroll To Task has been used to display Task 8's Gantt bar.

 Most beginning users are thrown by the fact that the chart portion of the Gantt view doesn't automatically show the Gantt bar for the selected task. Get in the habit of clicking Go To Task after you scroll the spreadsheet portion of the view and click another task. That will ensure you're always seeing the Gantt bar for the current task.

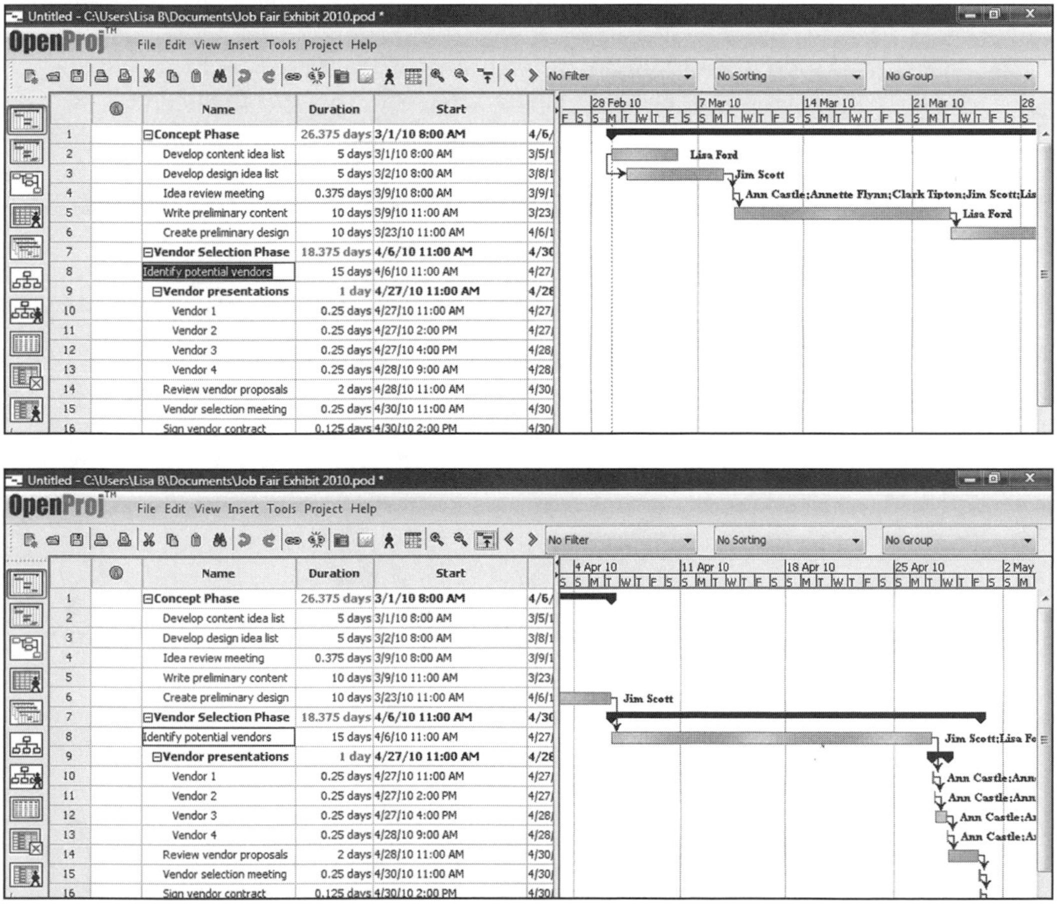

Figure 2.8 Scroll to Task was used to display Task 8's Gantt bar (bottom).

The Find feature enables you to jump to a task by entering information from any field. This process selects the task in the spreadsheet side of the Gantt view. You can then click the Go To Task button to display the task's Gantt bar in the graph side of the view. It can save a lot of time when you want to jump to a task that's either much later or much earlier in the project plan than the tasks you're currently viewing, because OpenProj will scroll vertically to the task. To Find a task:

1. Click the **Edit** menu and then click **Find**. (Shortcut: **Ctrl+F**.) The Find dialog box appears.

2. Open the Field drop-down list, and click the name of the field that holds the information to find.

3. Enter the matching information to find in the Find text box.

4. Click either **Find** button to find a task that's higher (up arrow) or lower (down arrow) in the list. As you can see in Figure 2.9, OpenProj finds the first task field that matches the find information you entered.

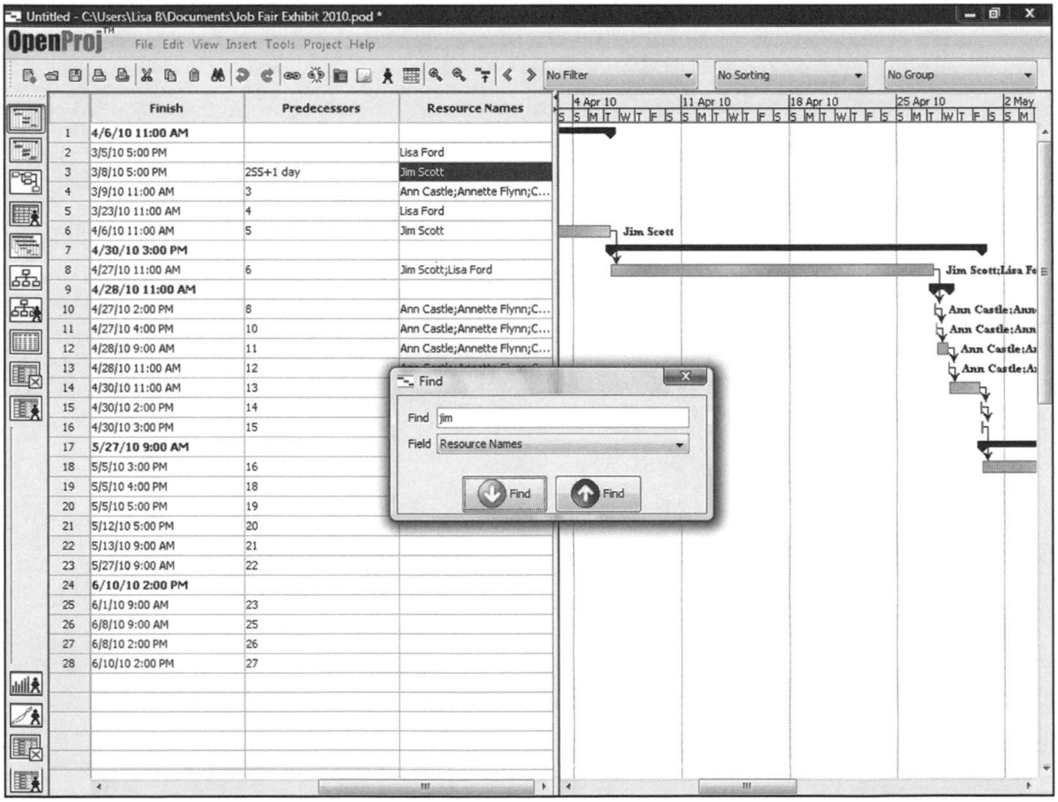

Figure 2.9 Find provides a fast way to jump to a task—based on information in a task field.

5. To find further matches, click either **Find** button again.

6. When you've finished finding information, click the **Close** (X) button in the upper-right corner of the Find dialog box to close it.

Changing Views

In my years of conducting training classes and working one-on-one with project management software users, I've learned that I can never emphasize finding and using views enough. The ability to display a view in OpenProj takes on a great deal of importance because:

■ OpenProj stores or calculates dozens and dozens of fields of information. No single view can show all of this information onscreen at one time. So, as project manager, you need to be able to find the view that shows the information that you need to track and make decisions about your project.

■ When you want to print information from OpenProj, OpenProj prints whatever view currently appears onscreen. So, as project manager, you need to be able to find the view that displays the information that team members and stakeholders need to see so that you can print and provide that information.

Although learning which view will work best for your needs in a given situation will take some time and exploration on your part, later parts of this book help by emphasizing what view to work in to perform project management activities and to find specific types of information. For example, when you want to see more detail about the tasks and schedules for individual resources, you can change to the Resource Usage view shown in Figure 2.10.

In addition to the view buttons along the left side of the screen, the View menu (see Figure 2.11) enables you to select the current view. Click **View** on the menu bar to open the View menu. The first 10 choices in the View menu represent the top views that you can show. The next four choices after the divider line are the bottom views. A radio button appears beside the name of the current view. You can click any of the views listed to display that view immediately. You also can use the Zoom In and Zoom Out choices to zoom the view.

 If you don't like having the view buttons at the left, you can drag the buttons using the hatched bar above them (Figure 2.12) to place the buttons in their own window that you can reposition. To return the buttons to their original position, click the **Close** (X) button in the upper-right corner of the floating window.

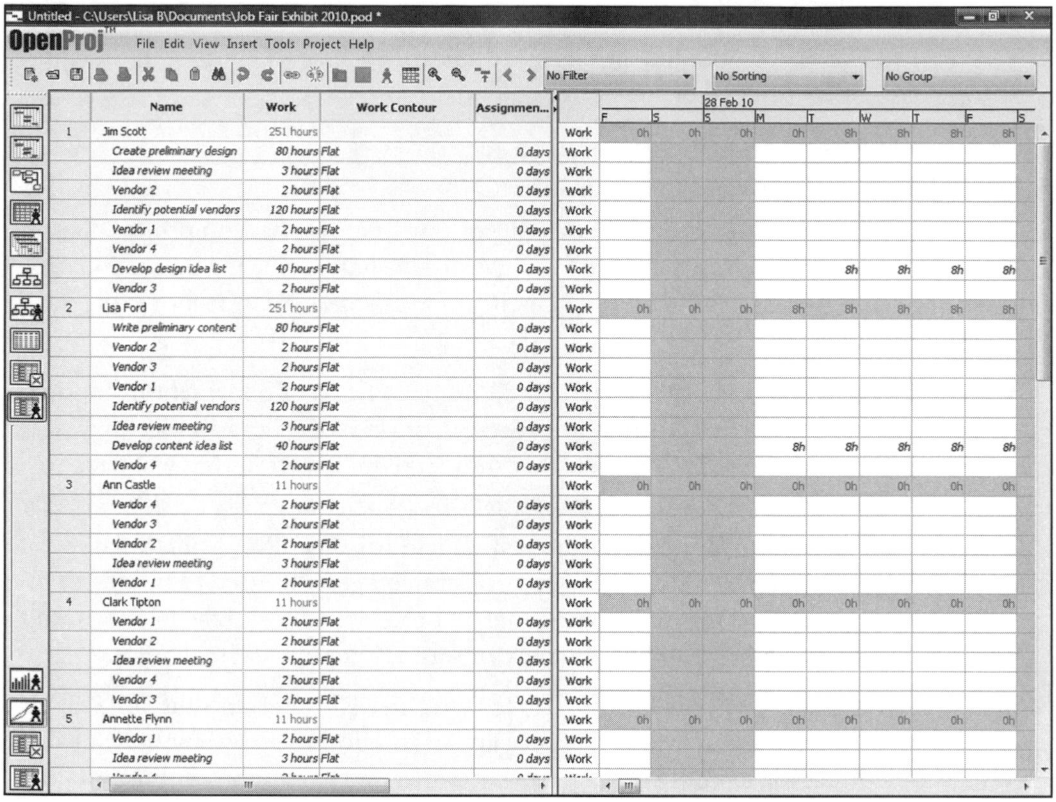

Figure 2.10 You can change to the view that shows desired information, such as this Resource Usage view.

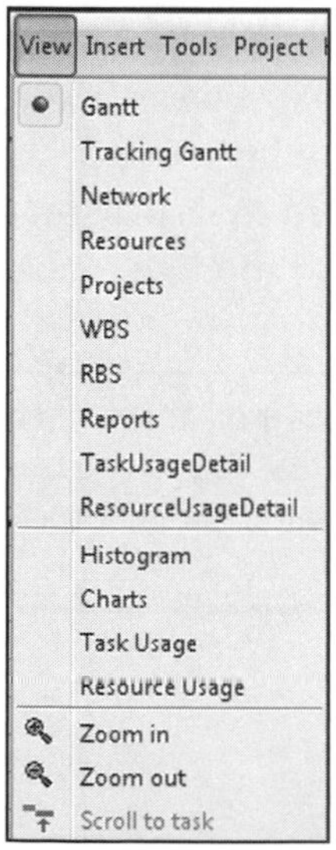

Figure 2.11
The View menu lists the top views, then the bottom views; click a view to display it.

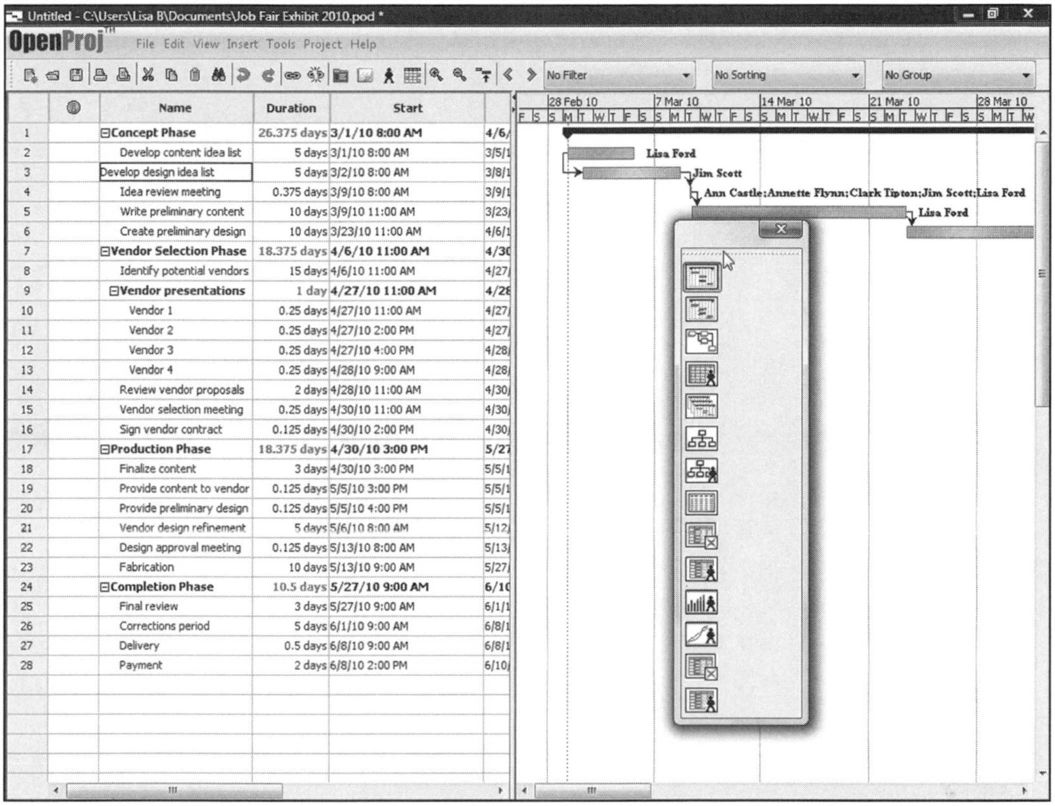

Figure 2.12 You can drag the view buttons to a location you prefer.

Changing Field Sets

One aspect of the spreadsheet in OpenProj differs significantly from working with a spreadsheet program: the issue of field sets. In OpenProj, a field set is a collection of different fields (columns) of information. For example, when you're entering new information about your tasks, you'll view an Entry field set with basic task information (see the top of Figure 2.13). When you later want to review cost information on a task-by-task basis, you will want to see the Cost field set (see the bottom of Figure 2.13). By offering different collections of fields as named field sets, OpenProj makes it easier for you to access and view the relevant fields (out of the dozens available) for particular project management tasks.

The *field set* controls which columns appear in a spreadsheet. (Sometimes the terms field set and spreadsheet are used interchangeably in OpenProj.) The default field set for any spreadsheet view is the Entry field set.

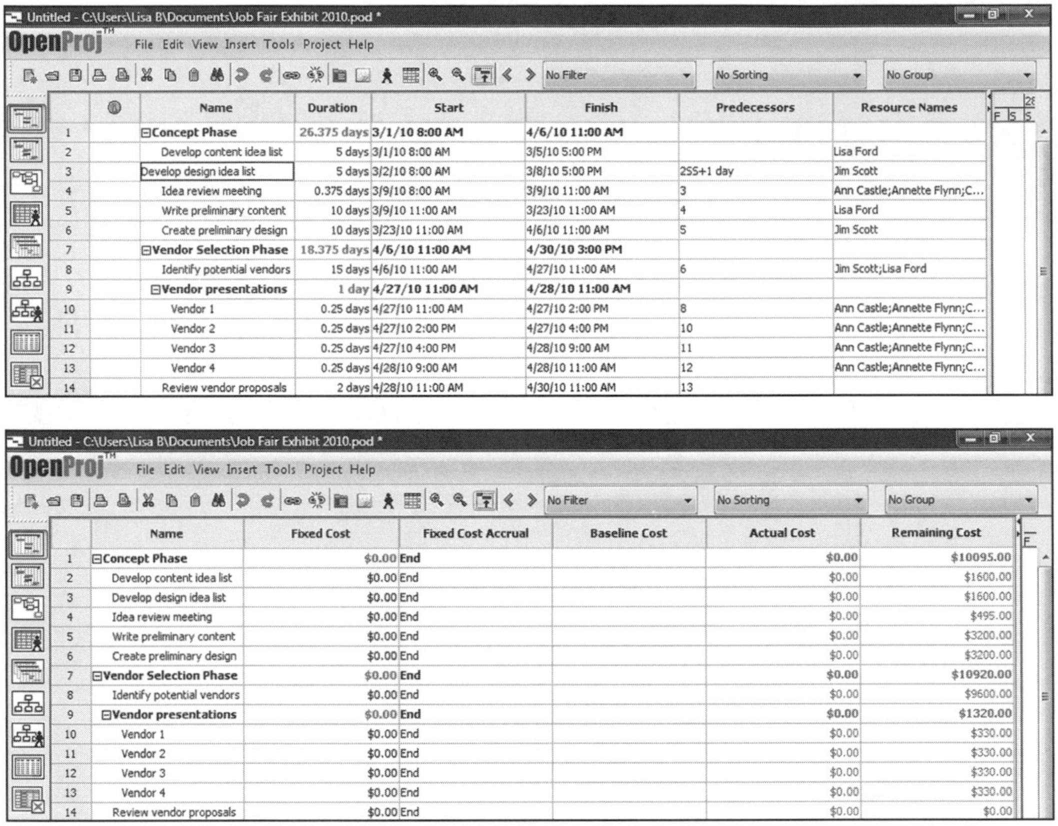

Figure 2.13 This example compares the Entry field set (top) and Cost field set (bottom).

You can move back and forth between the field sets at will, rather than having to customize the sheet view or hide and redisplay columns. To display the desired field set, right-click the **select all** button and then click the field set to display in the context menu that appears (see Figure 2.14).

Keep in mind that when you change to another field set (or make changes to the fields shown onscreen), those changes become part of the current view in the current file. So, if you will want to get back to the original view, keep notes about what changes you make, so that you can undo them later.

> Because the left portion of the Gantt view contains a spreadsheet, keep in mind that you can change the field set shown at the left in the Gantt view without affecting the contents of the graph side at the right.

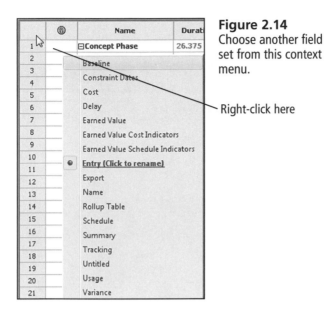

Figure 2.14
Choose another field set from this context menu.

Right-click here

Getting Help

Open source software like OpenProj is often a collaborative effort between many users who donate the time to bring the application to users for free or on a donation basis. This sometimes means that certain features aren't handled in the same way that they are for commercial software programs.

In the case of getting help about OpenProj, the open source approach has led to a help system that's strictly online and that is being built as a collaborative wiki on the Projity website.

To access the OpenProj online help, click the **Help** menu, then click **Projity Help**. In the Help Projity OpenProj dialog box that appears, click **Go To Online Help**. The list of available help topics appears as shown in Figure 2.15. You can click the OpenProj logo at the left if you want to see a list of other languages for which documentation is available.

Browse the documentation to find information, just as you would any other website. You also can enter a term to look for in the Search text box at the left and click the **Search** button to find matching information.

Click the logo to access
help in other languages

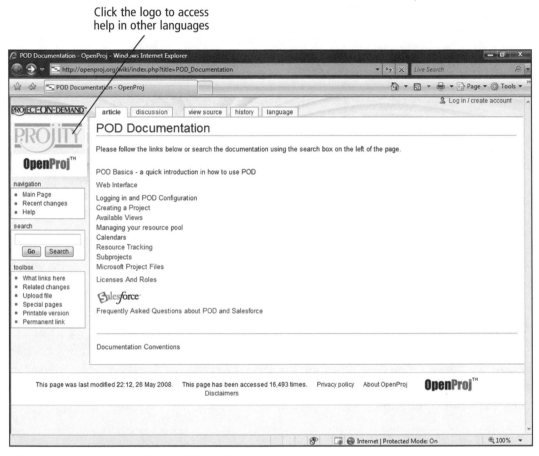

Figure 2.15 OpenProj offers its help online.

Chapter Review

This chapter gave you your first real look at the OpenProj 1.1 program. It showed you how to start and exit OpenProj, how to find your way around in the Gantt view, and how to change to another view. You also saw how to access the online Help system. Complete the Review Questions and Projects now to reinforce what you've learned before moving on to the next chapter.

Review Questions

Write your answers to the following questions on a sheet of paper.

1. Name one way each to start and exit OpenProj in Windows.

2. The _____ appears below the menu bar and offers buttons you can click to perform actions in OpenProj rather than having to choose menu commands.

3. To find the name of a tool, do this:

4. The _____ appears at the top of each column in a spreadsheet view.

5. When you add a task, its _____ appears in the row header cell to the left of the task name.

6. The default view in OpenProj is called the _____ view.

7. Access one of the 10 top views on the _____ menu.

8. When you click a task name, click the _____ button on the toolbar to scroll its Gantt bar into view on the graph at the right.

9. What is a field set in OpenProj?

10. Because OpenProj is open source, its online help was created as a collaborative _____.

Projects

Project 1

1. Start OpenProj.

2. Click **Close** to skip the Tip of the Day.

3. Leave **Create Project** selected and click **OK**.

4. Enter **Test** as the project name, and click **OK**.

5. Click in the first cell in the Task name field and type **Practice**. Notice how the row number (task ID number) appears to the left of the row.

6. Click **File** and then click **Exit**.

7. Click **No** when OpenProj asks whether to save your changes to the file.

Project 2

1. Open the Start menu in Windows.

2. Type **OpenProj**. A list of matching files and applications appears.

3. Press the **Esc** key to close the Start menu.

4. Double-click the new OpenProj shortcut on the desktop to start OpenProj.

5. Click **Close** to skip the Tip of the Day.

6. Leave **Create Project** selected and click **OK**.

7. Enter **Test** as the project name, and click **OK**.

8. Click in the first cell in the Task name field and type **Practice Again**. Notice how the row number (task ID number) appears to the left of the row.

9. Click **View** and then click **Network**. The Network view appears.

10. Click the **Resources** button in the view buttons at the left. The Resources view appears. Leave the file open for the next project.

Project 3

1. Click **Gantt** at the top of the view buttons to return to the default view.

2. Right-click the **select all** button and click **Tracking**. The Tracking field set appears.

3. Right-click the **select all** button again and click **Entry**. The Entry (default) table reappears in the Gantt view.

4. Choose **Help**, **Projity Help**, and then click **Go To Online Help**.

5. Browse the help as you prefer.

6. Exit your web browser and OpenProj using the method of your choice. Do not save changes to the practice file.

CHAPTER 3

JUMP START: CREATE AND MANAGE A PROJECT

This Chapter Teaches You How To:

- Make a custom calendar
- Set the project start date and calendar
- Add a list of tasks
- Outline and link tasks to build the schedule
- Add and assign resources in the schedule
- Save a baseline snapshot of the plan
- Track completed work
- Use views and reports to communicate

If you really, really can't wait to work through the contents of a book to get a grasp of how to work in OpenProj, then you might just like this chapter. Here you'll find a hands-on overview of how to use OpenProj to build and track a project plan. If you take the time to sit down and follow the steps presented here, you'll have a better sense of where OpenProj provides the greatest benefits to you as project manager and what you can expect in terms of using OpenProj to manage a live plan in your organization.

In the example project, you will be playing the role of the leader of a team that needs to develop and implement a process change in a manufacturing environment. You will set up the project plan file, add tasks (the right way!), determine the project schedule, and identify and assign resources. You will move on to save a record of the original plan, track work against the plan, and use views and reports to access information for control and communications. So, when you've got a free hour or two to have some quality time with this book and OpenProj, turn the page and get started!

 To see the finished solution file created by completing this chapter, go to www.courseptr.com, click the **Downloads** link in the navigation bar at the top, type **OpenProj** or this book's ISBN-10 number in the search text box, and then click **Search Downloads**.

Create Your Project Calendar

Every organization has its own working hours. Many organizations follow a 40-hour work week with 8 a.m. to 5 p.m. working hours. Other companies work on a 24/7 schedule, or have shifts with various starting times. For OpenProj to schedule work correctly in your project plan, you have to tell the program what working schedule your organization or the team involved in the project follows. This is called setting the ***base calendar*** for the project plan. OpenProj comes with three different calendars built in. However, none of these calendars have any holidays marked. So, *every* project plan file you create will require that you create a custom calendar reflecting scheduled nonworking days in your company.

You don't have to build a calendar from scratch. Because you can modify one of OpenProj's existing calendars, creating the custom calendar usually doesn't take long. We'll assume the fictional team members working on your example project for this chapter are all on a regular 40-hour work week, so we'll simply copy the Standard calendar in OpenProj and make our changes to the calendar copy.

So, time to start up OpenProj and save your new file; then you'll move on and create the custom calendar:

1. Click the **Start button**, click **All Programs**, click **OpenProj**, and then **OpenProj** to start the OpenProj program.

2. In the Welcome to OpenProj dialog box, make sure the **Create Project** option button is selected, and then click **OK**.

3. Type **Process Change** in the Project Name text box of the New Project dialog box, and then click **OK**.

4. Click **File** and then click **Save**. (Shortcuts: **Save Project** button on the Standard toolbar, **Ctrl+S**.) The Save dialog box appears.

5. If the file name doesn't appear automatically, type **Process Change** in the File Name text box, as shown in Figure 3.1. In this instance you are not changing the save location for the file. You are saving the file in the default *Documents* (Windows Vista) or *My Documents* folder on your system.

6. Click **Save**. OpenProj displays the new file name in the title bar.

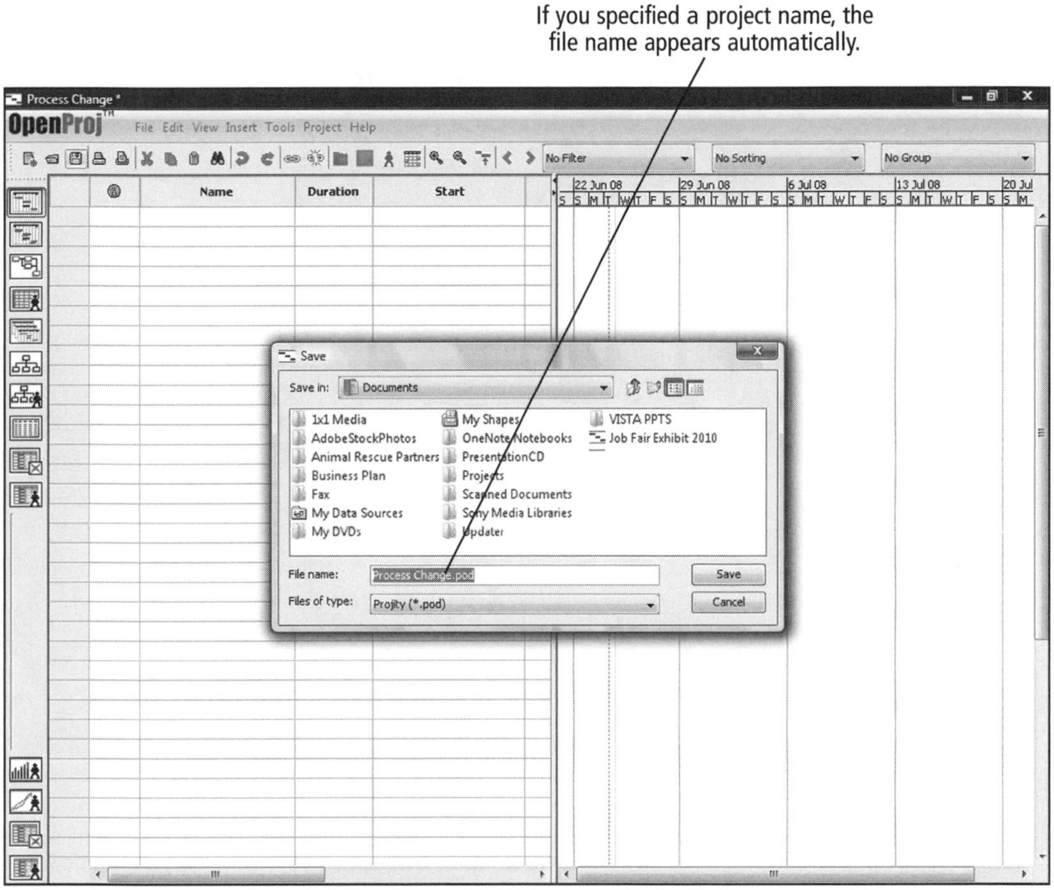

If you specified a project name, the
file name appears automatically.

Figure 3.1 Saving your new project plan in a file.

Now, make a copy of the Standard calendar in OpenProj and make changes to the custom calendar:

1. Click **Tools** and then click **Change Working Time**.

2. Click the **New** button in the lower-left corner of the Change Working Time dialog box.

3. In the New Base Calendar dialog box that appears, click the **Create a Copy of Calendar** option button, make sure that the calendar to copy is selected from the accompanying drop-down list (see Figure 3.2). If it's not, click the drop-down list and then click the calendar you want to copy, in this case, the Standard calendar.

4. Type **Process Change Calendar** into the **Name** text box. That is the name for your custom calendar.

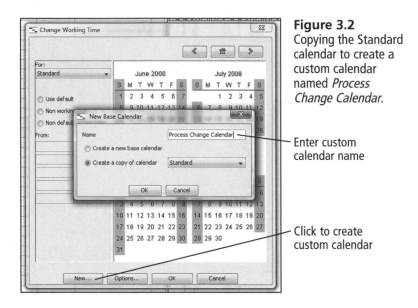

Figure 3.2
Copying the Standard calendar to create a custom calendar named *Process Change Calendar*.

Enter custom calendar name

Click to create custom calendar

5. Click **OK**. This takes you back to the Change Working Time dialog box. The For drop-down list now displays *Process Change Calendar*. The changes you make next will be saved into the custom *Process Change Calendar*.

6. Use the right arrow button above the calendar in the dialog box to scroll right (forward) to **May 2010**.

 This book assumes you are working prior to May 2010. If you are working at a later time, adjust all dates to refer to similar dates in 2011 or beyond.

7. Click the date May 31 (**31**) on the calendar.

8. Click the **Non Working Time** option button at the left. This marks May 31, 2010 as a nonworking day (see Figure 3.3) in the custom *Process Change Calendar*.

9. Scroll the calendar to **July 2010**.

10. Click July 5 (**5**) on the calendar.

11. Click the **Non Working Time** option button at the left. This marks July 5, 2010 (Figure 3.4) as a non working day.

12. Click **OK**. OpenProj finishes saving your custom *Process Change Calendar* in the *Process Change* file. The calendar isn't active in the file yet. You'll learn to apply the calendar in the next section.

Figure 3.3
May 31, 2010 has been marked a nonworking holiday.

Nonworking day marked on calendar

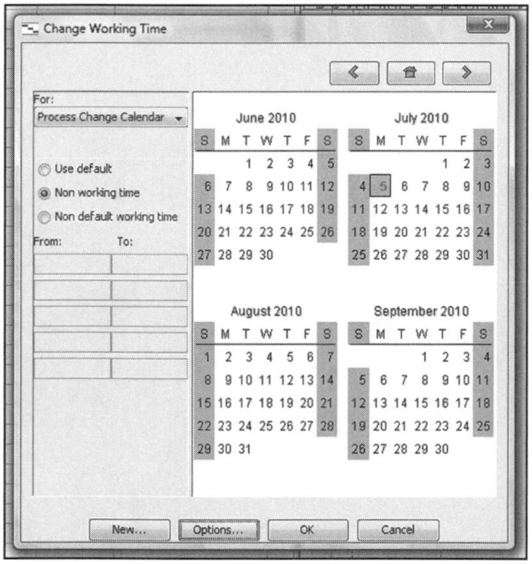

Figure 3.4
July 5, 2010 has been marked a nonworking holiday.

NOTE! If you choose a calendar or working hours that are different from a standard 40-hour, 8 a.m.–5 p.m. (17:00 hours) work week, you also need to change Duration Setting options in Open-Proj to ensure tasks will be scheduled correctly. To learn more about this, see Chapter 4.

Choose Overall Project Parameters

OpenProj assumes that, like any good project manager, you are planning your projects well in advance of the beginning of work, so you have time to thoroughly vet your plan and seek and receive the needed approvals for the schedule and budget.

Because you're planning in advance, you need to specify in a project file when the work will begin on the project—the project *start date*. Doing so enables OpenProj to build the schedule from the designated starting date automatically so that you don't have to enter later starting dates manually. You specify the starting date for every project plan file by using the Project Information dialog box. You also use this dialog box to specify the calendar that the project will follow.

The example process change project that you're creating will begin on May 3, 2010, the date that your imaginary boss specified. The project also needs to follow the *Process Change Calendar* custom calendar that you created earlier so that OpenProj takes into account the holidays that you marked when you created that custom calendar. Choose both of those settings for your project now:

1. Still working in your *Process Change* file in OpenProj, click **Project** and then click **Project Information**. The Project Information dialog box appears.

2. Click the drop-list arrow for the **Start** text box.

3. In the pop-up calendar that appears, click the arrow buttons beside the month and year as many times as needed to display **May, 2010** at the top of the calendar (see Figure 3.5).

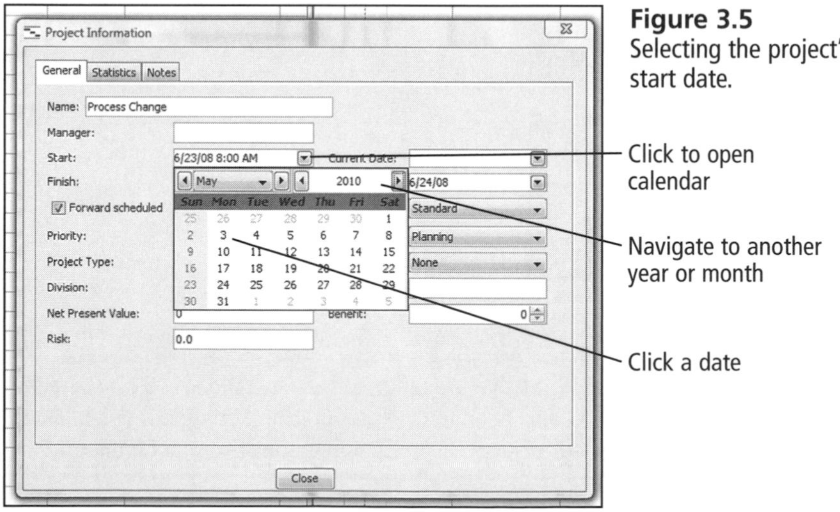

Figure 3.5
Selecting the project's start date.

Click to open calendar

Navigate to another year or month

Click a date

4. Click the **3** (for May 3, 2010) on the calendar. The calendar closes and **5/3/10 8:00 AM** appears in the Start text box in the dialog box.

Although you can type dates directly into text boxes, using the pop-up calendar ensures that you won't specify a weekend date accidentally.

5. Click the **Base Calendar** drop-down list arrow and then click **Process Change Calendar** (see Figure 3.6). Press **Tab** to finish the entry. This selects the custom calendar to be the calendar used by the project file.

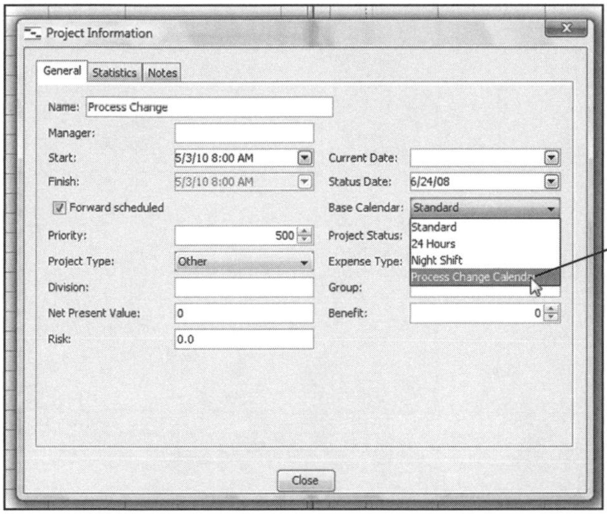

Figure 3.6
Assigning the custom calendar to the project file.

Choose the project calendar

6. Click **Close**. OpenProj applies the specified start date and your custom calendar to the project file. You can scroll the right side of the view to display the week including May 3, 2010, as shown in Figure 3.7.

You now have established the fundamental information that OpenProj needs to schedule your project plan correctly. You've told OpenProj that the *Process Change* project should be scheduled to begin on May 3, 2010, and that the project will follow the *Process Change Calendar* custom calendar that you created. Save your work, and then move on to start listing what will be done during the course of your project.

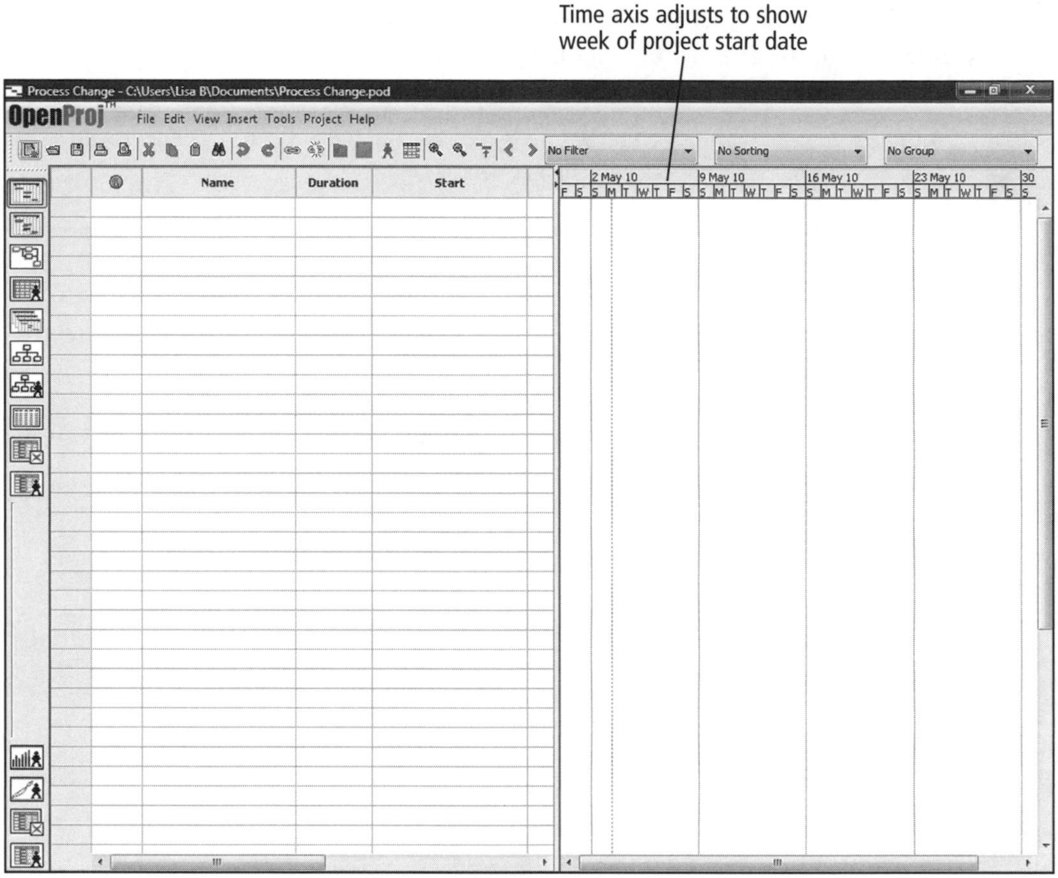

Time axis adjusts to show
week of project start date

Figure 3.7 Scroll to display the week including May 3, 2010.

Add Tasks

After you establish the project start date and calendar, you can begin to identify the specific work that will be completed in order to produce the goals and deliverables for the project. If the deliverable for our example project is "Implement a process change," then it's your job as project manager to determine whether it will take 10, 20, or 200 tasks to complete the job, and what each of those steps will consist of.

Each task should be as discrete as possible so that you can accurately track work against that completed task. For example, say part of a project involves writing a newsletter. If the newsletter consists of five articles and each is being written by a different person, then listing the individual articles as tasks gives you a clearer picture of the work than simply listing a single "Write Newsletter" task.

> When you're trying to break tasks down to an appropriate level, think ahead to how you might assign the work on that task. If your gut is telling you that several people will need to work on something you're thinking of as a "task," then look at that activity again to see if it needs to be broken down further so that one or two people can handle each smaller part.

You will build the list of tasks for the project in the spreadsheet in the left pane of the Gantt view. Even though the default table in the spreadsheet portion of the Gantt view contains multiple fields (columns), you will make entries for each task only in the *Name* and *Duration* fields.

Repeat: make entries ONLY in the *Name* and *Duration* fields.

While Chapter 5 provides more details about entering tasks, trust me for now that you'll be taking better advantage of OpenProj's capabilities if you avoid typing in dates for tasks. The *Name* field identifies the name of each task, and the *Duration* field indicates how much time you think each task will take to complete in hours, days, or weeks, for example.

The example *Process Change* project requires that you enter a number of tasks into the spreadsheet at the left side of the Gantt view. Table 3.1 lists the entries you should make for each task in the *Name* and *Duration* columns, starting from the first row of the sheet. Type the *Duration* entries exactly as shown. Note that some of the tasks will not have *Duration* field entries. You'll see why that is in the next section.

For now, make the entries listed in Table 3.1 into the *Process Change* file. You can press **Enter** or **Tab** after you make each cell entry, and use the arrow keys to move around between cells, as well. If the table shows no *Duration* field entry for a task, leave that field blank. Note that OpenProj also may change each duration to display in days after you make a *Duration* field entry.

When you finish, your file should look like Figure 3.8. After you verify that it does, save your work and move on to the next section.

> The Gantt bar turns red for any task that is part of the **critical path** for the project. Chapter 10 will discuss the critical path and why it's an important tool for you as project manager.

Table 3.1 Task Entries for *Process Change* File

Name Field	Duration Field
Preliminaries	
Identify affected departments	1w
Identify department representatives	1d
Planning meeting to discuss process change	4h
Development	
Review existing process	2w
Develop list of proposed process changes	2w
Send proposal to department representatives	2h
Incorporate feedback	1w
Implementation planning	
White board new process	1d
Role play new process	3d
Refine new process adding role play changes	2d
Develop implementation schedule	1w
Provide implementation plan to department representatives	2h
Resolve open issues or questions	3d
Document new process	
ISO procedures	2w
Work instructions	3w
Establish training schedule	2d
Perform employee training	2w
Launch new process	2d
Adjust documentation	1w
Retrain	1w
Quality Dept. audit	1w
Completion	0

If you're struggling with breaking down tasks and are ending up with durations that seem out of scale (multi-week tasks versus tasks that take only a few hours), perhaps some of the detail work needs to be broken out into a separate project file. This will keep the management of the main project from becoming burdensome, while having the details covered by a second project.

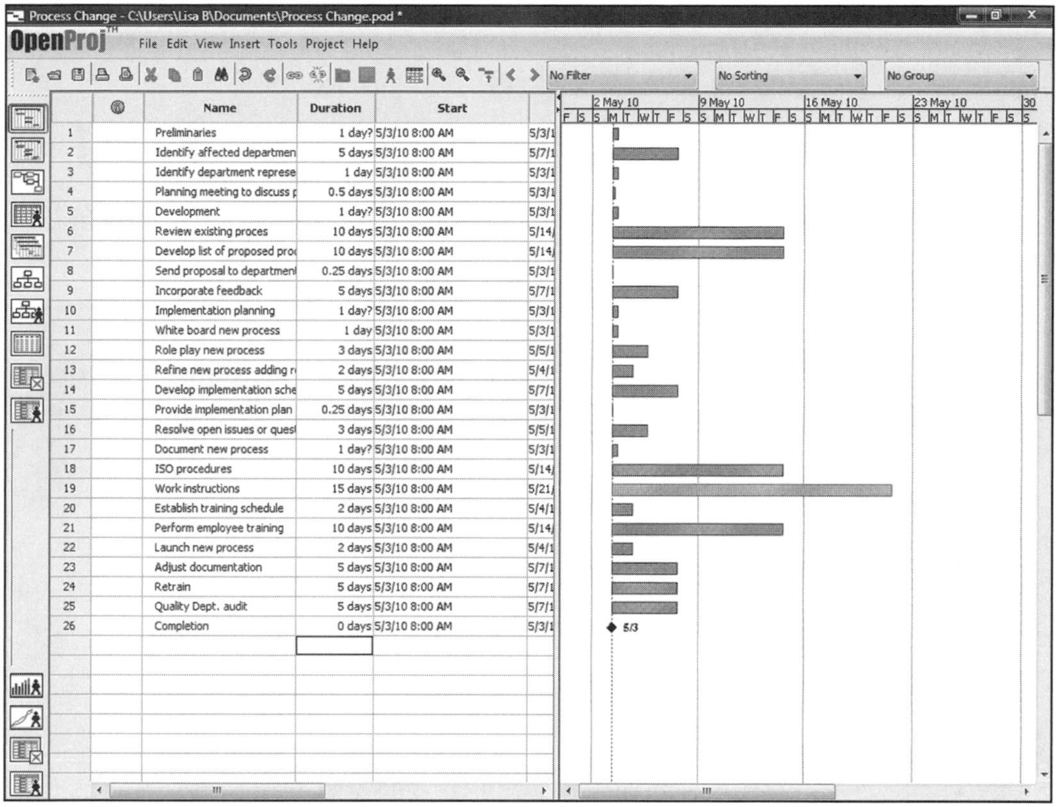

Figure 3.8 Tasks typed in to the *Process Change* project plan.

Organize and Schedule Tasks

If you looked closely at your project plan (or Figure 3.8), you might have noticed two key points:

- All the tasks start on the same date.
- That date is the project start date you specified earlier—May 3, 2010.

That's exactly right. By default, OpenProj schedules every new task you add to begin on the project start date specified in the Project Information dialog box. OpenProj will then reschedule tasks to build out the actual schedule based on the relationships you establish between tasks.

But first, you should organize tasks in the plan into logical groups of related tasks. This process creates a type of task called a ***summary task***. The summary task summarizes (adds up) the information about all the tasks in a summary group. The tasks where you left the

Duration field blank will become summary tasks when you complete the steps in this section. Their estimated *Duration* field entries will be replaced with the summed *Duration* entries for the tasks (called **subtasks** or **detail tasks**) in each group.

 A question mark in a *Duration* field entry—as in 1 day?—indicates an *estimated* duration. The question mark reminds you that you may need to revisit and finalize that Duration entry at a later time. If you enter a duration that you're not confident about, type a question mark in with your entry to remind yourself to update it when you have better information.

When you organize your list of tasks, you use techniques resembling outlining in other programs. You will *indent* (demote) tasks to make them subtasks using the Indent button on the toolbar.

In addition, you can improve your list of tasks by adding any tasks you might have forgotten, such as a summary task, or by moving other tasks around.

It's generally a better practice to organize tasks before scheduling them. Because scheduling involves creating relationships between tasks, you need those tasks in place before defining the relationships.

Organize the Project Outline

So, pick up where you left off with the *Process Change* file. Use these steps to organize (or outline) and complete the list of tasks:

1. Drag over the row numbers for **tasks 2 through 4** to select those tasks. (Remember, the row numbers that appear at the left are also the task ID numbers.) A selection highlight appears over the rows.

2. Click the **Indent** button on the toolbar. The button looks like a right arrow button. As shown in Figure 3.9, OpenProj immediately indents the tasks and identifies task 1, *Preliminaries*, above as a summary task. You can tell that it's a summary task because its name now appears in bold and has a minus icon (for collapsing the group), and the task's Gantt bar changes to a black, summary task Gantt bar. Finally, the task's duration has changed from 1 day?, an estimated duration entered by OpenProj because you did not make a *Duration* entry for task 1, to **5 days**, the current total duration for the indented subtasks: from the Start date of the earliest subtasks to the Finish date of the latest subtask.

3. Select and indent **tasks 6 through 9**.

4. Select and indent **tasks 11 through 20**.

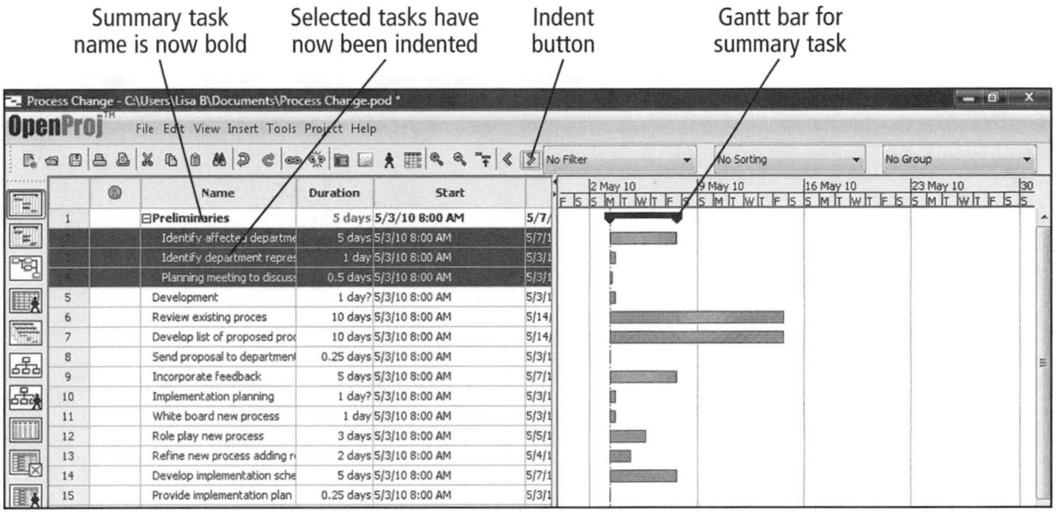

Figure 3.9 Indenting tasks establishes the summary tasks and project outlining.

5. Click any cell to deselect tasks 11 through 20.

6. Select **tasks 18 and 19** and indent them again. You can have multiple levels of tasks within the outline for a project. Use as many as needed to reflect the task organization.

7. Click **task 21**. You realize that you need a new summary task to head the last several tasks, so add it now.

8. Click **Insert**, and then click **New Task/Resource** (Shortcut: **Ctrl+K**). A blank, new task appears.

9. Type **Implementation** as the task name for the new task and press **Enter**.

10. OpenProj automatically indents the new task (task 21) to the level of the task above it. Because you want the new task to be a summary task, click the **task 21** row number and then the **Outdent** button on the toolbar. The task moves to the highest level, as shown in Figure 3.10.

11. Select and indent **tasks 22 through 27**.

12. Click on any **Name** cell to remove the selection.

13. Taking one last look at the list of tasks, you realize that task 26, *Quality Dept. audit*, should appear earlier, before task 24, *Adjust documentation*. To fix the problem, click the row number for task 26. This selects the entire task. Right-click the task and click **Cut**, or click the **Cut** button on the toolbar. Click the row number for task 24, *Adjust documentation*. Right-click the selection and click **Paste** (see Figure 3.11), or click the **Paste** button on the toolbar.

The new task has been
outdented to the highest level

Outdent
button

	ⓘ	Name	Duration	Start
1		⊟Preliminaries	5 days	5/3/10 8:00 AM	5/7
2		Identify affected departme	5 days	5/3/10 8:00 AM	5/7/1
3		Identify department repres	1 day	5/3/10 8:00 AM	5/3/1
4		Planning meeting to discuss	0.5 days	5/3/10 8:00 AM	5/3/1
5		⊟Development	10 days	5/3/10 8:00 AM	5/14
6		Review existing proces	10 days	5/3/10 8:00 AM	5/14/
7		Develop list of proposed pr	10 days	5/3/10 8:00 AM	5/14/
8		Send proposal to departme	0.25 days	5/3/10 8:00 AM	5/3/1
9		Incorporate feedback	5 days	5/3/10 8:00 AM	5/7/1
10		⊟Implementation plannin	15 days	5/3/10 8:00 AM	5/21
11		White board new process	1 day	5/3/10 8:00 AM	5/3/1
12		Roleplay new process	3 days	5/3/10 8:00 AM	5/5/1
13		Refine new process adding	2 days	5/3/10 8:00 AM	5/4/1
14		Develop implementation sch	5 days	5/3/10 8:00 AM	5/7/1
15		Provide implementation pla	0.25 days	5/3/10 8:00 AM	5/3/1
16		Resolve open issues or que	3 days	5/3/10 8:00 AM	5/5/1
17		⊟Document new process	15 days	5/3/10 8:00 AM	5/21
18		ISO procedures	10 days	5/3/10 8:00 AM	5/14/
19		Work instructions	15 days	5/3/10 8:00 AM	5/21/
20		Establish training schedule	2 days	5/3/10 8:00 AM	5/4/1
21		Implementation	1 day?	5/3/10 8:00 AM	5/3/1
22		Perform employee training	10 days	5/3/10 8:00 AM	5/14/
23		Launch new process	2 days	5/3/10 8:00 AM	5/4/1
24		Adjust documentation	5 days	5/3/10 8:00 AM	5/7/1
25		Retrain	5 days	5/3/10 8:00 AM	5/7/1
26		Quality Dept. audit	5 days	5/3/10 8:00 AM	5/7/1
27		Completion	0 days	5/3/10 8:00 AM	5/3/1

Figure 3.10 Outdenting tasks moves them to a higher outline level.

21	⊟Implementation	10 days	5/3/10 8:00 AM
22	Perform employee training	10 days	5/3/10 8:00 AM
23	Launch new process	2 days	5/3/10 8:00 AM
24	Adjust documentation	5 days	5/3/10 8:00 AM
25	Retr...	5 days	5/3/10 8:00 AM
26	Com...	0 days	5/3/10 8:00 AM

> ▷ Indent
> ◁ Outdent
> ▦ New
> 🗑 Delete
> 🗈 Copy
> ✂ Cut
> 📋 Paste
> ▶▶ Expand
> ◀◀ Collapse

Figure 3.11
Paste a cut task into a
new position.

Figure 3.12 shows how your project plan looks now that you've organized it by outlining,
adding a missing task, and moving a task to the proper location in the list. There are now
four tasks identified as top-level summary tasks, and one additional task that summarizes
at a lower level. The problem is that all the tasks still start on May 3, 2010.

The last task, for which you entered a 0 duration, is a **_milestone_**. The Gantt view shows a
milestone as a black diamond.

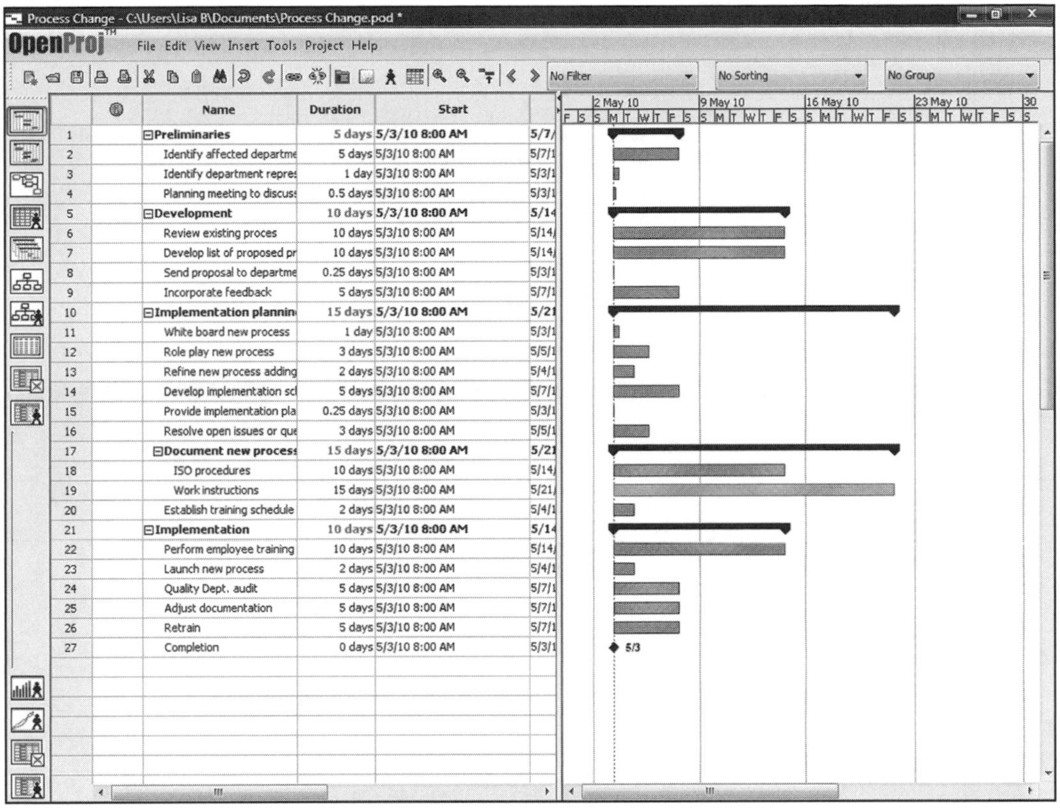

Figure 3.12 The project plan now includes an organized list of tasks.

> **NOTE!** After you've created a task with more than 0 duration and have assigned a resource to it, you can convert the task to a milestone. This preserves the duration, schedule, and work information associated with the task, but displays it as a milestone on the Gantt chart. To make this change, double-click the **task's name** in the spreadsheet side of the view to display the Task Information dialog box, click the **Advanced** tab, click the **Mark Task as Milestone** check box to check it, and then click **Close**.

Use Links to Schedule the Project

To enable OpenProj to calculate the full project schedule, you need to establish the relationships between tasks. Tasks in a project occur in a particular order and are normally related. One task must finish so that the next task can begin, for example. To establish these relationships between tasks, you *link* the tasks in the project plan. By default, OpenProj creates Finish-to-Start links, which schedule tasks one after the other. (Chapter 6 covers links and link types in more detail.) Add links into the *Process Change* file now to have OpenProj calculate the project schedule:

1. Drag over the task row numbers for **tasks 2 through 4** to select those tasks.

2. Click the **Link** button on the toolbar. The button looks like a chain link. You also can choose **Edit, Link**. As shown in Figure 3.13, OpenProj links the tasks and changes the *Start* and *Finish* dates for tasks 3 and 4 to reflect the new sequence in the schedule.

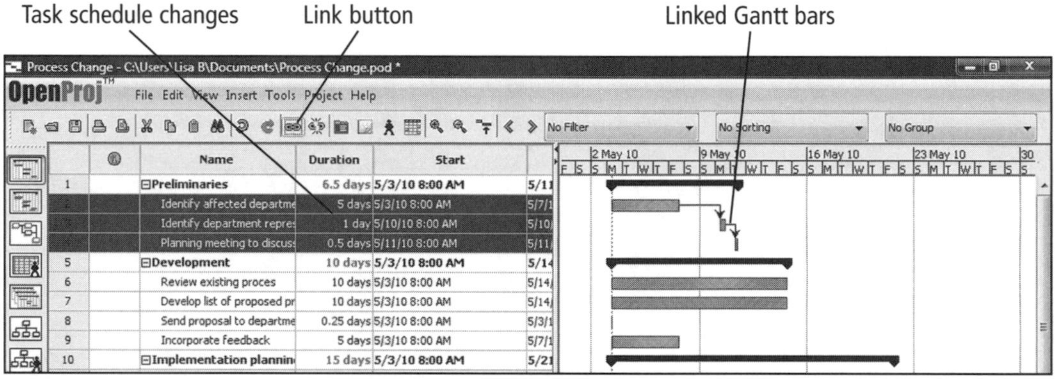

Figure 3.13 Linking tasks builds the schedule.

3. Click the task row number for **task 4**, press and hold the **Ctrl** key, click the task name for **task 6**, and then release the **Ctrl** key. Now click the **Link** button. As shown in Figure 3.14, OpenProj reschedules task 6 accordingly, but it also adjusts the *Development* summary task to reflect the change to task 6. You should not link summary tasks because they don't reflect specific work. Generally speaking, only link the detail or subtasks so that OpenProj can accurately recalculate the schedule when individual tasks' schedules change.

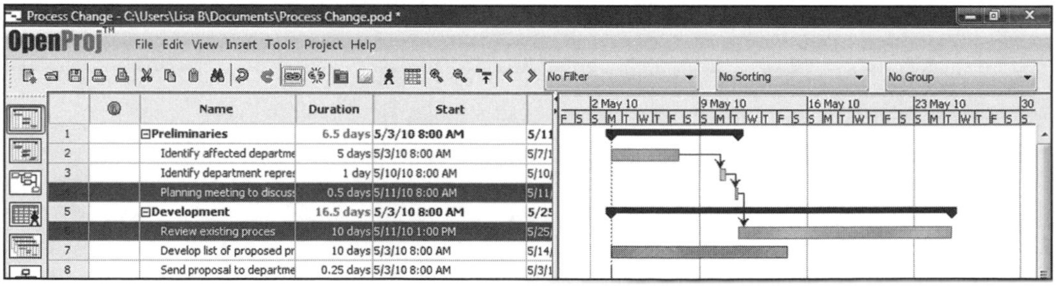

Figure 3.14 Don't link the summary tasks.

4. Select and link **tasks 6 through 9**.

5. Use the Ctrl+click method you learned in Step 3 to select **tasks 9 and 11** and then link them.

6. Select and link **tasks 11 through 16**.

7. Use Ctrl+click to select **tasks 16 and 18** and then link them.

8. Select and link **tasks 18 and 19**.

9. Use Ctrl+click to select **tasks 16 and 20** and then link them. This step illustrates that linked tasks don't necessarily follow one after the other in the task sheet. You may need to link tasks that are relatively far apart in the list if their work and schedules are related.

10. Use Ctrl+click to select **tasks 20 and 22** and then link them.

11. Finally, select and link **tasks 22 through 27**.

12. Look at the *Finish* field entry for task 27, the last task. Based on the links you've created, OpenProj has calculated a finish date of 8/17/10 5:00 PM.

13. Now scroll the chart pane to the right until you can see the Gantt bars for tasks 18 and 22. Looking at your schedule, you realize that some of the links don't make sense because the new procedures need to be documented before employee training can begin.

14. Use the Ctrl+click method to select **tasks 16 and 20**. Click the **Unlink** button, which looks like a broken chain link. (Or choose **Edit, Unlink**.) OpenProj moves the Gantt bars for the later tasks to reflect the fact that task 20 no longer has a task linked in before it, so it is rescheduled back to the project start date.

15. Select and link **tasks 19 and 20**. OpenProj reschedules the last several tasks based on the new link. The *Finish* field entry for task 27 now shows a recalculated finish date of 9/21/09 5:00 PM.

16. Click the **Name** field for task 1, and click the **Scroll To Task** button on the toolbar. OpenProj scrolls the Gantt bars for the early tasks back into view.

17. Click **Project** and then click **Project Information**. Click the **Statistics** tab. OpenProj displays calculated summary information about the whole project, as shown in Figure 3.15. After reviewing the information, click the **Close** button.

18. Now say that you are concerned that 9/21/10 is too late as the project finish date. Let's move the project start date earlier to see the impact on the finish date. Click **Project** and then click **Project Information**. Click the **General** tab if needed. Use the **Start** calendar to choose a date of **April 20, 2010** and then click **Close.**

19. Review the newly calculated finish date for task 17, *Completion*. The new finish date is 9/8/10 5:00 PM.

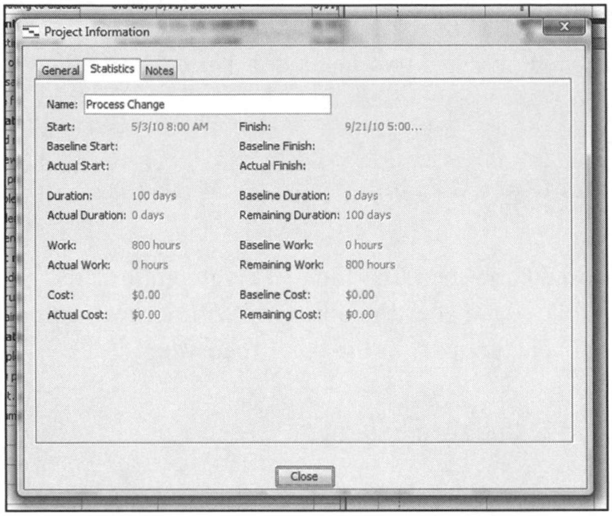

Figure 3.15
Use the Project
Information dialog
box to see a summary
of the project's
schedule.

20. Click the **Undo** button on the toolbar. (Shortcut: **Ctrl+Z.**) This returns the project to the previous May 3 start date, with a finish date of 9/21/10.

The last three steps illustrate why you don't want to type start and finish dates for tasks. Allowing OpenProj to calculate dates based on links means that OpenProj retains the ability to recalculate linked tasks based on earlier changes like changing the project start date. Typing in dates removes that flexibility, which would force you to have to retype dates to change the schedule. When you later mark work as complete on a task, OpenProj will stop recalculating the task start, because the completed work set an actual start date.

21. Save the *Process Change* file.

List Resources

So, the *Process Change* project will take nearly four months to complete, as currently scheduled. You now have mapped out what needs to be done. The next question is who will do the work and what materials will they need? In other words, what resources will you need to accomplish the project tasks? You'll use an OpenProj view called Resources to enter resource information. Resources view offers a number of different fields of information. You can make entries in all of or some of the fields, depending on your project planning and tracking requirements. (See Chapter 7 to learn about the Resources view fields in more detail.)

For now, follow these steps to list the resources for the example project:

1. Working in the *Process Change* file, click **View** and then click **Resources** or click the **Resources** button at the left. The Resources view, which looks like a spreadsheet, appears.

2. Type the resource information listed in Table 3.2. You can press **Tab** and use the **arrow keys** to move between the cells, and simply skip any field not mentioned in the table. In the *Standard Rate* field, you may have to press the **Backspace** key to delete the placeholder entry completely before typing your new entry. The work around for this is to click the cell rather than pressing Tab to move to it; clicking the cell automatically highlights the cell's contents, so you can simply type replacement contents.

 You must click the *Base Calendar* field for each resource, open the drop-down list, and select the *Process Change Calendar*.

Table 3.2 Resource Entries for *Process Change* File

Name	Standard Rate	Base Calendar
Jim Maxwell	45	Process Change Calendar
Jane Riggs	45	Process Change Calendar
Sandy Paulson	40	Process Change Calendar
Len Wilkins	40	Process Change Calendar
Jane France	35	Process Change Calendar
Alan Lewis	30	Process Change Calendar

3. Now you need to add a last resource of a different type. This is a ***material resource***—an item or consumable that will be used in some quantity during the course of the project. In the next blank cell in the *Name* field, type **Binder** and press **Tab** twice. To set the Binder resource up as a material resource, click the selected cell in the *Type* field to open the drop-down list, and then click **Material**. Press **Tab** twice to move to the *Material Label* field and type **dozen**. Press **Tab** four times, click to select the existing entry in the *Standard Rate* field, type **36**, and then press **Enter** or **Tab** to finish. (The *Material Label* and *Standard Rate* entries correlate, in this instance meaning binders cost $36 per dozen.) Your finished Resources view entries should look like Figure 3.16.

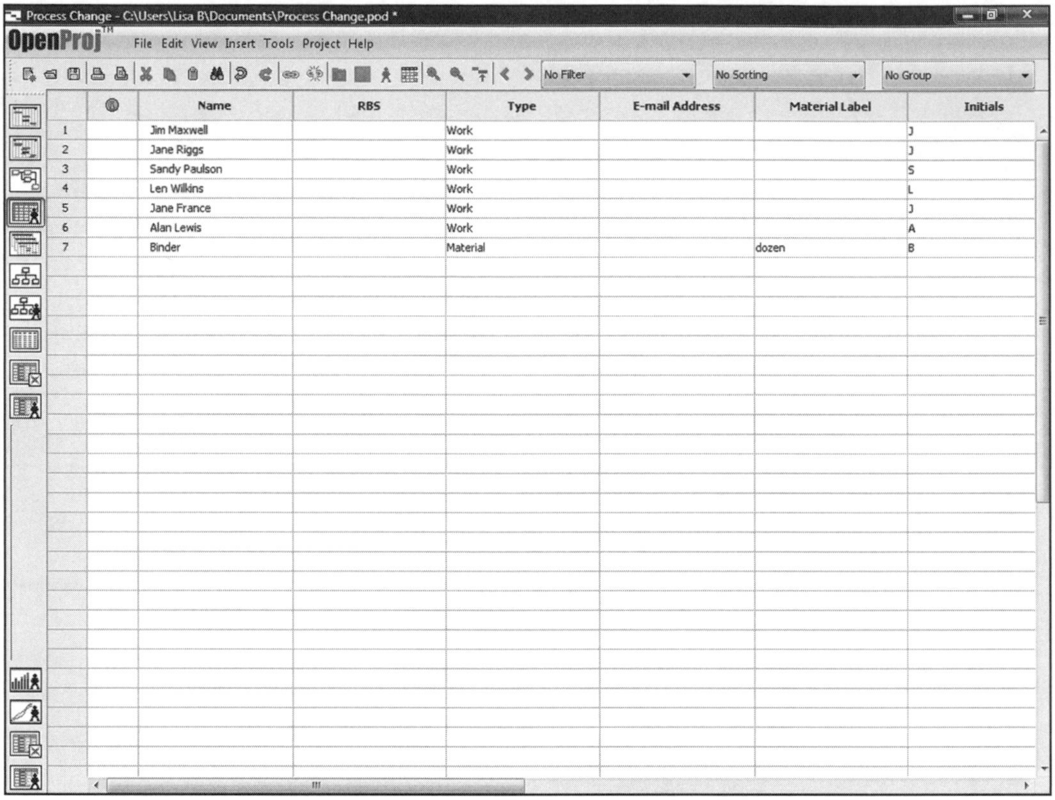

Figure 3.16 Enter information about resources in the Resources view.

> **NOTE!** Notice that there is a *Base Calendar* field in the Resources view. If a resource follows a different calendar—such as when a person has vacation days—you should choose the other calendar or identify the resource's time off before proceeding with your planning. Chapter 7 explains how to adjust the calendar for an individual resource.

Assign Resources

In the next phase of planning the project, you get specific about exactly who will be performing each particular task. You will **assign** resources to tasks.

When you assign the first resource(s) to a task, OpenProj leaves the *Duration* field entry you made for the task the same. So, if you assign one resource to each task, the schedule will stay the same. However, OpenProj uses a method called **effort driven scheduling**; the program assumes that if you add more resources to a task, the task's duration should decrease because more resources can get the work done faster. (I'll go into the math behind how OpenProj changes durations later in Chapter 8.) So, the assignments you make—how you as project manager choose to deploy resources—can dramatically affect the schedule in your project.

So, assign resources in the example *Process Change* file now. You'll start by changing back to the default Gantt view because you need to be working in a view where you can see the tasks in order to make assignments.

1. Click **View** and then click **Gantt** or click the **Gantt** view button at the left.
2. Click **task 2**, *Identify affected departments*. Notice that the task has a 5 days (1 week) duration.

 As with linking, assign resources only to detail tasks (the level at which the work actually occurs), not summary tasks. Rare exceptions exist when you might assign a resource to a summary task to account for administrative work, but remember that is the exception, not the norm.

3. Click the **Assign Resources** button on the toolbar. (Shortcut: **Alt+F10**.) The button has a picture of a person on it. The Assign Resources dialog box appears. If the button is inactive, clicking a cell in the spreadsheet portion of the view should reactivate it.
4. Click **Jim Maxwell** in the Name list of the Assign Resources dialog box and then click **Assign**. Jim Maxwell's name appears beside the Gantt bar for task 2 and the row with his name is highlighted in the dialog box. Notice that the task retains its original duration of 5 days (see Figure 3.17).
5. Leaving task 2 selected, click **Jane France** in the Assign Resources dialog box and then click **Assign**. Now both resource names appear beside the task bar in the Gantt chart and the task's duration has decreased to 2.5 days. This is effort-driven scheduling in action.
6. Assume in this case that you do not want the task duration to decrease. Click **Jane's name** again in the Assign Resources dialog box, if needed, and then click **Remove**. The task duration returns to 5 days. However, you want to assign both Jim and Jane to the task without affecting its duration. To do so, you need to remove Jim from the task, too, so click **Jim Maxwell** in the Assign Resources dialog box and click **Remove**.
7. Now use Ctrl+click to select both **Jane France** and **Jim Maxwell** in the Assign Resources dialog box and then click **Assign**. This time, both their names appear beside the task but the task retains its 5 days duration.

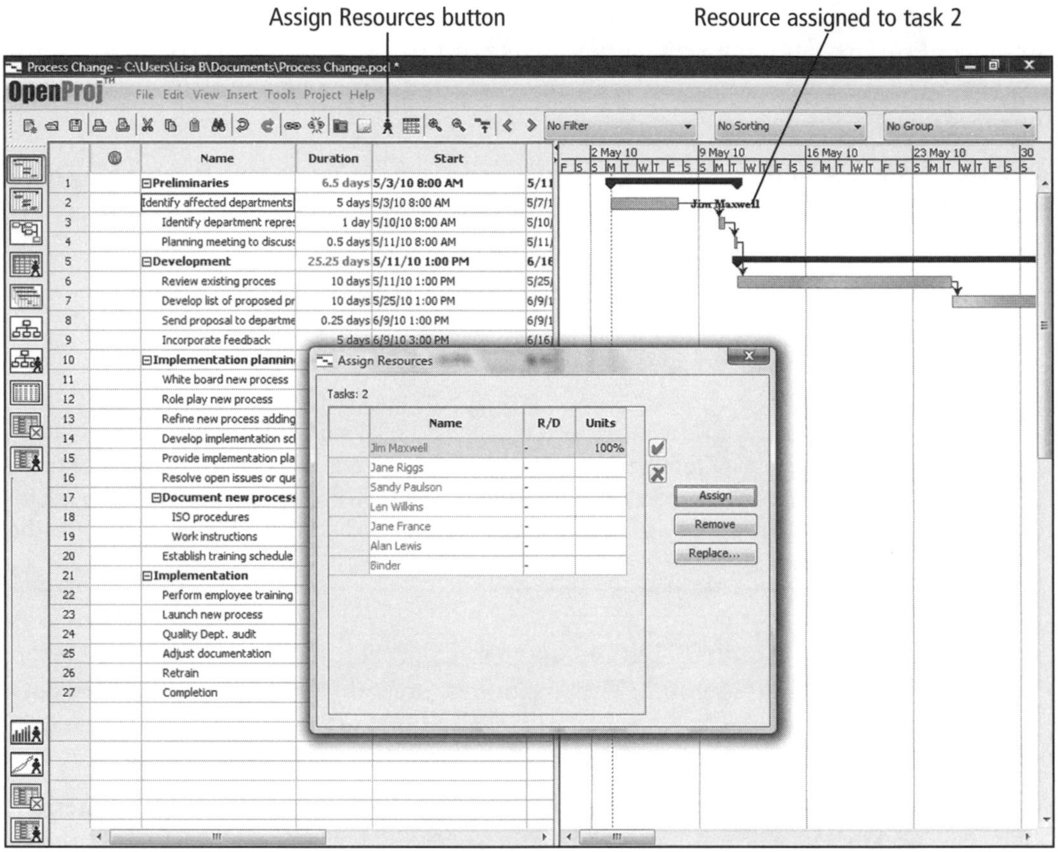

Assign Resources button   Resource assigned to task 2

Figure 3.17 Add resources to tasks with the Assign Resources dialog box.

8. Click **task 3** in the task spreadsheet and then assign **Alan Lewis** to the task using the Assign Resources dialog box. Notice that you can leave the Assign Resources dialog box open and move between using it and the task spreadsheet.

9. Click **task 4** in the task spreadsheet, use Ctrl+click to select all resources except the Binder resource, and click **Assign**. This assigns all the resources to the meeting task without changing the task duration.

10. Click **task 6**, *Review existing process.* Say that you want to assign Len Wilkins to the task; you want to allow him the full two-week duration to complete the task, but you know he'll only be working on the task about 25% of the time. So, you don't want OpenProj to calculate his costs and working hours as if he were working full time on the task. To get this right, click the Name cell for **Len Wilkins** in the Assign Resources dialog box, double-click the **Units** cell to the right of the selected resource name to select the existing entry, type **25**, and then click the **green check mark** button. Then click **Assign**. Figure 3.18 illustrates that Len is now assigned to work on that task 25% of his time over two weeks.

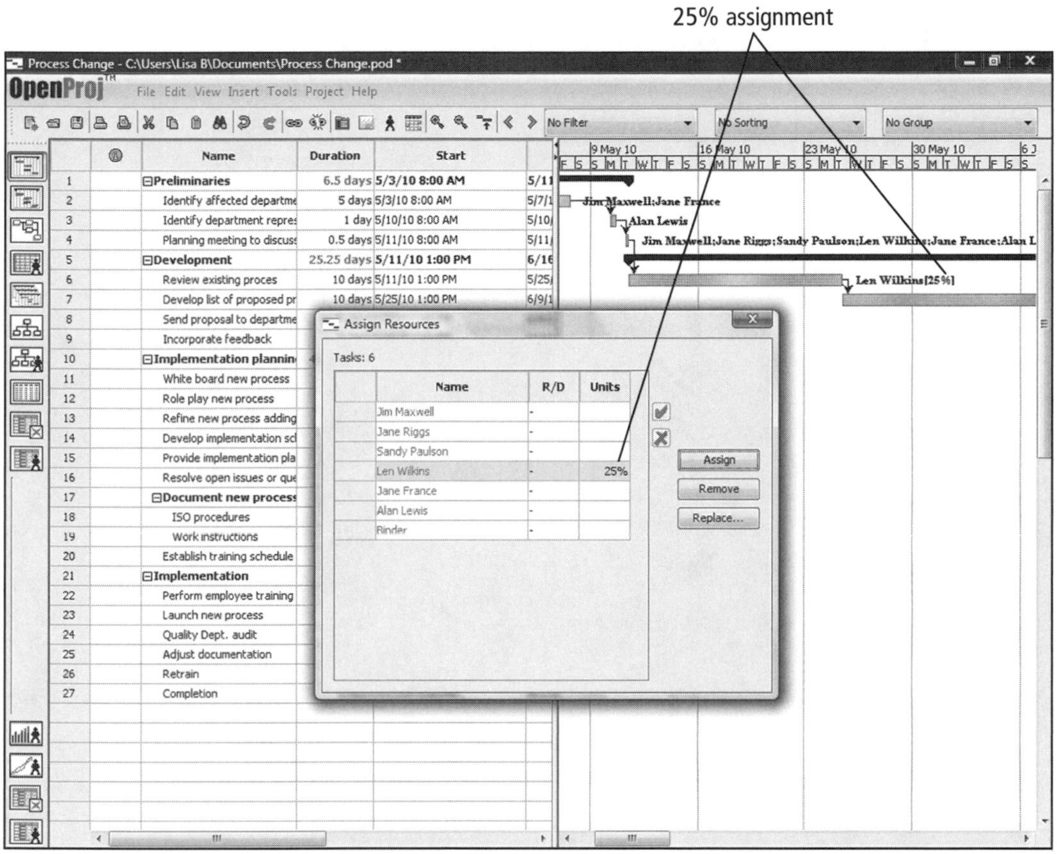

Figure 3.18 Assigning a resource to work part time on a task.

11. Assign the resources as listed in Table 3.3 to the remaining tasks. Where the table lists multiple resources, use the Ctrl+click method to select all the resources and assign them at the same time. All of the assignments are full time.

12. Assume that you've reviewed the plan and you want to accomplish task 22, *Perform employee training*, more quickly and to help Jim Maxwell with his workload near the end of the project. Click **task 22** and assign **Sandy Paulson** to the task, too. Adding the second resource reduces the task's duration to 5 days.

13. You also realize that the training will require a binder for each employee trained, and 48 (4 dozen) employees will be trained. With task 22 still selected, click the **Binder** resource in the Assign Resources dialog box, click the **Units** cell to the right of the selected resource, type a **4**, click the **green check mark** button, and then click **Assign**. As shown in Figure 3.19, OpenProj assigns the specified number of binders to the task.

Table 3.3 Remaining Resource Assignments for *Process Change* File

Task ID	Task Name	Resource(s)
7	Develop list of proposed process changes	Jane France Jim Maxwell
8	Send proposal to department representatives	Len Wilkins
9	Incorporate feedback	Jane France Jim Maxwell Len Wilkins
11	White board new process	All except Binder
12	Role play new process	Alan Lewis Jane Riggs Sandy Paulson
13	Refine new process adding role play changes	Jane Riggs Sandy Paulson
14	Develop implementation schedule	Alan Lewis
15	Provide implementation plan to department representatives	Alan Lewis
16	Resolve open issues or questions	Jane Riggs
18	ISO procedures	Jane France
19	Work instructions	Jim Maxwell
20	Establish training schedule	Sandy Paulson
22	Perform employee training	Jim Maxwell
23	Launch new process	All except Binder
24	Quality Dept. audit	Jane France
25	Adjust documentation	Jim Maxwell
26	Retrain	Jim Maxwell

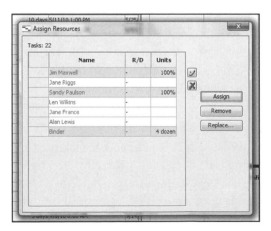

Figure 3.19
Use the Units cell to assign a quantity of a material resource.

14. Click the **Close (X)** button in its upper-right corner to close the Assign Resources dialog box.

15. Save your changes to the *Process Change* file.

Save the Baseline

At this point in the real world, you would perform a thorough review of your project plan to make sure that it is complete, accurate, and realistic. You would check assignments to ensure that the resources have the bandwidth to handle the tasks assigned, and you would circulate the plan and budget to secure the necessary sign-offs. After you and other stakeholders have given the plan the "thumbs up," you can consider it final and ready for kick off.

To manage any plan, you need to see your progress versus that original plan. In OpenProj, you can save your original plan as a *baseline*, or snapshot of the original schedule and budget. Later, as task schedules change based on actual work, OpenProj will be able to show you how the actual schedule varies from the original schedule.

Follow these steps to set and view the baseline:

1. Click **any cell** in task 1 to move back to the beginning of the *Process Change* file, and then click the **Scroll To Task** button on the toolbar to display its Gantt bars in the right portion of the view.

2. Click **Tools**, point to the **Tracking** choice, and click **Save Baseline** in the submenu that appears.

3. In the Save Baseline dialog box (see Figure 3.20), make sure that the Baseline and Entire Project options are selected and then click **OK** to save the baseline.

4. Save the *Process Change* file. In this case, saving also preserves the baseline information in the file.

Figure 3.20
These settings save the baseline for the entire project plan.

Right away, you should see that the Gantt chart changes slightly. As Figure 3.21 illustrates, a second thin Gantt bar appears for each of the summary and detail tasks. The top original bar represents the current schedule for the task. The bottom thin bar, which is gray, represents the baseline (original) schedule for the task. As you mark work as complete and adjust task schedules in the next section, you'll see how the bars compare progress to the original plan.

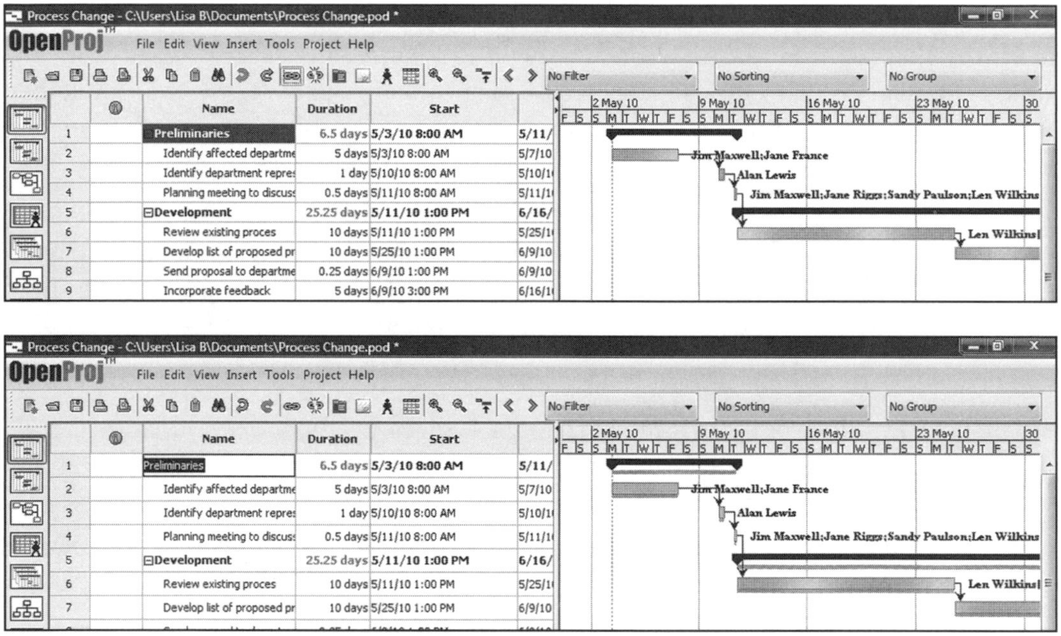

Figure 3.21 The Gantt bars before saving the baseline (top) and after (bottom).

Track Completed Work

After setting your plan and saving the baseline, it's off to the races! Work begins on the project, and you establish regular communications between yourself and all the resources to gather information about the amount of work completed on each task. You will need to enter the information about work completed into the project plan so that OpenProj can calculate data such as the hours of work completed for the project as a whole and the portion of the budget now expended. You also will need to make adjustments to task schedules as needed so that OpenProj can recalculate the schedules for linked tasks accordingly.

The Tracking Gantt view provides an excellent location to track progress, given that its field set enables you to enter actual completion information and see calculations such as actual versus remaining statistics. To enter completion percentages, you also can use the Update

Task dialog box. Follow these steps to track part of the work completed for the *Process Change* project:

1. Click **View** and then click **Tracking Gantt**, or click the **Tracking Gantt** view button at the left. The field set changes.

2. Click **task 2**, *Identify affected departments*, press **Tab** three times, type **100** in the *Percent Complete* field, and then press **Enter**. (If you need to use the Delete or Backspace key to delete a current entry in the *Percent Complete* field, do so as needed throughout the steps.) As shown in Figure 3.22, a few dramatic changes occur in the Tracking Gantt view. *Actual Start* and *Actual Finish* dates have been entered for the task. The top Gantt bar for the task has a black bar all the way through the middle, indicating that it is 100% complete. Plus, the first summary task shows a calculated entry in the *Percent Complete* field.

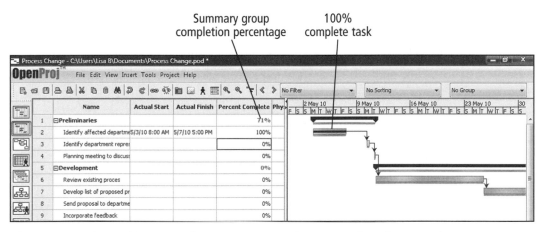

Figure 3.22 The Tracking Gantt illustrates progress when you mark work as complete.

 The field sizes in the field sets in OpenProj often can be too wide. In Figure 3.22, the widths of a few fields have been reduced so more fields can appear in the figure. To change the size of a field, move the mouse over the boundary to the right of the field heading, and drag left or right to size the field as desired.

3. Click **task 3**, *Identify department representatives*. This task is finished, but it started and finished a day later than scheduled, so you need to enter the actual start and finish dates that occurred. To do so, click **Tools**, point to **Tracking**, and click **Update Tasks**. In the Actual area of the Update Task dialog box (Figure 3.23), type **5/11/10** into both the *Actual Start* and *Actual Finish* text boxes, pressing **Tab** to finish each entry. (You also could use the text box drop-down calendars to specify the

dates, if desired.) Click **Close**. As shown in Figure 3.24, the Tracking Gantt changes even more dramatically this time. The top Gantt bar for task 3 and the one for each subsequent linked task move to reflect the fact that task 3 occurred later than originally scheduled. The gray baseline bars remain in their original positions, giving you a graphic indication of the schedule change.

 OpenProj keeps three sets of dates for you: the saved *baseline* dates, the evolving *current* dates, and the *actual* dates based on when work was completed. Marking some work as complete on a task sets the Actual Start date, and marking the task as 100% complete sets the Actual Finish date. Once an actual date has been set, OpenProj will no longer reschedule the corresponding current date, because it then must match the actual date.

4. In the row for task 4, enter **100** in the *Percent Complete* field.

5. In the row for task 6, *Review existing process*, enter **25** in the *Percent Complete* field. Notice that its top Gantt bar remains red; only a portion of it is marked with a black bar to indicate the completion percentage.

6. Let's assume that that's all the work you need to track for now. So, save the *Process Change* file.

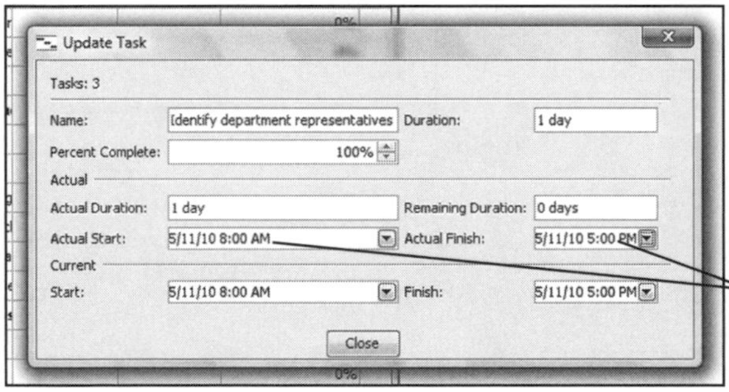

Figure 3.23
Enter actual dates in the Update Task dialog box.

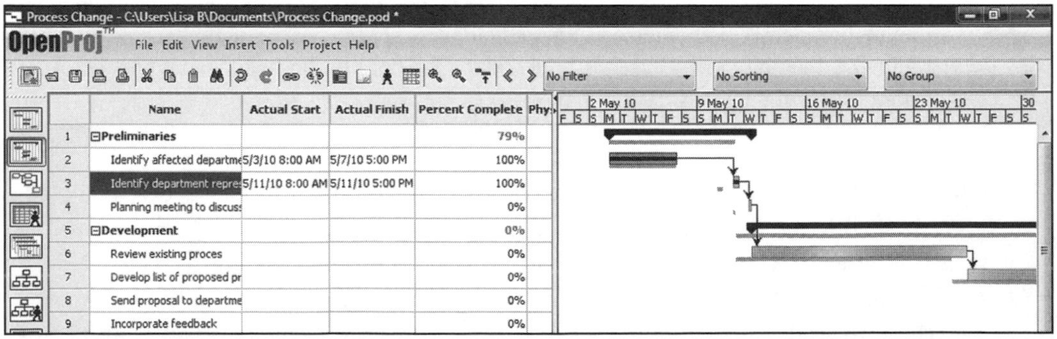

Figure 3.24 Here's how the actual dates entered in Figure 3.23 affect the Tracking Gantt bars.

As is the case for many OpenProj features, you can use a number of different techniques and get much more detailed about tracking completed work. Chapter 11 gets into the nitty-gritty about that.

Share the Results Through Views and Reports

Chapter 2 explained how to select any of the various views available in OpenProj. To share the information onscreen in a view, you can print the view. OpenProj prints whatever view currently appears onscreen.

Print your file now, which is still in Tracking Gantt view, for example:

1. With the *Process Change* file still onscreen, click **File** and then click **Print Preview**. A preview view of the file appears onscreen.

2. Click the right arrow button at the top of the preview to scroll to page 2 of the printout. You should then be able to see the bars for tasks, as shown in Figure 3.25.

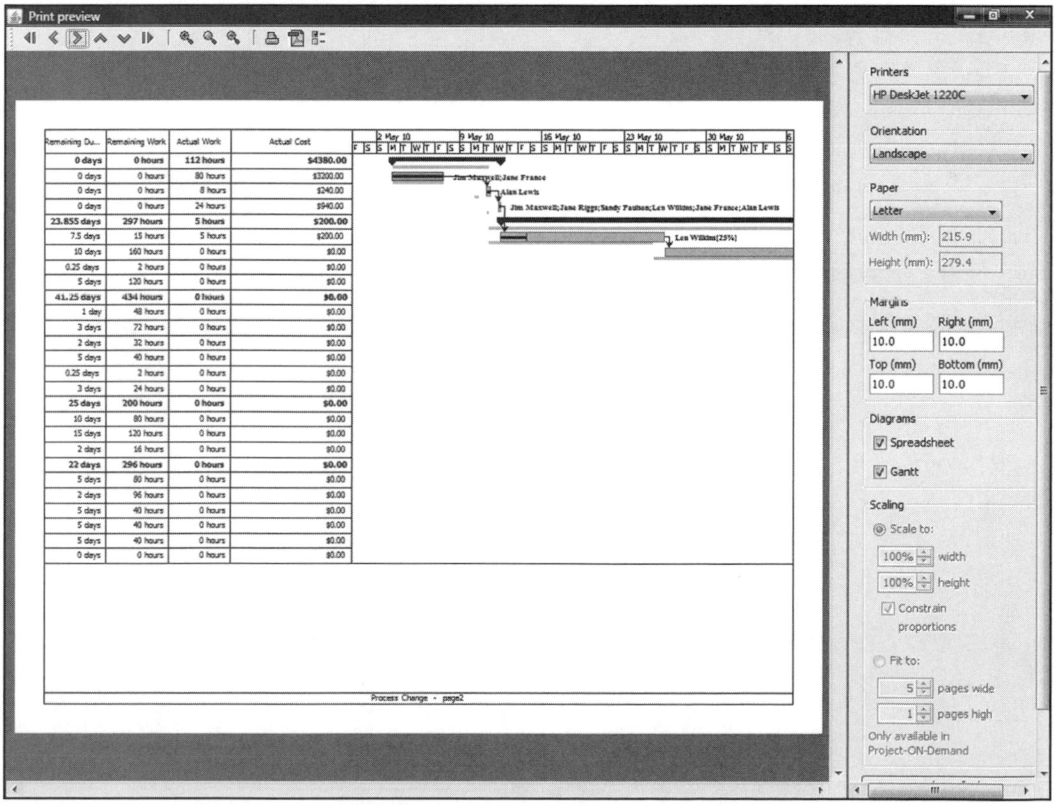

Figure 3.25 A print preview of the *Process Change* file in Tracking Gantt view.

3. Review the print setup choices in the pane at the right, making any changes as needed.

4. Click the **Print** button on the toolbar, and then click **OK** in the Print dialog box to print the view and close the print preview. (Note that you could click **File**, and then **Print** to print without displaying the Print Preview.)

5. Click the preview window **Close (X)** button to close the window if needed.

That's it. In a few mouse clicks, you can have a hard copy of any view to distribute to any stakeholder.

OpenProj also offers a number of reports that present the information from your project in nicely formatted layouts. Here's how to find and print a report of the information in your *Process Change* file:

1. Click **View** and then click **Reports**, or click the **Reports** view button at the left.

2. Open the **Report** drop-down list at the top of the preview, and click **Who Does What**. Then open the **Columns** drop-down list and click **Tasks Assigned**. The report appears in a print preview (see Figure 3.26).

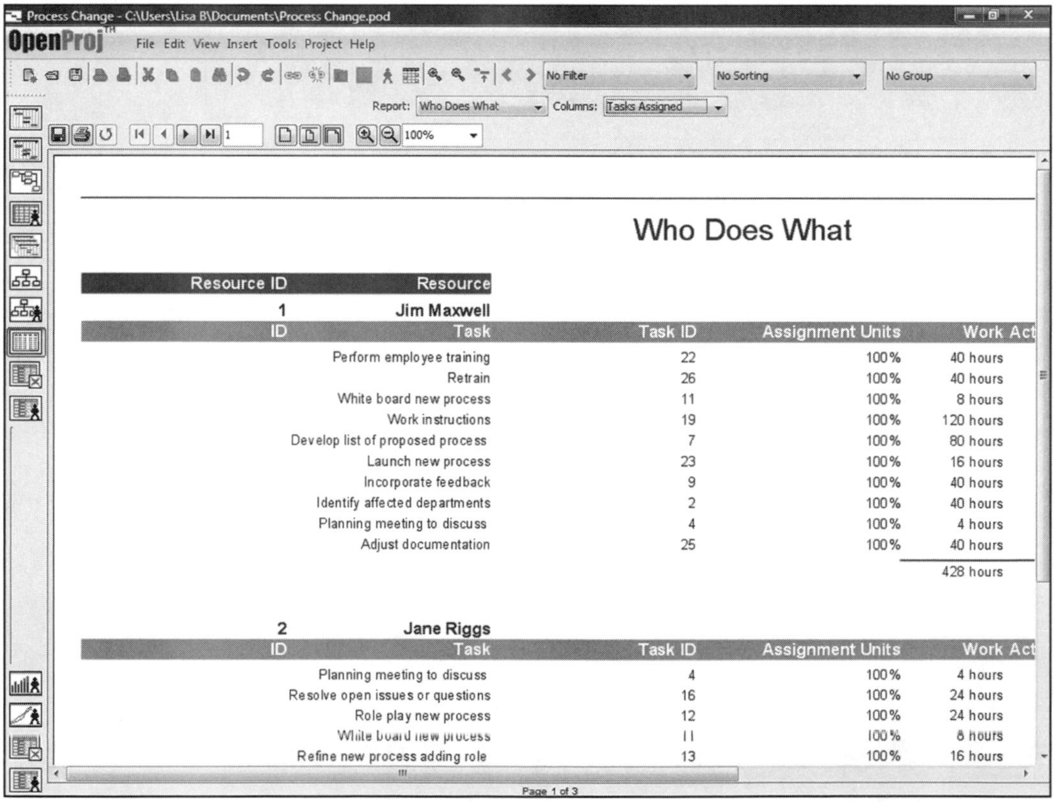

Figure 3.26 View and adjust a report before printing it .

3. To print the report, click the **Print** button above the preview and then **OK**.

4. Click **View** and then click **Gantt**, or click the **Gantt** view button at the left.

5. Resize columns as needed by dragging the right column header border for any column.

As shown in Figure 3.27, in the default Gantt view, a green check mark indicator appears in the indicators field for any task that you've marked as 100% complete.

6. Save and close the *Process Change* file.

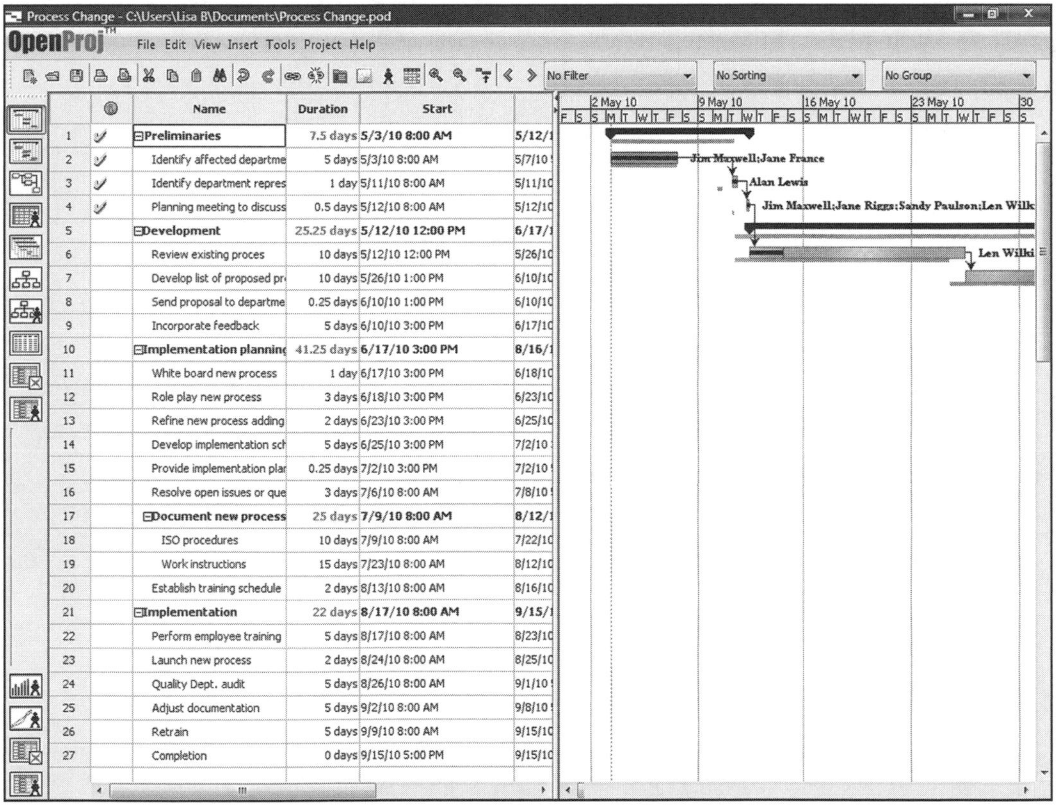

#	⊘	Name	Duration	Start	
1	✓	⊟Preliminaries	7.5 days	5/3/10 8:00 AM	5/12/1
2	✓	Identify affected departme	5 days	5/3/10 8:00 AM	5/7/10
3	✓	Identify department repres	1 day	5/11/10 8:00 AM	5/11/10
4	✓	Planning meeting to discuss	0.5 days	5/12/10 8:00 AM	5/12/10
5		⊟Development	25.25 days	5/12/10 12:00 PM	6/17/1
6		Review existing proces	10 days	5/12/10 12:00 PM	5/26/10
7		Develop list of proposed pr	10 days	5/26/10 1:00 PM	6/10/10
8		Send proposal to departme	0.25 days	6/10/10 1:00 PM	6/10/10
9		Incorporate feedback	5 days	6/10/10 3:00 PM	6/17/10
10		⊟Implementation planning	41.25 days	6/17/10 3:00 PM	8/16/1
11		White board new process	1 day	6/17/10 3:00 PM	6/18/10
12		Role play new process	3 days	6/18/10 3:00 PM	6/23/10
13		Refine new process adding	2 days	6/23/10 3:00 PM	6/25/10
14		Develop implementation sch	5 days	6/25/10 3:00 PM	7/2/10
15		Provide implementation plar	0.25 days	7/2/10 3:00 PM	7/2/10
16		Resolve open issues or que	3 days	7/6/10 8:00 AM	7/8/10
17		⊟Document new process	25 days	7/9/10 8:00 AM	8/12/1
18		ISO procedures	10 days	7/9/10 8:00 AM	7/22/10
19		Work instructions	15 days	7/23/10 8:00 AM	8/12/10
20		Establish training schedule	2 days	8/13/10 8:00 AM	8/16/10
21		⊟Implementation	22 days	8/17/10 8:00 AM	9/15/1
22		Perform employee training	5 days	8/17/10 8:00 AM	8/23/10
23		Launch new process	2 days	8/24/10 8:00 AM	8/25/10
24		Quality Dept. audit	5 days	8/26/10 8:00 AM	9/1/10
25		Adjust documentation	5 days	9/2/10 8:00 AM	9/8/10
26		Retrain	5 days	9/9/10 8:00 AM	9/15/10
27		Completion	0 days	9/15/10 5:00 PM	9/15/10

Figure 3.27 Checked tasks are marked as 100% complete.

Chapter Review

If you've followed the steps in this chapter, you've now created and managed your first project plan in OpenProj. You've now seen how to set up and choose a project calendar, specify a project start date, list tasks, outline and link tasks, list resources, assign resources, save the baseline, track work, and print a view or report. And you survived the experience! Reinforce your new skills now by answering the review questions and handling the practice projects.

Review Questions

Write your answers to the following questions on a sheet of paper.

1. True or False: The calendars that come with OpenProj have holidays marked.

2. The information you specify to define overall project parameters include the _____ and the _____.

3. To define each task, enter its _____ and _____.

4. To enable OpenProj to calculate task schedules, _____ the tasks.

5. Change to the _____ view to enter resources.

6. What is a material resource?

7. What is effort-driven scheduling?

8. Use the _____ dialog box to add resources to tasks.

9. Save the _____ so that you can track work against the original schedule.

10. For each task, the Tracking Gantt view shows:

    a. A regular bar for the current or actual task schedule

    b. A thin bar for the baseline task schedule

    c. Neither of the above

    d. Both a and b

Projects

To see example solution files created by completing the projects in this chapter, go to www.courseptr.com, click the **Downloads** link in the navigation bar at the top, type **Open-Proj** or this book's ISBN-10 number in the search text box, and then click **Search Downloads**.

Project 1

1. Click the **New Project** button on the toolbar to create a new, blank file.

2. Type **Market Opportunity Report** in the Project Name text box of the New Project dialog box, and then click **OK**.

3. Click **Tools** and then click **Change Working Time**.

4. Click the **New** button.

5. Type **35 Hour Week** in the Name text box, click the **Create a Copy of Calendar** option button and select **Standard** from the drop-down list, and then click **OK**.

6. Click the **Options** button, change the Hours Per Day entry to **6**, change the Hours per week entry to **35**, and click **OK**.

7. Press and hold the **Shift** key, and click each day heading (**M, T, W, T, F**) on any month of the calendar. This selects every work day through the year.

8. Click the **Non Default Working Time** option button at the left.

9. In the To column, change the 17:00 entry to **16:00** and press **Tab**. Click **OK** immediately to apply the change and close the Change Working Time dialog box.

10. Click **Project** and then click **Project Information**. Click the **General** tab if needed.

11. Specify a Start Date of **January 1** of the next calendar year.

12. Open the **Base Calendar** drop-down list and click **35 Hour Week**. Press Tab to make sure the entry finishes.

13. Click **Close**.

14. Click the **Save Project** button on the toolbar, and save the file as *Market Opportunity Report*.

You can create a folder named *OpenProj Exercises* in your *Documents* or *My Documents* folder and save your exercise practice files there.

Project 2

1. Enter the following tasks into the *Market Opportunity Report* file (numbers are in days):

Name	Duration
Research	-
Market size	2
Competing companies	2
Competing products	3
Ideas	-
Test competing products	10
Develop prototype ideas	15
Secure manufacturing quotes	10
Business Plan	-
Write business case	5
Develop financials	10
Finalize	2
Deliver	0

 If you enter only a number in the *Duration* field, OpenProj assumes you are entering the duration in *days*.

2. Use the **Indent** button on the toolbar to indent these tasks:

   2 through 4

   6 through 8

   10 through 13

3. Use the **Link** tasks button on the Standard toolbar (and Ctrl+click if needed) to link these tasks:

   2 through 4

   4 and 6

   6 through 8

   8 and 10

   10 through 13

4. Click **View** and then click **Resources**.

5. Enter **Craig** and **Janet** in the first two *Resource Name* cells.

6. Assign the **35 Hour Week** calendar to both resources in the *Base Calendar* field.

7. Click **View** and then click **Gantt**.

8. Click the **Assign Resources** button, and then use the Assign Resources dialog box to make the following assignments (assign both resources simultaneously when instructed to add both):

Task ID	Resource
2	Janet
3	Craig
4	Both
6	Craig
7	Both
8	Janet
10	Craig
11	Janet
12	Both

9. Click **Close** to close the Assign Resources dialog box.

10. Save your changes to the *Market Opportunity Report* file.

Project 3

1. Click **Tools**, point to **Tracking**, and then click **Save Baseline**.

2. Click **OK** to save the baseline for the entire project.

3. Click **View** and then click **Tracking Gantt**.

4. Mark **task 2** as **50%** complete.

5. Click **View** and then click **Gantt**.

6. Click **File** and then click **Print**. Click **OK** to print the file.

7. Save and close the *Market Opportunity Report* file.

PART TWO

BUILDING A
PROJECT PLAN

CHAPTER 4

CREATING A PROJECT PLAN FILE AND CALENDAR

This Chapter Teaches You How To:

- Create a blank project file
- Save a file
- Switch to another file window
- Close a file
- Understand the project calendar, as well as calendars for tasks and resources
- Set up your own calendar that reflects holidays and a custom work schedule
- Match the calendar options to the calendar
- Apply a calendar and set the project start date

Common sense dictates the first steps of planning any project: establishing the overall schedule the project will follow and when the work on the project will actually start.

After you create your new project plan file, you need to take those two steps to ensure that OpenProj will calculate accurate schedule information, including an actual finish date for the project. This chapter shows you how to create a project file, establish and assign a calendar, and set the start date to ensure your planning will be accurate from the get-go.

Making a New File for Your Project Plan

In introducing you to projects and project management, Chapter 1 explained how every project must have discrete tasks, specific deliverables, and a distinct starting and ending time for the project as a whole. Based on those facts, it makes sense to place the information about each project plan in a separate file in OpenProj. Doing so ensures that OpenProj can calculate accurate schedule, completion, and budget information about each specific project.

OpenProj only offers the ability to start from scratch with a blank file. However, a little later I'll show how you can work around this limitation by creating a file with some "starter" information that you can reuse for other projects.

Creating a Blank File

You saw in Chapter 2 that when you start OpenProj, it immediately prompts you to open an existing file or create a new file. You enter some basic information about the file and then begin your work. If, for some reason, you no longer have a blank project file open but want to use one for a new project, you can create a new blank file at any time using one of the following methods:

- Click the **New Project** button (which looks like a sheet of paper with a starburst on it) at the left end of the toolbar.
- Press **Ctrl+N**.
- Click **File** and then click **New Project**.

No matter which of those methods you choose, the New Project dialog box opens immediately. As shown in Figure 4.1, you can enter Project Name, Manager, Start Date, and Notes information. Then click **OK** to finish creating the file. Note that entering the Start Date at this point is optional. You also can change it later using the Project Information dialog box.

Saving a File

If you've ever had a power surge or some other incident cause you to lose your work in a computer file, then you've learned the hard way that, in most instances, none of your work can be retrieved unless you saved it to a disk. Better to play it safe by saving early and often.

The first time you save a file, OpenProj by default assumes you want to assign it the same name as the name you entered in the Project Name text box of the New Project dialog box. Obviously, the file's name should reflect the nature of the project that you're planning. Given that you can use more than 200 characters in a file name, you can be quite descriptive and embellish further beyond the basic project name you specified earlier. Just keep in

Click the New Project
button to create a blank file

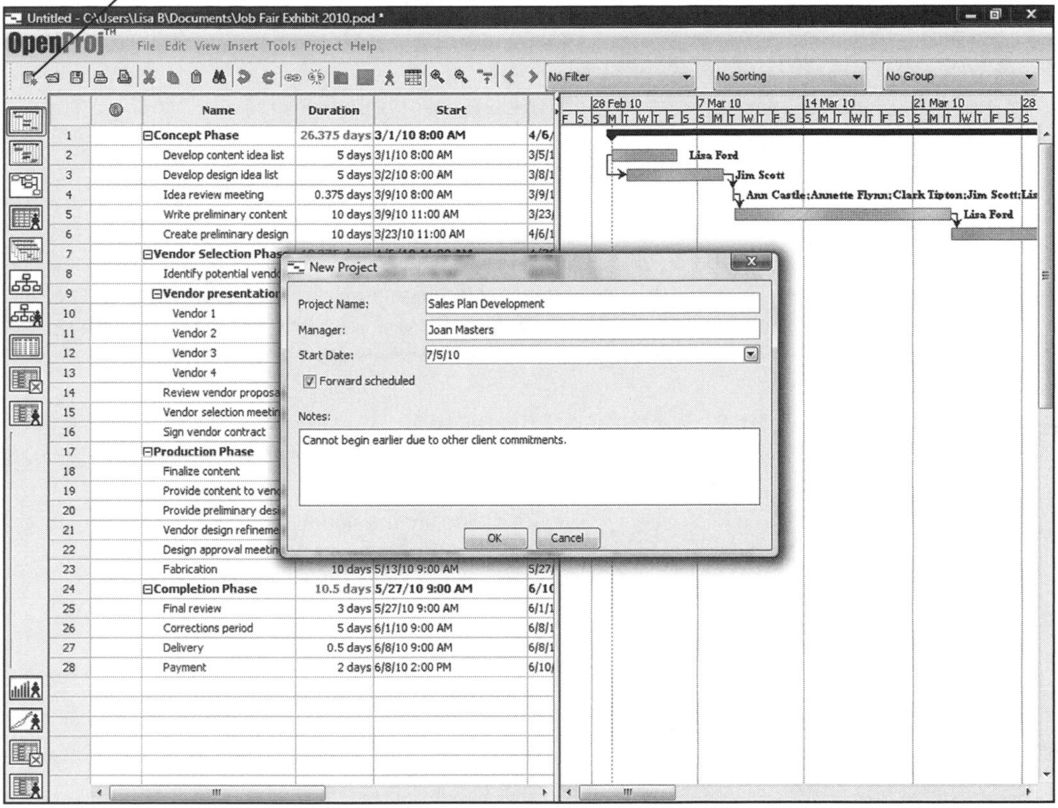

Figure 4.1 Enter overview information about the newly-created file.

mind that in most cases, folder windows only can display the first several words in a file name. If it's possible that you will be creating multiple versions of the file over time, consider including the date you save the file in the file name. For example, if you first save a file as *Brochure Plan 2010-05-01*, saving the file later as *Brochure Plan 2010-06-01* creates a copy of the file that you can instantly identify as the most recent version.

Windows Vista includes a version tracking feature that periodically saves versions of files and folders. Don't rely on this feature to be able to backtrack to an older version of a project plan, as you may not be able to retrieve the information from the precise date or time you want. If you need older versions of a file for backup and record keeping, use Save As to create and date multiple versions of a project plan file, as advised above.

To save a project plan file for the first time and give it a file name, use the process below, which is probably familiar to you from your experience with other programs:

1. Click **File** and then click **Save**. (Shortcuts: **Save Project** button on the toolbar, **Ctrl+S**.) The Save dialog box appears.

2. Use the **Save In** drop-down list and the list of available folders to select the disk and folder where you'd like to save your file.

Resist the temptation to save your project files to removable media like a USB flash drive (thumb drive) only. Hard disks are still the more stable storage location, and if you lose the removable media, then (ouch!) your project plan file will be gone for good. Always save to a hard disk first and then copy the file to a removable disk such as a CD-R or USB flash drive.

3. If desired, edit the suggested name for the file in the File Name text box (Figure 4.2).

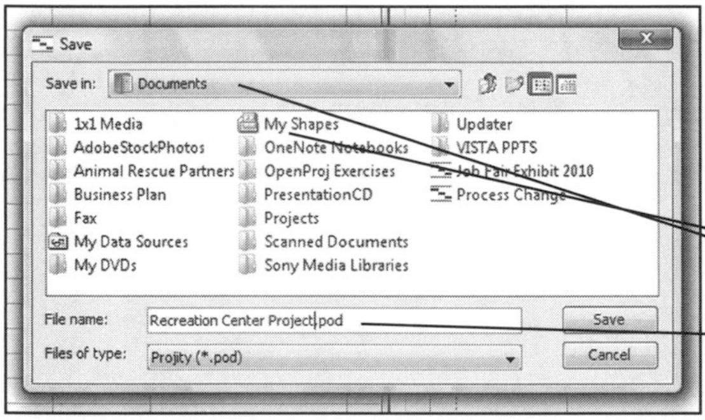

Figure 4.2
Specify the name and location where you'd like to save a file.

4. Click **Save**. OpenProj displays the new file name and path (disk and folder location) in the title bar.

The figures in this book show OpenProj being used with the latest Windows Vista operating system. If you're running OpenProj under Windows XP or another operating system, some features, such as the Save As and Open dialog boxes, might look a little different.

From that point on, to save your further changes to a file, click the **Save Project** button or press **Ctrl+S**. If you need to save a copy of the current file and give another name to the copy, click **File** and then click **Save As**. Then repeat the process from Step 2, above, to indicate the save location and new file name.

Other File Skills

Because OpenProj works much like other Windows applications, you should be able to get up to speed quickly moving around, choosing commands, and so on. Here's just a brief reminder of three other skills for working with existing project files:

- **Opening an existing file.** When you need to open an existing file, choose the **File, Open** command; click the **Open a Project** button on the toolbar; or press **Ctrl+O**. Then in the Open dialog box that appears, use the **Look In** and folders list to navigate to the desired file. Click the file and click **Open**. If you have just started the OpenProj program, you need to click the **Open Project** option button (Figure 4.3), and then click **OK** to display the Open dialog box.

Figure 4.3
Click **Open Project** if you want to open a file after starting OpenProj.

 Throughout the book, you may see command selections abbreviated. For example, rather than saying "Click **File**, and then click **Open**," a step might say "Choose **File, Open**."

- **Switching between windows.** If you have more than one project plan file open, you can use the Project menu to move between the open files. Click **Project** and then click the name of the file that you want to view and use (see Figure 4.4).

- **Closing a file.** If you've finished working with a file, click **File** and then click **Close** to close it. OpenProj will prompt you to save any changes that you made to the file, so click **Yes** to do so.

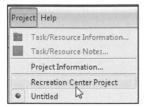

Figure 4.4
Click the name of an open file in the Project menu to switch to that file.

Do I Have to Do All of This over Again Every Time?

OpenProj does not offer a template feature like many other programs. That doesn't mean you have to start every project plan file from scratch, however. You can create your own "starter file" that has a custom calendar set up, a list of resources that you use commonly, a list of common tasks for a particular type of project, and so on. You can open the starter file and use the **File**, **Save As** command to save it under a new name. Then, you can change the project start date using the **Project**, **Project Information** command. OpenProj will automatically reschedule any starter tasks (assuming you have them properly linked and no work is marked as complete).

Opening a Microsoft Project or Other File

If you or a colleague has project plan information that's stored in one of a few other file formats, OpenProj enables you to reuse that data. In addition to its own Projity *.pod file format, Open Proj can open files in these formats:

- Microsoft Project *.mpp and *.mpx files.
- Microsoft Project 2008 XML *.xml files.
- Gnome Planner *.planner files.

Opening a file in another format is nearly as fast as opening a native OpenProj file:

1. Click **File** and then click **Open**. (Shortcuts: **Open a Project** button on the toolbar, **Ctrl+O**.) The Open dialog box appears.

2. Use the **Look In** drop-down list and the list of available folders to select the disk and folder where the file to open is stored.

3. Open the **Files of Type** drop-down list (Figure 4.5), and click the file type for the file to open.

 Note that when the default **Projects** choice is selected for Files of Type, the Open dialog box lists both OpenProj and Microsoft Project files. Selecting a specific file format from the Files of Type drop-down list makes the Open dialog box list only files of the matching type, perhaps making the file you need a bit easier to spot.

4. Click the name of the file to open, and click **Open**. OpenProj converts the file directly and opens it, so you can begin working with it immediately.

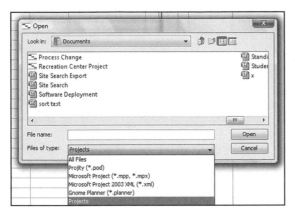

Figure 4.5
Use the Files of Type
list to select another
file format for the file
to open.

Making the Project Calendar

Although project management involves many subtle and intangible factors and skills, realizing project goals and deliverables on time serves as one of the most visible and tangible ways to measure success. An unrealistic plan is likely unachievable and can leave you looking like a less-than-competent project manager in the end.

Using OpenProj for accurate planning requires that you first choose and likely even customize the calendar that OpenProj will use to schedule tasks. This section discusses calendars and how they impact OpenProj's calculations.

Understanding the Project Calendar

Every project plan file you create in OpenProj follows a *project calendar* or *base calendar*. OpenProj schedules the work for each task during the working hours specified by the assigned base calendar. For example, if the calendar calls for eight-hour workdays, OpenProj will schedule a 12-hour task over the span of two days: eight hours on the first day and four hours on the second day.

OpenProj offers three default calendars, any one of which you can assign to be the project calendar as described in the later section, "Choosing the Project Calendar and Start Date." The default calendars are:

- **Standard.** This calendar specifies a typical (U.S.) office work calendar: a Monday through Friday work week with eight hours of work per day: 8:00 hours to 17:00, with a one-hour lunch break starting at noon (your basic 8:00 a.m. to 5:00 p.m. work day).

- **24 Hours.** This calendar specifies a 24/7 schedule like that followed in three-shift manufacturing environments. It schedules work from 0:00 to 0:00.

- **Night Shift.** This calendar schedules an eight-hour night schedule six days a week (Monday through Saturday). The shift runs from 23:00 (11 p.m.) in the evening to 8:00 the following morning, with a break for lunch from 3:00 to 4:00. Because by default OpenProj assumes that each new day begins at 0:00 (12 a.m.), it actually lists the working hours for each shift in this calendar in three segments: 0:00 to 3:00, 4:00 to 8:00, and then 23:00 to 0:00 (the beginning of the next shift on the next day).

None of the default calendars include holidays! So, unless your employer offers zero holidays, at the very least you need to identify holidays in the base calendar, even if you choose to use one of the default calendars. If you're managing multiple projects over time, it makes the most sense to create a custom calendar as described next.

OpenProj uses military time, also called the 24-hour clock, to specify working hours. The clock starts at 0:00 (midnight) through 23:59 (just before midnight). This system is believed to be less confusing because there's no ambiguity between noon and midnight and thus no need to include the a.m. and p.m. suffixes. It also happens to be an easier system for computers to sort and there's no need to convert time values to display, so it makes OpenProj more efficient. As well, most countries throughout the world have adopted the 24-hour clock as their timekeeping standard. It may take a bit of getting used to, to instinctively know that 8:00-17:00 is an 8:00 a.m. to 5 p.m. work schedule, but like anything else, you'll get there after a little practice.

Also note that a trick or two applies when you speak in military time. "6:00" can either be said as "six hundred" or "six hundred hours." Times with minutes generally leave off the "hours;" for example, "14:30" is usually spoken as simply "fourteen thirty."

Setting Up a New Calendar

Creating a custom base calendar in OpenProj requires three activities: copying an existing calendar, marking holidays and other days off (called non working time), and making any necessary changes to the daily working hours.

To create a new, custom calendar by copying an existing calendar, start here:

1. Click **Tools** and then click **Change Working Time**.
2. Click the **New** button in the lower-left corner of the Change Working Time dialog box.
3. In the New Base Calendar dialog box that appears, first click the **Create a Copy of Calendar** option button to select it and make sure that the calendar to copy is selected from the accompanying drop-down list (see Figure 4.6). If it's not, click the drop-down list and then click the calendar to copy.

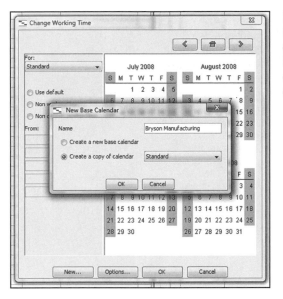

Figure 4.6
Copying a default calendar gives you a head start when you create a custom calendar.

4. Type the desired calendar name into the **Name** text box.

5. Click **OK**. This takes you back to the Change Working Time dialog box, where you can modify the calendar, as described next.

6. After you've made the desired modifications, click **OK** to close the Change Working Time dialog box.

Naming and Marking a Holiday

OpenProj considers any day without working hours to be a non working day. Non working days include holidays and other days during which no work occurs, such as a scheduled plant closing. To customize a calendar, you must mark the non working days for your company or project. (You even can mark partial non working days.) Then, OpenProj will not schedule any hours of work to occur on the non working days.

To mark a non working day in a calendar, follow these steps:

1. If the Change Working Time dialog box isn't open, click **Tools** and then click **Change Working Time**.

2. If the calendar you want to edit doesn't appear as the **For** choice (see Figure 4.7), open the drop-down list and click the calendar to edit.

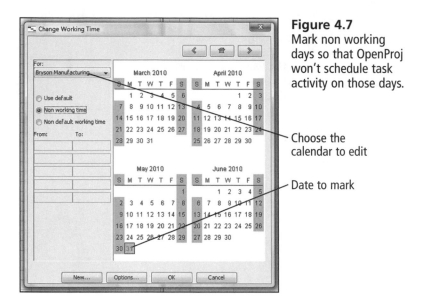

Figure 4.7
Mark non working days so that OpenProj won't schedule task activity on those days.

Choose the calendar to edit

Date to mark

3. Scroll the calendar in the middle of the dialog box by clicking the left and right arrow buttons at the top until you see the date to mark and then click the date.

To select multiple consecutive days, click the first day, and then Shift+click the latest day. You also can Ctrl+click to select non-contiguous days. Or, click the column heading for a day to select that day of the week throughout the entire calendar (all months and years). Shift+click or Ctrl+click column headings to select additional days of the week throughout the year.

4. Click the **Non Working Time** option button near the upper-left. This finishes marking the date for the exception. If you click another date on the calendar, you will see the non working day's box has been shaded and its date changed to bold red.

5. Repeat Steps 3 and 4 to mark additional non working days.

6. Click **OK** to close the Change Working Time dialog box and save your calendar changes.

7. Save your change to the file you're working in to ensure your calendar changes are preserved there.

If you want to mark a date that's only partially non working, select the date on the calendar as you would when marking it as non working time. Click the **Non Default Working Time** option button, and then enter the desired working times (see Figure 4.8).

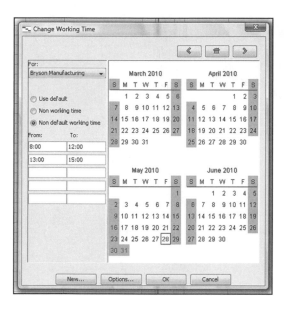

Figure 4.8
You can change the working hours for a single date, as well.

Changing the Work Week Schedule

If your project follows a special schedule, such as having a 7:00 to 16:00 (7 a.m. to 4 p.m.) schedule, you can change the default work week settings in the Change Working Time dialog box, as follows:

> Use the steps described here *before* you mark holidays in your calendar. Changing the daily working schedule as described here reapplies those hours to any dates previously marked as non working.

1. If the Change Working Time dialog box isn't open, click **Tools** and then click **Change Working Time**.
2. If the calendar you want to edit doesn't appear as the **For** choice, open the drop-down list and click the calendar to edit.
3. Click the **M (Monday)** column heading for the days on any month of the calendar.
4. Ctrl+click the remaining column headings. (Using Shift+click to select a contiguous range doesn't work for column headings.)
5. Click the **Non Default Working Time** option button at the left, and then edit the working times as desired (see Figure 4.9).
6. Click **OK** to close the Change Working Time dialog box and save your calendar changes, and save the file.

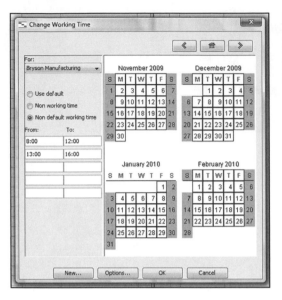

Figure 4.9
The days selected at
the right will be set to
the working hours
entered at the left.

Synching Calendar Options with the Calendar

One last step will ensure that OpenProj schedules the tasks correctly in your new project plan file. You need to change settings in the Duration Settings dialog box, accessible via the Change Working Time dialog box, to ensure that they match the settings you've created in the custom calendar. This is particularly important if you've altered the number of working hours per day. It also applies if your company schedules and tracks more than 20 days of work per month.

For *every* calendar that you create that follows non-standard working hours (or variations of the Night Shift or 24 Hours calendar), follow these steps to set duration options that match the calendar:

1. If the Change Working Time dialog box isn't open, click **Tools** and then click **Change Working Time**.

2. If the calendar you want to work with doesn't appear as the **For** choice, open the drop-down list and click the desired calendar.

3. Click the **Options** button at the bottom of the dialog box.

4. In the Duration Settings dialog box, change the **Hours Per Day**, **Hours Per Week**, and **Days Per Month Values** as needed to match the calendar that you've created (Figure 4.10).

5. Click **OK** to close the Duration Settings dialog box.

6. Click **OK** to close the Change Working Time dialog box and save your calendar changes, and save the file.

Figure 4.10
Defaults for working hours and days need to match the settings for the calendar you created.

Reviewing Other Calendars

If you've jumped ahead and poked around in OpenProj on your own, you might have noticed text boxes or fields for a *task calendar* and/or *resource calendar*. Indeed, in addition to assigning a calendar to the overall project, you can assign alternate calendars for resources and tasks.

For example, every human resource probably has a scheduled vacation in addition to the company holidays. Adjusting the resource's calendar tells OpenProj not to schedule the resource to work during the vacation period. Chapter 7 explains how to adjust a resource calendar. Likewise, a task might follow a different schedule than the rest of a project. Your project might, for the most part, follow an eight-hour workday but might include a testing task that runs continuously for 24 hours. Chapter 9 shows you where to change a task's calendar, if needed.

In general, both task and resource calendars override the project base calendar. Whenever both the task and the assigned resource have a specific calendar, OpenProj schedules work only during the periods allowed by both the task and resource calendars. The only exception is if you specify that a task should ignore the calendars for assigned resources, another choice you'll learn about in Chapter 9.

Choosing the Project Calendar and Start Date

You've already learned how to create a custom calendar, but that process doesn't apply the calendar to the current file. (Yes, even though the calendar is saved in the file.) So, now, you must not only assign the desired calendar to your project plan file but also specify the *project start date*.

What's the deal with the start date? This is another instance where OpenProj assumes that you are following professional project management practices. In that case, you're planning your projects well in advance to allow ample time to have the plan and budget approved, as well as to ensure that the resources you need will be available. The specific approval process and timing varies widely from organization to organization. One company might approve plans within weeks, while a larger company or government agency might have a lengthy, strict vetting process. At any rate, be sure you're planning far enough in advance to secure any needed planning, budgetary, and resource approvals and to get buy-in from all the stakeholders for your project.

You MUST select the project calendar and change the calendar options as described next BEFORE you add tasks into the project plan. Otherwise, OpenProj will schedule those tasks according to its defaults, which may not reflect your needs. You have to delete those tasks, apply the right calendar, and then add the tasks back in to reschedule them.

Follow these steps to assign the project start date and calendar in the current (open) project file:

1. Click **Project** and then click **Project Information**.
2. Working on the General tab of the Project Information dialog box, enter the desired project start date in the **Start** text box (see Figure 4.11). Also edit the starting time if required to match the calendar or a desired starting time for the project.

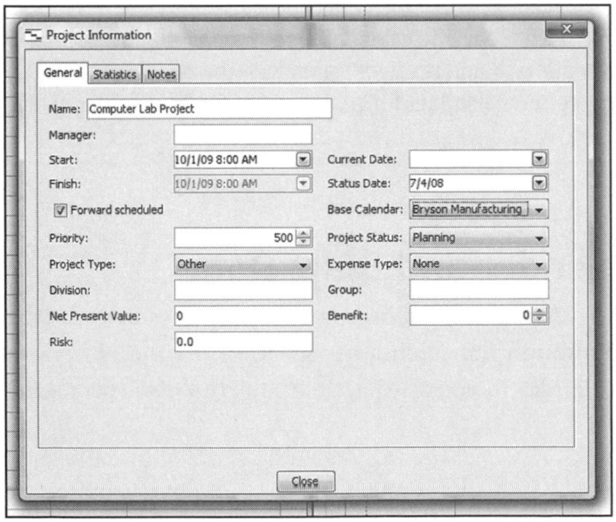

Figure 4.11
Enter the project start date and select the project base calendar here.

For any field or cell where you need to enter a date in OpenProj, click the cell. You then can type a date or click the drop-down arrow that appears to use a calendar to choose a date.

3. Leave the **Forward Scheduled** check box checked.

4. Open the **Base Calendar** drop-down list and click the desired project base calendar.

5. Click **OK** to close the dialog box.

6. Save your file.

Help! I Need to Schedule Backward from a Finish Date.

So, the organization muckety-mucks have dictated that your project has to be completed by a particular date, and you want to work backward from that date. To do so, click the **Forward Scheduled** check box to clear the check in the Project Information dialog box. Then enter the desired project finish date in the **Finish** text box. After you click **OK**, OpenProj will schedule all tasks you enter to end on the specified finish date, and linking (see Chapter 6) will schedule the tasks back into the present, as needed.

 If you used a template to create your project plan, change the start date to snap the first task and any linked tasks out to the desired schedule.

Other Project Information Settings

The General tab of the Project Information dialog box offers a number of other settings, some of which are used for specific purposes you'll learn about later in the book, and others which represent optional information you may want to capture about a project plan. Here's a rundown of those additional settings and how to use them:

- **Priority.** Specify an overall priority setting of 0 through 1000 for the project. If you later export the plan as a Microsoft Project plan, this setting can be used for rescheduling work between projects.

- **Project Status.** Choose one of six available status settings to identify the status of the project. At this stage of initial planning, you can leave Planning selected, and then later progress through the Pending Approval, Active, Completed, Cancelled, and On Hold settings as needed.

- **Project Type.** If you want to further classify the nature of the project, select one of the available settings shown in Figure 4.12.

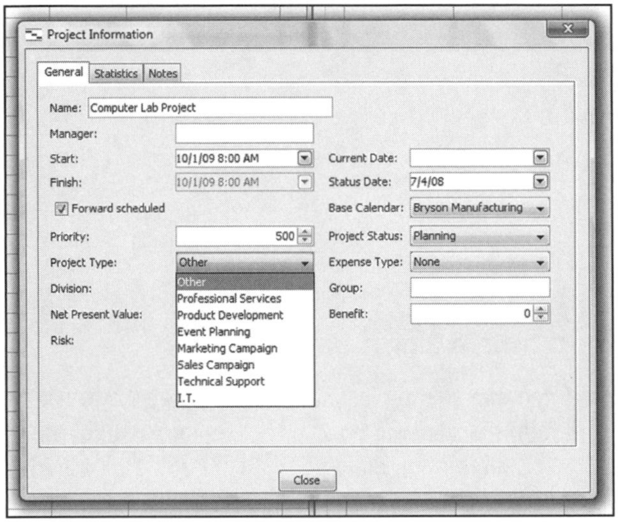

Figure 4.12
Setting Project Type and other overall project settings.

- **Expense Type.** Accounting rules require that organizations account for the expenses from different types of projects in different ways. Use the Expense Type drop-down list to select the method that applies to your project, if any. For example, if the project creates a new asset for the business, you could choose Capitalize. For a project like a moving project, the correct choice would be Expense. Other choices include Overhead, Indirect, and Direct.

- **Division.** Enter the name of the division in/by which the project is being performed.

- **Group.** Enter the name of any specific group or team performing the project.

- **Net Present Value.** If you want to enter an estimate of the net present value of cash flows for the project, enter it here. Net present value indicates how much value a project adds to the organization.

- **Benefit.** Specify a value of 0-10 that you believe reflects the value of the project to the organization.

- **Risk.** Managing risk is a key function of project management. Enter a value here that reflects your perception of the riskiness of the project as a whole. You can use your own subjective scale or any type of risk valuation system that your organization has in place in choosing the value to enter.

Chapter Review

This chapter taught you the key skills you need to establish a project plan: creating a file to hold project information, setting up a calendar for work scheduling, and assigning that calendar and a start date to the project plan file. Review that information in more detail and get some hands-on practice before moving on to the next chapter.

Review Questions

Write your answers to the following questions on a sheet of paper.

1. Why do you store each project plan in a separate file?
2. Do I have to start every new project from scratch?
3. My employer doesn't follow an 8 a.m. to 5 p.m. schedule. How do I match my project schedule to the real work schedule?
4. Why do I enter a project start date?
5. True or False: Duration Settings options must match the custom calendar applied.

Projects

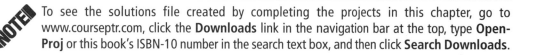

To see the solutions file created by completing the projects in this chapter, go to www.courseptr.com, click the **Downloads** link in the navigation bar at the top, type **Open-Proj** or this book's ISBN-10 number in the search text box, and then click **Search Downloads**.

Project 1

1. Start OpenProj.
2. Reopen the *Market Opportunity Report* file you created in the projects at the end of Chapter 3.
3. Create a new, blank file with *04Proj01* as the Project Name.
4. Use the Project menu to redisplay the *Market Opportunity Report* file.
5. Close both files without saving any changes.

Create a folder named *OpenProj Exercises* in your *Documents* or *My Documents* folder and save your exercise practice files there.

Project 2

1. Create a new, blank project file with the Project Name *Bryson File Reorganization*.

2. Use the Change Working Time dialog box to create a new calendar named *Afternoon Job Share*. Change its default work week to have working hours of 13:00 to 17:00, Monday through Friday. Also mark at least two holidays in calendar year 2009 and use the **Options** button to choose the appropriate Duration Settings choices.

3. Assign the *Afternoon Job Share* calendar to the file and set a project start date early in 2009, editing the start time to 13:00 (1 p.m.) to match the assigned calendar.

4. Save the file as *Bryson File Reorganization*.

Project 3

1. Reopen the Project Information dialog box.

2. Change the Project Type to **Professional Services**. Enter **1.2** as the Risk setting.

3. Save your changes to the file, and close the file.

4. Close OpenProj.

CHAPTER 5

ADDING AND ORGANIZING TASKS

This Chapter Teaches You How To:

- Break down the work for a project into task-sized chunks
- Enter task information the right way
- Understand and use task durations
- Create milestones
- Move, add, and delete tasks
- Undo one or more changes
- Organize the schedule with outlining
- Collapse and expand the outline
- Display a task that summarizes the project schedule

You can be a more successful project planner if you have the discipline to consider all the details. In building your project plan, you need to map out what activities need to happen and when. This chapter teaches you how to build a list of project tasks in OpenProj, thereby yielding a more complete and well-developed project plan. You'll learn what task information to enter, and how to re-order and identify tasks. You will learn to further develop your plan by undoing changes, applying outlining, and using the outlining to hide and redisplay schedule information.

Understanding the WBS (Hierarchy)

If you've ever felt stuck in the face of a complex challenge, you might have gotten this good advice from a friend or colleague: "Take it one step at a time." Breaking a large undertaking down into deliverable parts enables you to focus on and complete activities, contributing to overall completion.

As a project manager, you need to take the same approach toward planning any project. You need to break the project down into a list of deliverables or outputs that fall into groups and organize those items in the order in which they need to be done. This is called creating the **Work Breakdown Structure** (or hierarchy of outcomes) for the project. The Work Breakdown Structure, also called the **WBS**, should organize the scope for the project—project goals, outcomes, and deliverables.

You might diagram the WBS on paper using a flowchart or organization chart structure, or create an outline of the planned outcomes in the WBS. The WBS can then serve as a starting point for identifying and entering specific activities in a project plan file.

After creating the WBS, you can use it for reference as you break the project down into tasks that have the right level of granularity (detail level) for your tracking purposes. If a "task" is too general and encompasses several activities, you won't really be able to track the completion of the individual activities. If you go too far in the other direction and break the schedule down into components that are too small, you risk putting yourself in a situation where you spend too much time tracking and maintaining tiny parts of the schedule.

 Like the project as a whole, each task should have a specific starting point and ending point. Generally, each task also represents a fairly discrete action (*research article*, *write article*, and so on), rather than a more general undertaking or outcome from the WBS (for example, *newsletter*). Identifying activities with specific starting and ending points can help you distinguish between what's a task and what's an overall phase or part of a project plan.

Consider the three examples shown in Figure 5.1. In the example on the left, the tasks lack enough detail to allow for useful tracking. The far right example goes to the other extreme, breaking down the activity into an unnecessary and cumbersome level of detail. Goldilocks in the middle is "just right," giving the project manager enough information to know which specific activities to check on, while not breaking the schedule down into tiny activities. The construction manager needs to know when the electrical work will be completed on each level of the house, but he doesn't need to know exactly when electrical outlets versus lighting fixtures will be installed.

 You can display a field of WBS codes that identify where each task falls in the hierarchy of the project. The section called "Hiding and Reinserting a Field" in Chapter 9 illustrates how to display another field like the WBS field onscreen.

	⑩	Name
1		⊟Electrical
2		Rough In
3		Finish

	⑩	Name
1		⊟Electrical
2		⊟Rough In
3		Basement
4		1st Floor
5		2nd Floor
6		⊟Finish
7		Basement
8		1st Floor
9		2nd Floor

	⑩	Name
1		⊟Electrical
2		⊟Rough In
3		⊟Basement
4		Lighting
5		Outlets
6		Switches
7		⊟1st Floor
8		Lighting
9		Outlets
10		Switches
11		⊟2nd Floor
12		Lighting
13		Outlets
14		Switches
15		⊟Finish
16		⊟Basement
17		Lighting
18		Outlets
19		Switches
20		⊟1st Floor
21		Lighting
22		Outlets
23		Switches
24		⊟2nd Floor
25		Lighting
26		Outlets
27		Switches

Figure 5.1 The left task breakdown is too general and the right one too detailed, but the center example breaks the project down to the right level.

If you want to use OpenProj to lay out even small details for a project or to manage a project plan from the "10,000 feet" level, that's okay, too. Create the level of detail that suits your planning needs. The maintenance engineers at a manufacturing company might need to break a machine maintenance schedule into lots of small tasks and track them on an hour-by-hour basis, while the COO of a company might just want to track overall phases for a project. However, most projects are managed at a level somewhere in between.

People have different working styles when it comes to getting thoughts and ideas in order. The method that you use to build a list of project tasks doesn't really matter, as long as you've first carefully determined the scope, so that you can make sure you include all the needed activities and no unneeded ones. OpenProj can accommodate any style you use to build the list of tasks from there:

- **Top-down planning.** You like to map out overall phases or parts of a plan, and then break those phases down level by level.
- **Bottom-up planning.** You like to list all the tasks or activities that need to happen in order to meet an overall goal or deliverable, and then identify what phase or group the individual activities fit into.
- **Brain dump.** You like to list everything that needs to take place in a project, and then go back and rearrange it into a logical or chronological order.

Entering Basic Task Information

In OpenProj, you enter and organize a list of tasks to create the WBS. As you learned in Chapter 1, *tasks* are the discrete actions or activities that need to be completed to meet the goals and deliverables of your project plan. Building the list of tasks is one of most essential parts of the planning process.

You type task information in the spreadsheet in the left portion of the Gantt view. To create a task, you need to make entries into only two fields:

- **Name.** Type in the name or label that you want to use to identify the task. As a rule you should stick with names that are as brief and descriptive as possible. Your organization might prefer to use a special convention for task names, such as including both subject and verb, as in "Program Module 1" rather than simply "Module 1."

- **Duration.** Enter the span of time between the start and finish for the task. If you type a number such as **4**, OpenProj assumes you are entering the duration in days and adds *days* beside the value, as shown in Figure 5.2. ("Working with Durations," next in the chapter, explains how to work with other duration entries.) If you enter no duration, OpenProj assumes a default duration of one day (1 day?, where the question mark indicates that the duration is estimated). If you are entering a task that's the name for a phase or group of other tasks, you don't need to enter the duration. OpenProj will calculate that duration for you when you later outline and schedule the tasks.

Mi STEP You should enter information ONLY into *Task Name* and *Duration*. If you type a date into the *Start* or *Finish* field for a task, OpenProj adds a **constraint** to the task, which limits OpenProj's ability to reschedule the task and recalculate the schedule. "Using a Task Constraint if Needed," in Chapter 9, describes what constraints are, when to use them, and how to apply the right type of constraint.

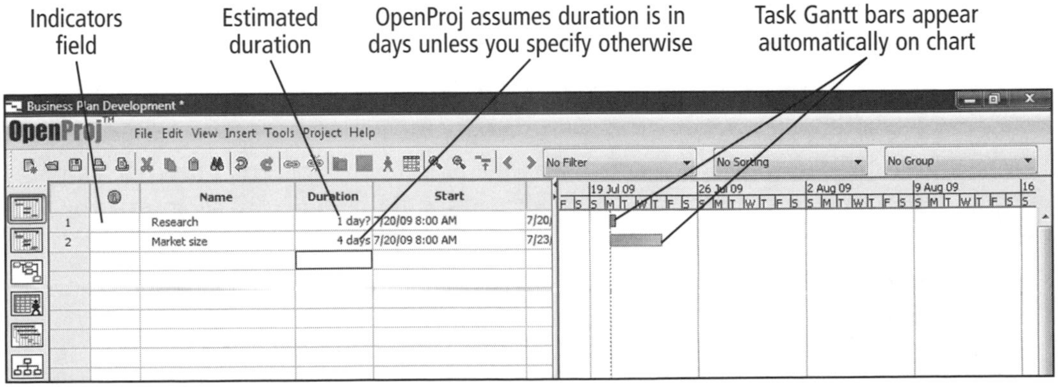

Indicators field   Estimated duration   OpenProj assumes duration is in days unless you specify otherwise   Task Gantt bars appear automatically on chart

Figure 5.2 Enter the task's name and duration only.

If you've ever used a spreadsheet program, entering tasks in the task sheet will come naturally. Follow these steps to create the list of tasks in your project plan:

1. Click on first empty cell in the *Name* column.
2. Type the name for the task.
3. Press **Tab** to move to the *Duration* column.
4. Type the task duration value, such as **3** for 3 days (see Figure 5.3).

Enter a value

	ⓘ	Name	Duration	Start		19 Jul 09	26 Jul 09	2 Aug 09	9 Aug 09	16
1		Research	1 day	7/20/09 8:00 AM	7/20					
2		Market size	4 days	7/20/09 8:00 AM	7/23					
3		Competing products	5	7/20/09 8:00 AM	7/20					

Business Plan Development — OpenProj™ — File Edit View Insert Tools Project Help — No Filter — No Sorting — No Group

Figure 5.3 Typing the *Duration* field entry to finish a task.

5. Press **Enter** and then press **Shift+Tab** to move the cell selector to the *Name* cell.
6. Repeat Steps 2 through 5 to add more tasks as needed.

After you enter each new task name, a number for the task appears in the gray row heading area at the left side of the task sheet. This row number is also the **task ID** number that OpenProj uses to identify the task when you link it or perform some other activities. So, remember to check the row header area to find the task ID number for a task when needed.

Although you won't use it to enter basic task information, you should be aware that the Task Information dialog box provides another location where you can work with task values such as the task *Name* and *Duration* field entries. If you double-click a task in the spreadsheet portion of the Gantt view, the Task Information dialog box (see Figure 5.4) opens. You can use the tabs in this dialog box to view and change task information. (Later chapters will cover specific instances when you use the settings here.) After you make the desired changes, click **OK** to close the dialog box.

At one manufacturing company where I've taught project management software classes, many of the users make Task Name entries in ALL CAPITAL LETTERS for purposes of matching output from another planning system used in the company. While you might think that typing in all caps makes the tasks more readable, in reality the opposite tends to be true because the capital letters all have the same height. Lowercase letters vary more in shape and are thus easier for the brain to recognize.

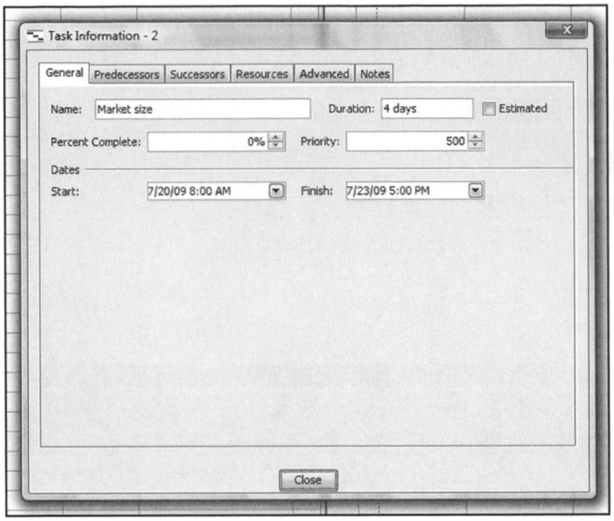

Figure 5.4
You also can use the Task Information dialog box to work with task settings.

Working with Durations

You've already learned that when you type a number into the *Duration* field for a task, OpenProj assumes the entry is in days. But the definition of a day depends on the calendar you've assigned to the project and the hours per day specified in the Duration Settings dialog box.

In real life and under the Standard calendar in OpenProj, a day means a typical eight-hour workday. So, a 1 day task will have a schedule of eight hours from 8:00 (8 a.m.) to 17:00 (5 p.m.), not counting an hour for lunch. However, if you've chosen the 24 Hours calendar and have changed the Duration Settings dialog box settings to reflect a 24-hour working schedule, then a 1 day task will have a 24-hour schedule.

Not every task lasts a full day (no matter what the calendar), such as a two-hour planning meeting, and some tasks last longer and might even exceed the daily working hours. For example, running your company's booth at a trade show or running a software test are tasks that might take 16 hours on a single day during a project that otherwise has eight-hour working days.

OpenProj enables you to schedule the exact amount of time a task will take to finish based on the abbreviation or duration label that you include with the numeric value in the *Duration* column of the task sheet.

Table 5.1 lists the abbreviations or duration labels. The far right column of the table includes an example entry and what it means in terms of how OpenProj schedules the task.

Table 5.1 Duration Labels (Abbreviations)

Time Unit	Abbreviations	Example
Minutes	M Min Mins	**30m** means 30 working minutes
Hours	H Hr Hrs Hour	**30h** means 30 working hours
Days	D Dy Day	**30d** means 30 working days
Weeks	W Wk Week	**30w** means 30 working weeks
Months	Mo Mons Month	**2mo** means 2 working months

If you enter a number only in the *Duration* field, OpenProj assumes you are entering the duration in days.

To use one of the duration labels:

1. Click the ***Duration*** cell for the task.

2. Type the numeric value for the duration.

3. Type the desired duration label, as in the top example in Figure 5.5.

4. Press **Enter**. The Gantt bar for the task adjusts to reflect the new duration, as in the bottom portion of Figure 5.5. Also note that OpenProj automatically converts the entry into an equivalent number of days, for consistency.

You do not have to type a space between the duration value and label. OpenProj automatically inserts the space and may adjust the duration label displayed, for example changing a 16h duration entry to 16 hrs. Throughout the book, I'll refer to durations using the shortest label and omitting the space, as in 16h.

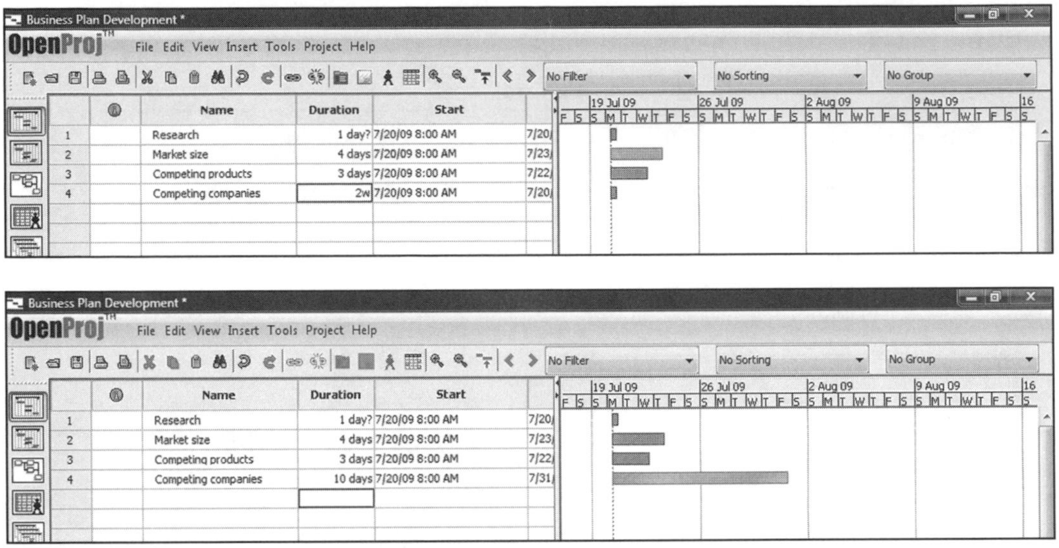

Figure 5.5 Use a duration label to express durations in time periods other than days.

But How Do I Know What the Duration Should Be?

Even though the tools in OpenProj automate your ability to build and track the project plan, they aren't a substitute for the human expertise of yourself and your team. Generally speaking, use your experience to judge what the duration of each task in the plan should be. If you don't have enough expertise, you can use these methods to better identify a task's likely duration:

- Ask a team member or someone from another department who has more expertise with a particular type of task or has managed a similar project to help you develop the task estimate.

- If the task will be handled by an outside vendor and you have multiple vendors bidding for the work, be sure to have the competing vendors supply duration estimates, and then base your duration on that information.

- Think through the task requirements and develop optimistic (O), pessimistic (P), and most likely (M) durations. (Use consistent units such as hours or days.) Then, plug the estimates into the following PERT analysis formula: (O+4M+P)/6=Estimated duration. This analysis gives more weight to the most likely duration, while still considering the extremes, in producing an estimate.

- If you've used OpenProj to track a similar task or project, refer back to your previous project plan file. The valuable history recorded in any OpenProj file, including whether a task happened on or off schedule and notes about why that was the case, can help you identify more accurate durations the next time around.

Adding a Milestone

When you've got a few years of life or career experience under your belt, you may look back at a particular occurrence and think, "Wow, that was really a milestone for me." While you may have invested a lot of time and sweat in pursuit of your milestone, the achievement itself—receiving the diploma or contract, for example—flies by in an instant.

OpenProj enables you to add a *milestone* task to your project plan to mark a significant point or event. To mark a task as a milestone, simply enter **0** (zero) in the *Duration* field for the task. As shown in Figure 5.6, OpenProj charts a milestone task with a diamond marker rather than a Gantt bar.

> **GOTTA KNOW**
>
> Any task for which you enter 0 (zero) duration is a *milestone* task.

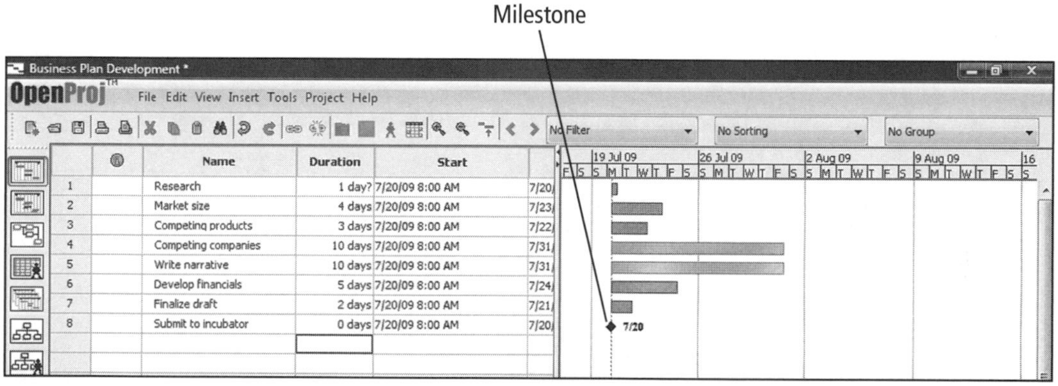

Figure 5.6 Use a milestone task (with a 0 duration) to mark an important point in the project schedule.

You enter milestones with a 0 duration because they have no actual work associated with them. For example, you may not be able to initiate work on a project until you receive a signed copy of the contract from the client. Although the contract receipt doesn't require any work on your part, it does trigger work on other tasks when it actually occurs. So, the milestone task enables you to track that event and use it to trigger the other work in your project plan. Some project managers use milestones to mark particular dates when they want to status the project, or particular dates that might be significant checkpoints in the project, such as the day when 50% of the overall project duration has passed. You can even use a milestone to tell OpenProj to prevent schedule changes from delaying the project finish date. You'll learn that trick in Chapter 9.

You also can mark a task with a longer duration as a milestone after entering the task duration. Double-click the task, click the **Advanced** tab of the Task Information dialog box, click the **Mark Task as Milestone** check box to check it, and then click **Close**. This changes the task's appearance on the Gantt graph to that of a milestone bar (diamond), but it does not reduce the duration or amount of work assigned. Because that might cause confusion when reviewing the plan, it may be a better practice to stick with milestones that have a 0 duration.

Moving Tasks Around

If you tend to use a "brain dump" style of planning where you type all the tasks that come to mind and then rearrange them later, you need to know how to move the tasks into the proper order when the time comes.

The process for moving a task begins with selecting the task. To select the whole task, click the **task row number** (task ID number) in the gray row heading area at the left. As shown in Figure 5.7, OpenProj highlights the entire task.

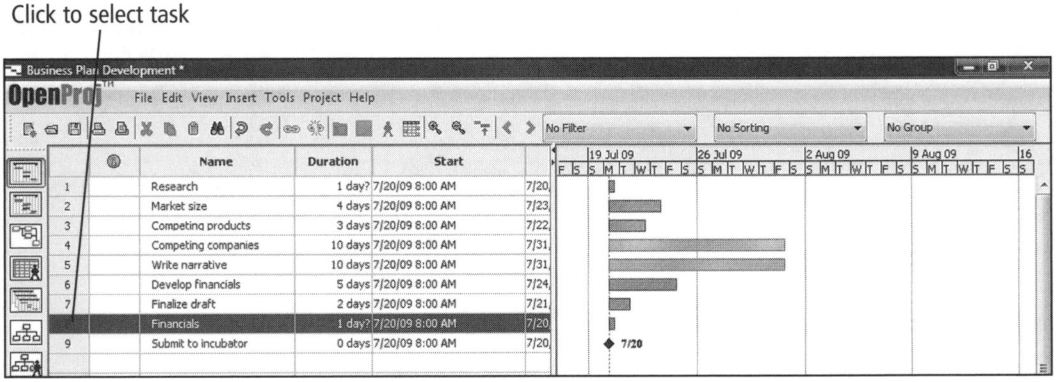

Click to select task

Figure 5.7 Click the task row number to select the whole task.

Clicking the task name does *not* select the whole task. If you click the task name and then try to cut and paste, you will move the task *Name* cell entry only, not the task.

After you select a task, you can use cut and paste to move it. Click **Edit** and then click **Cut** (Shortcut: **Ctrl+X** or **Cut** button on toolbar). Click a cell to specify the paste destination; the task you just cut will be inserted in the row below that cell. Click **Edit** and then click **Paste** (Shortcut: **Ctrl+V** or **Paste** button on toolbar). The task appears in the new location.

If the Cut button isn't active when you try to cut the task, try clicking another task and then reselecting the task by clicking its task ID (row) number.

Be careful about moving tasks later in the process, after you've linked tasks to establish the project schedule. (Chapter 6 describes that process.) Moving tasks around at that point can disrupt or even remove links, which can undo a significant portion of your planning. Also keep in mind that moving tasks permanently changes task ID (row) numbers to reflect the new order.

Adding and Deleting Tasks

A thorough project manager typically calls on colleagues and team members to help build the project plan and ensure that the plan includes all the activities required to produce the project deliverables. After receiving some input, the project manager will typically need to add more tasks to the project plan, or possibly to delete unneeded tasks.

To add a task to the project plan:

1. Click a cell in the task above which you want to insert a new task.
2. Click **Insert** and then click **New Task/Resource** (Shortcut: **Ctrl+K**). The new, blank task row appears, as shown in Figure 5.8.
3. Add the task *Name* and *Duration* entries as you normally would.

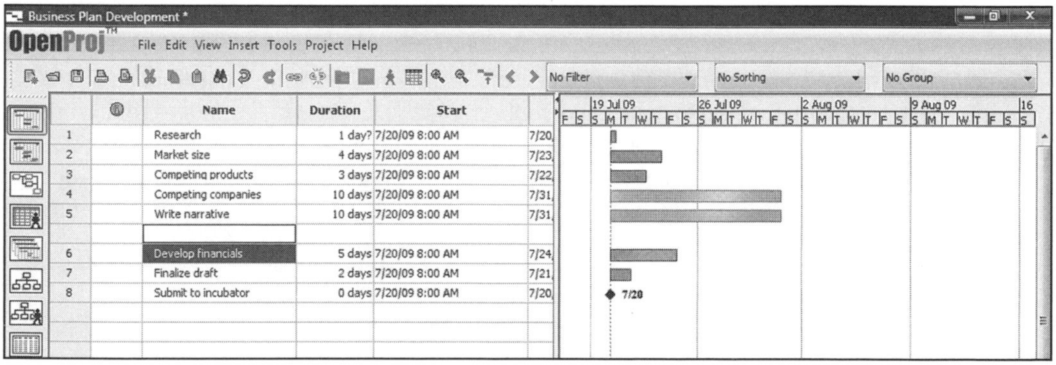

Figure 5.8 A new, blank task row has been inserted.

If you select the entire task by clicking the task ID, you sometimes can insert a row by pressing the **Insert** key on the keyboard. This method doesn't always work, but its functionality will likely be improved in later OpenProj releases. You also can right-click the task ID, and click **New** in the context menu that appears to insert a new, blank task.

OpenProj also enables you to delete tasks, but you should of course use caution when doing so, especially if you've already applied linking in your project plan. To delete the entire task, you have to:

1. Click the **task ID** number (row header).
2. Click **Edit**, and then click **Delete**. The task row disappears immediately.

The alternate method for deleting a task is to right-click the **task ID** and click **Delete** in the context menu. No matter which method you use, OpenProj does not prompt you to confirm the deletion.

Note that if you click the task *Name* cell for the task and then press **Delete**, OpenProj deletes the task name only. This method therefore doesn't delete the entire task, but does enable you to delete and retype a new task name.

If you delete a task accidentally, you can press **Ctrl+Z** immediately to undo the deletion. The section called "Using Undo" later in this chapter provides more information about undoing changes you make to the project plan file. In addition, keep in mind that when you add and delete tasks, OpenProj permanently changes the task ID numbers, so if a task addition or deletion has unwanted renumbering consequences, make sure you undo the change.

 Although you can add and delete tasks even after you've started tracking work on a project, it's best to take the time to build a thorough list of tasks before you've outlined or linked any tasks. That's because OpenProj can't produce an accurate calculation of the project's duration without all the tasks being present. In such a scenario, missing tasks will mean that you've underestimated the schedule and work involved in your project, making the project plan unrealistic.

Editing a Task

As you refine your project plan, you may need to make changes to task information that you've previously entered. For example, when touching base with a vendor you might learn that you overestimated the duration for a particular task, so you need to change the

Duration field entry for the task. Or, you might want to get more specific about the names you've assigned to tasks, or even replace temporary "code names" with live names for tasks.

Just like working in a spreadsheet program, you can change the entry in any cell in the spreadsheet portion of the Gantt view. Start by clicking the cell to edit in the task, and then simply begin typing to replace the entire entry in the cell. Press **Enter** to finish the change.

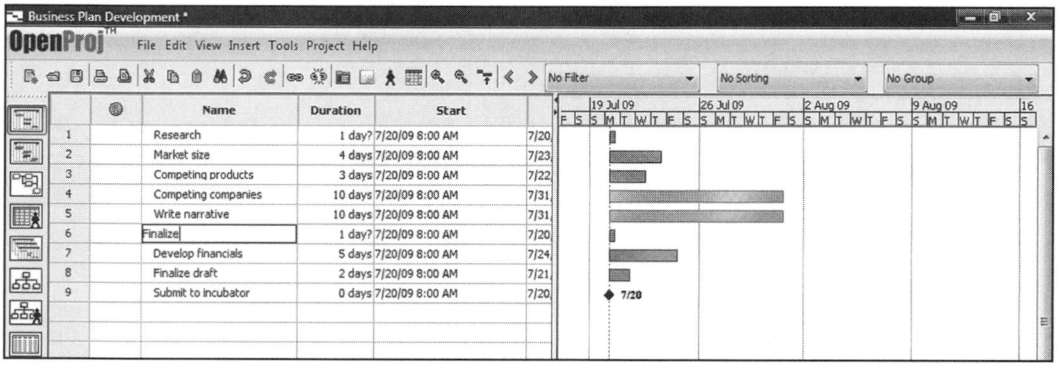

Figure 5.9 Click a cell and type replacement information.

 If you start editing a cell but realize that you no longer want to make the change, press **Esc** on the keyboard to cancel the edit.

Using Undo

The calculations that occur behind the scenes in OpenProj are highly complex. A duration change to a single task can ripple all the way through a lengthy project, making it difficult to reverse all the calculations resulting from even more changes. Despite the challenges of dealing with such complex calculations, you can undo the most recent changes that you made to your project file.

After you make the first change in your project plan file during the current work session, the Undo button becomes active on the toolbar. Click that button to undo the most recent change that you've made. Click the button again to undo additional changes. Once you've used undo, you can redo actions. Click the **Redo** button to redo a change. See Figure 5.10 to check out these buttons.

The Edit menu offers equivalents of the Undo and Redo buttons: Undo and Redo, of course. As in many other familiar applications, the keyboard shortcuts for the Undo and Redo commands are Ctrl+Z and Ctrl+Y, respectively.

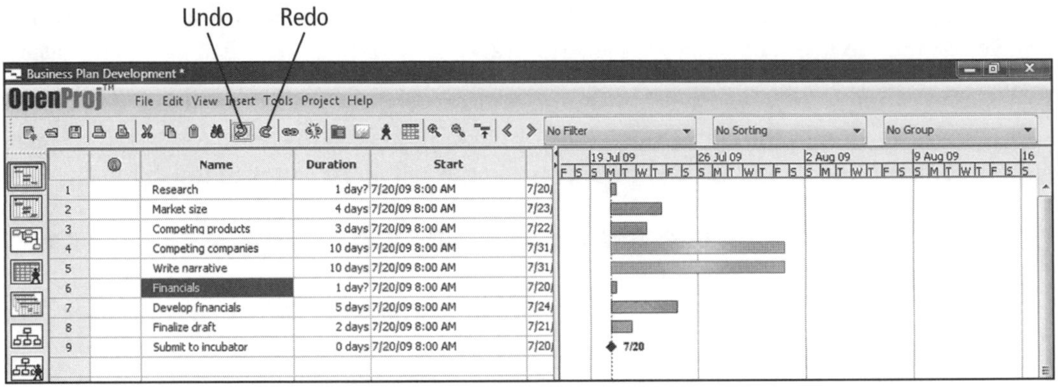

Undo   Redo

Figure 5.10 Taking advantage of undo.

  NOTE! Redo is another feature that's not always working properly in the OpenProj version available as of this writing, so be sure you check the impact of any redo action to ensure it's a change that you want.

  MISTEP Saving the file typically clears the stack or history of changes, eliminating the ability to undo. So, as you work, you'll have to balance your desire to keep undo changes available with the need to save your work from time to time to make sure that you don't lose anything given a power fluctuation or other system problem.

Using Outlining to Structure the Work

Outlining in OpenProj helps you organize tasks related by function or chronology. For example, many projects fall into logical phases or stages of activity, so outlining the tasks by phase or stage makes the project easier to follow. OpenProj actually enables you to apply multiple levels of outlining within a project plan, but as a practical matter, you'll want to limit the outline to two or three levels for smaller project plans.

Outlining also enables you to hide and redisplay tasks by collapsing and expanding the outline. This enables you, in your role as project manager, to view project overview information when needed or to focus on specific tasks at other times.

Finally, outlining enables OpenProj to summarize information. Outlining creates ***summary tasks*** and ***subtasks*** (or ***detail tasks***). You indent subtasks to convert the task above to a summary task that calculates information about the indented subtasks. For example, as you track work in the project plan, the summary task can calculate an overall completion percentage for the tasks in the group, which gives you as project manager a better idea of overall areas where the project is on track or off track.

Indent *subtasks* (*detail tasks*) to make the task above them into a ***summary task***. The summary task calculates information about all the subtasks within the summary group, such as the overall duration for the group. Use the Outdent and Indent buttons on the toolbar to apply outlining. A context menu offers Expand and Collapse commands for working with the outlined tasks.

If you applied outlining to a list in Word or Excel and copy that information into the OpenProj spreadsheet, the pasted information doesn't retain its outlining. You need to reapply the outlining in OpenProj.

Creating Subtasks

OpenProj's toolbar provides the tools you need to apply outlining in the project plan: the Outdent and Indent buttons at the far right end of the toolbar. You select the tasks to which you want to make an outlining change and then click one of the buttons. Clicking the Outdent button *promotes* the selected tasks to the next higher outline level, while clicking the Indent button *demotes* the selected tasks to the next lower outline level, making them into subtasks.

Even though OpenProj offers two buttons, most novice users have an easier time outlining the project plan by working from the top down and thus only use the Indent button to demote tasks into subtasks. So, here's the easiest way to outline your project plan:

1. Identify the first task that you want to be a summary task and drag over the task ID (row) numbers for the tasks below that you want to demote into subtasks. You also can select a range of tasks to demote by clicking the *Name* **cell** for the first cell in the range and Shift+clicking the bottommost task in the range.

2. Click the **Indent** button on the toolbar. Or, if you've selected the task rows, you can right-click the row headings and click **Indent**. The selected tasks become subtasks and the task above them becomes a summary task, as illustrated in Figure 5.11. The summary task's cells in the task sheet appear in bold, and the Gantt bar for the summary task changes to a summary task bar.

3. Repeat Steps 1 and 2 to demote other groups of tasks and thus finish creating all the top-level summary tasks, as shown in Figure 5.12.

4. Create subsequent lower outline levels by selecting and demoting subtasks as needed.

If you do need to outdent (promote) one or more tasks to a higher level, select the task and click the **Outdent** button on the toolbar or, if you've selected the tasks by dragging over the task ID numbers, right-click the ID numbers and click **Outdent**.

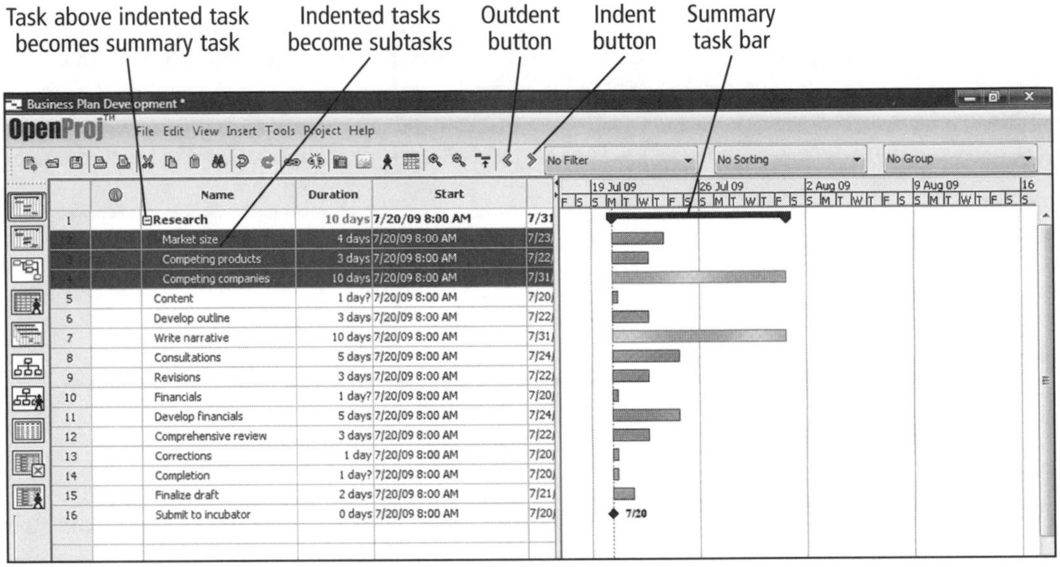

Task above indented task
becomes summary task   Indented tasks   Outdent   Indent   Summary
                            become subtasks   button   button   task bar

Figure 5.11 Demote tasks to make them into subtasks and promote the task above into a summary task.

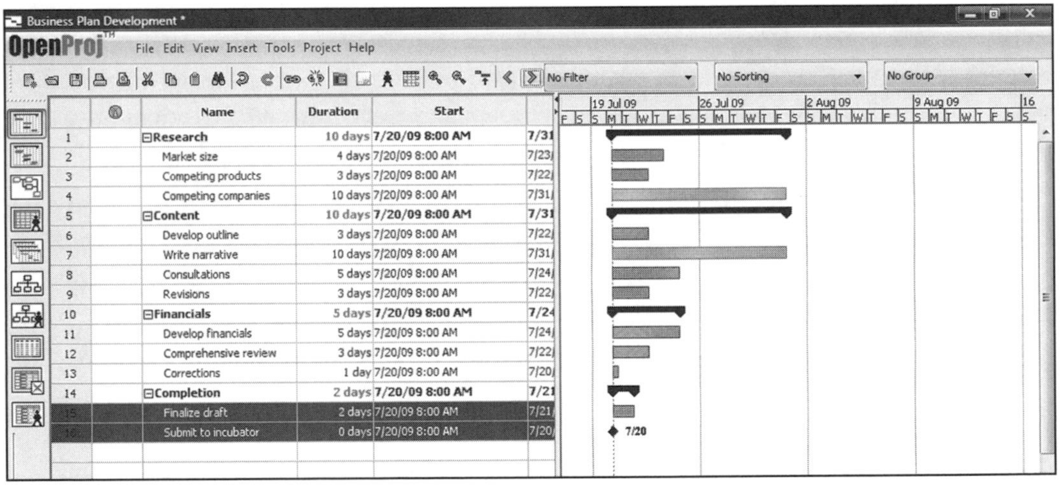

Figure 5.12 All the top-level summary tasks created in a project plan.

Keep in mind that you can still insert new tasks into the project plan after applying outlining. An inserted task typically takes on the subtask outline level of the nearest tasks, rather than the summary task outline level. For that reason, look carefully at how OpenProj treats the inserted task (as well as any tasks you move) and promote or demote it as needed.

Indenting a summary task typically also indents its subtasks. So, if you realize that a summary task needs to be at the same level as its subtasks, select and *demote* the summary task and then select and *promote* the subtasks.

Also, if you've already applied linking to schedule the project as described in Chapter 6, promoting a task and then demoting the tasks beneath it can break the link between the new summary and subtasks, creating unwanted scheduling changes. So you should, as much as possible, try to build and organize a thorough task list before linking. If that's not possible, be sure to examine the impact of every outline change on task links and scheduling.

Hiding and Redisplaying Subtasks

If you have a project plan that includes hundreds of subtasks—and believe me, many project managers do—you may neither need nor want to see all of the subtasks onscreen at all times. Outlining enables you to *collapse* (hide) subtasks when you don't need to see them, and then *expand* (redisplay) the subtasks at any later time. Examples of when you may want to collapse one or more summary groups of tasks include:

- **When you want to zero in on the activity in a single phase of the project.** You can collapse all the other summary groups and view only the subtasks for the phase under discussion.

- **When you need to discuss the "10,000 feet" level with stakeholders.** Stakeholders outside your project team often don't need to see information about every task in the project plan. Collapsing the outline to top-level summary tasks provides a framework for review while hiding details not presently needed.

- **When you want a schedule printout that includes some subtasks but not others.** OpenProj prints the current view as it appears onscreen. If you've collapsed one or more summary groups onscreen, the same summary groups will be collapsed in the printout. This can save paper and help you deliver only the information needed by particular team members or stakeholders.

You can use either context menu commands or the outline symbols (buttons) beside the task name for each summary task to collapse or expand subtasks. Figure 5.13 shows how these various controls and a collapsed summary group look.

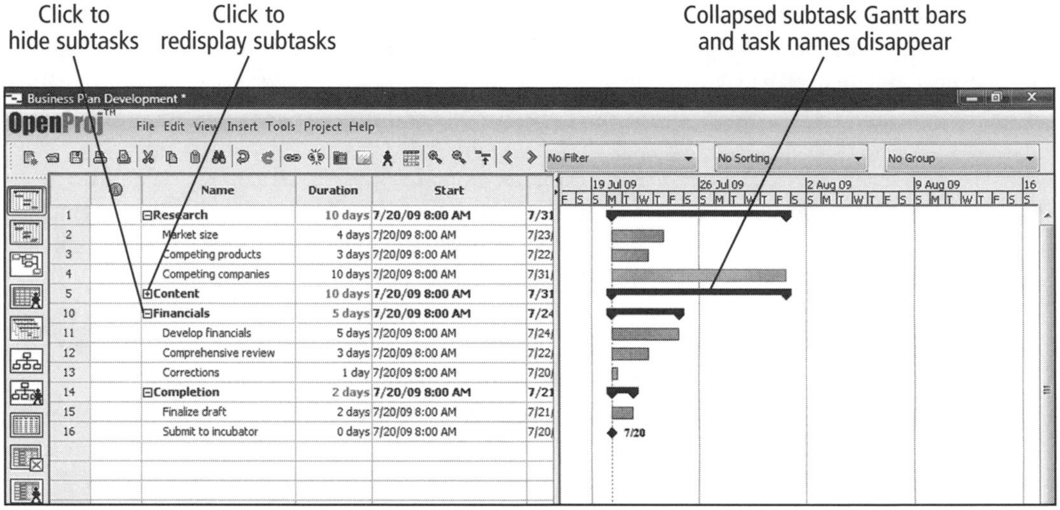

Click to   Click to   Collapsed subtask Gantt bars
hide subtasks   redisplay subtasks   and task names disappear

Figure 5.13 Collapsing a summary task hides its subtasks.

Use one of these techniques to collapse or expand subtasks:

- **Collapse (hide) tasks in a summary group.** Click the **minus (-) outline symbol** to the left of the summary task name, or right-click the **summary task ID (row)** number and then click **Collapse** in the context menu. The subtasks for the summary group collapse, hiding both the task names and the Gantt bars.

- **Expand (redisplay) tasks in a summary group.** Click the **plus (+) outline symbol** to the left of the summary task name, or click the **summary task ID (row)** number and then click **Expand** in the context menu. The subtasks for the summary group expand, redisplaying both the task names and the Gantt bars.

- **Collapse or expand all the subtasks.** In a lengthy project plan, it could be quite time-consuming to collapse and expand summary groups one by one. To collapse or expand all of the subtasks in the plan, drag over the task ID (row) numbers for all the tasks in the project plan. Then right-click a task ID number and click **Collapse** in the context menu to hide all the subtasks (see Figure 5.14) or the **Expand** command to redisplay all the subtasks.

If you have a lengthy list of tasks, making selecting tasks by dragging over row numbers difficult, you can click the gray **select all** button, which is the blank gray box where the row and column headings intersect at upper-left. Then right-click any task ID number to display the context menu so you can collapse or expand subtasks.

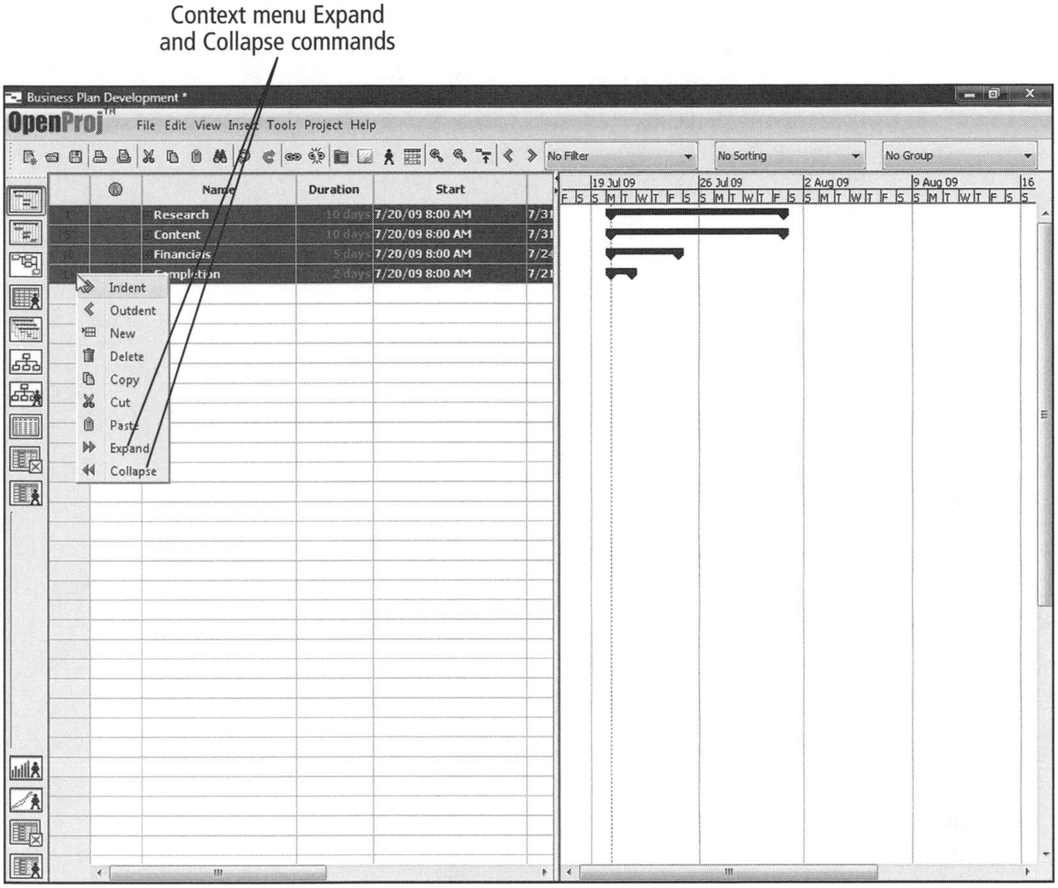

Context menu Expand
and Collapse commands

Figure 5.14 Select all the tasks and then use the context menu to hide (shown here) all subtasks or redisplay them.

Note that the outlining you apply appears in other views such as Tracking Gantt view, too, and you can collapse and expand information in those views using the same techniques. The Task Usage and Resource Usage views also use similar outline symbols for assignments, which you can collapse and expand, too.

Creating and Displaying WBS Codes

Unlike some other project management programs, OpenProj does not create WBS codes for you. This is in part because many organizations use custom WBS code schemes, and the custom codes need to be set up manually. A typical WBS code numbering system resembles an outline numbering scheme you may have seen used in an academic paper, report, or technical white paper. For example, if the project plan has five top-level summary tasks, they are numbered 1 through 5. The next level of subtasks below use a decimal followed by the subtask number. So, if summary task 2 has three subtasks, their WBS codes are 2.1, 2.2, and 2.3. In this way, WBS codes can give you a better sense than the task ID number of how a particular task fits in to the overall scheme for the project.

The most-used views do not show the WBS codes by default. One way that you can view and enter a WBS code for a particular task is to double-click the task in the task spreadsheet to open the Task Information dialog box for the task. Click the **Advanced** tab and then enter the desired code in the **WBS Code** text box, as in the example in Figure 5.15. Click **OK** to close the dialog box when you finish.

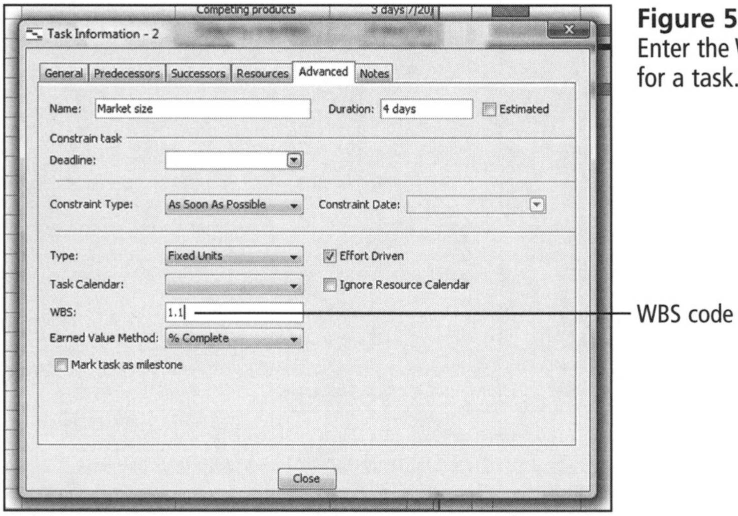

Figure 5.15
Enter the WBS code for a task.

If, however, you need to see and edit the WBS codes for all the tasks in the project plan, you can add a WBS code field to the task spreadsheet in the Gantt view by following these steps:

1. Right-click a gray field column heading, such as the *Name* field column heading, and click **Insert Column** in the context menu that appears.

2. Open the **Field** drop-down list in the Insert Column dialog box, press **W** on the keyboard to scroll down, and then click **WBS** to select it and close the drop-down list (see Figure 5.16).

3. Click **OK** to close the dialog box and add the field. As shown in Figure 5.17, the field shows existing WBS numbers and lets you specify or edit the numbers for each task.

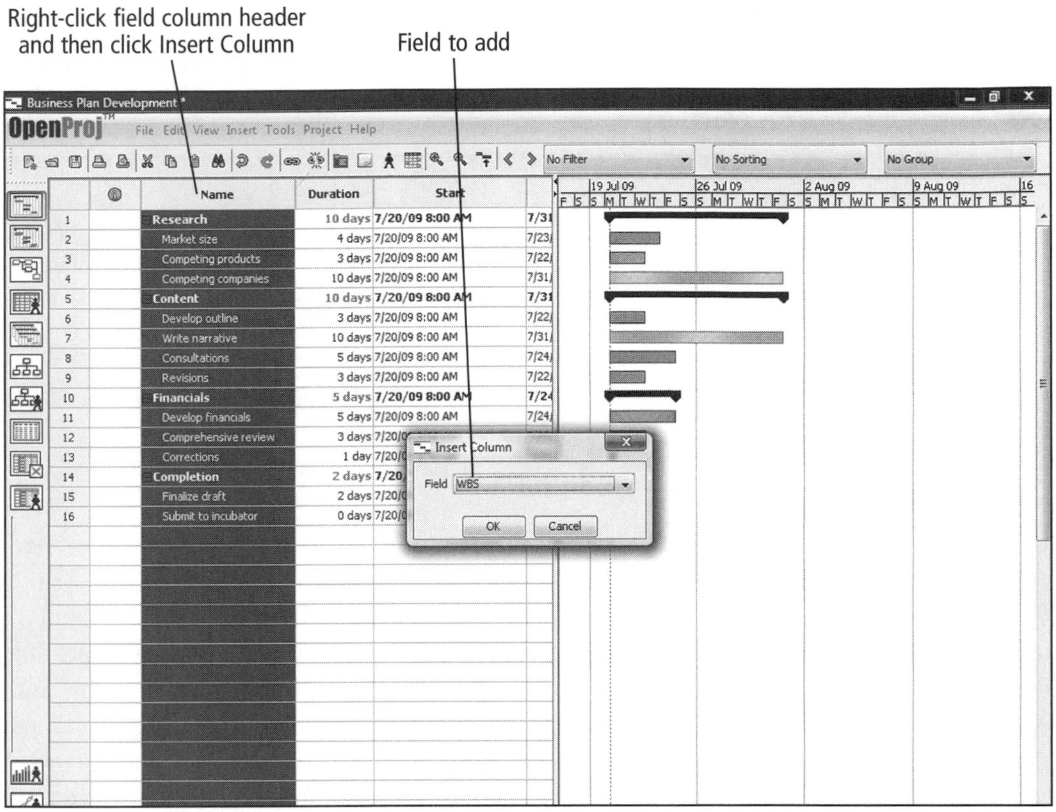

Right-click field column header
and then click Insert Column

Field to add

Figure 5.16 Adding the WBS code field.

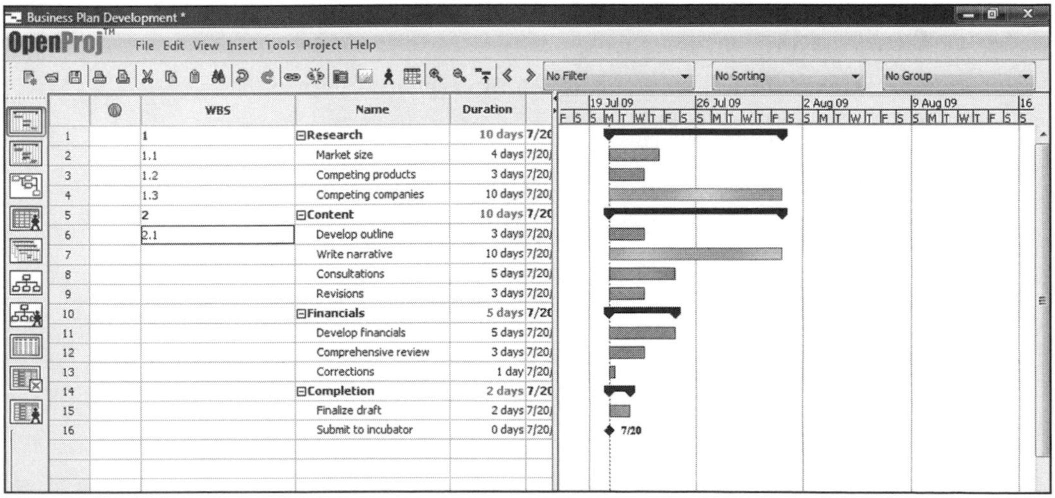

Figure 5.17 The WBS code field appears where inserted on the task spreadsheet.

The changes made to the task sheet of the Gantt view using the steps in this section apply to the current file only. Chapters 9 and 12 provide more details about working with fields, tables, and views.

If you reopen a file and don't see the field you've added, the wrong field set might be displayed. Right-click the **select all** button (where the row and column headers intersect at upper left), and click the appropriate field set. Often when you add a field such as the WBS field and save the file, OpenProj automatically creates a new field set to store your changes, and gives the field set the same name as the OpenProj file.

Chapter Review

In Chapter 5, you have covered some crucial skills for building any project plan. You learned the right way to create a task without compromising OpenProj's ability to recalculate the task's schedule at a later time. You learned how to use duration labels to gain precision in task scheduling and to create a special-purpose task called a milestone. Because planning itself is a process, you saw how to refine your schedule by moving, adding, deleting, and editing tasks, as well as how to undo changes that you decide you don't need. You learned the ins and outs of using outlining to organize the schedule, show and hide information, and identify tasks by WBS code rather than task number. Try the Review Questions and Projects now to ensure you've got a handle on the "need to know" stuff that you've just taken in.

Review Questions

Write your answers to the following questions on a sheet of paper.

1. Where do you enter the list of tasks?
2. What two pieces of information should you enter to create each new task?
3. Why should you not type dates for a task in the *Start* or *Finish* fields?
4. What's the duration you enter to have OpenProj mark a task as a milestone, and when would you use a milestone?
5. What is the task ID number for the task named *Competing products* in Figure 5.7?
6. Click the _____ to select the entire task.

7. In an outline, _____ tasks summarize the data for the _____ tasks under them.

8. Use the _____ button on the toolbar to demote tasks to the next lower outline level.

9. _____ subtasks hides their task names and Gantt bars.

10. What tab in the Task Information dialog box shows the WBS code?

Projects

To see the solution file created by completing the projects in this chapter, go to www.courseptr.com, click the **Downloads** link in the navigation bar at the top, type **Open-Proj** or this book's ISBN-10 number in the search text box, and then click **Search Downloads**.

Project 1

1. Create a new, blank project file with the Project Name *Site Search*.

2. Use the Project Information dialog box (**Project, Project Information**) to set a project Start Date of **2/2/10**. Leave **Standard** selected as the Calendar setting and click **Close**.

3. Save the file as *Site Search*.

Create a folder named *OpenProj Exercises* in your *Documents* or *My Documents* folder and save your exercise practice files there.

4. Make the following entries in the *Name* and *Duration* fields (leave *Duration* fields blank where indicated):

Assess Needs

Infrastructure   4d

Space   1w

Parking   3d

Expansion   2w

Document   1w

Interview Realtors   2w

Hire Realtor   2d

Identify Site	
Review Listings	3d
Visit Listings	2w
Purchase Site	
Write Offer Contract	4h
Negotiate Contract	6d
Secure Financing	1w
Schedule Closing	0
Final Site Review	2h
Closing	4h
Possession	0

5. Right-click the task ID for **task 7**, *Interview Realtors*, and click **New**.

6. Enter **Identify Realtor and Site** as the name for the new task.

7. Right-click the task ID for **task 13**, *Purchase Site*, and click **New**.

8 Enter **Select Site** and **0** as the name and duration for the new task.

9. Select **task 19** and cut (**Edit, Cut**) and paste (**Edit, Paste**) it to move it above task 14.

10. Click the **Undo** button to return task 19 to the prior location.

11. Save your changes to the file.

Project 2

1. Working in the *Site Search* file, use the **Indent** button on the toolbar to convert the following groups of tasks to subtasks:

   Tasks 2 through 6

   Tasks 8 through 13

   Tasks 15 through 16

   Tasks 18 through 21

2. Use the **Undo** button on the toolbar to undo your two most recent changes.

3. Use the **Indent** button on the toolbar to once again indent tasks 15 through 16 and tasks 18 through 21.

4. Demote task 17.

5. Demoting task 17 caused an unwanted demotion of tasks 18 through 21, so use the **Outdent** button on the toolbar to promote tasks 18 through 21.

6. Save your changes to the file.

Project 3

1. Use the - (**minus**) outline symbol to collapse the subtasks under the *Assess Needs* summary task.

2. Collapse the tasks under the other two summary tasks.

3. Use the + (**plus**) outline symbol to expand the subtasks under the *Identify Realtor and Site* summary task.

4. Drag over all the task ID numbers, right-click an ID number, and click **Expand**.

5. Right-click the **Name** field header and then click **Insert Column**.

6. Open the **Field** drop-down list, press **W**, and then click **WBS**.

7. Click **OK** to finish adding the WBS code field to the task spreadsheet.

8. Save your changes to the file and then close the file.

 If you reopen the *Site Search* file and don't see the *WBS* field, the wrong field set might be displayed. Right-click the **select all** button (where the row and column headers intersect at upper left), and click **Site Search** in the menu that appears.

CHAPTER 6

SCHEDULING THE PROJECT BY LINKING TASKS

This Chapter Teaches You How To:

- Link tasks to build the project schedule
- Link two tasks or many tasks at one time
- Understand the four different types of links
- Use the Task Information (or Resource Information) dialog box
- Change the link type
- Unlink tasks
- Use lead time or lag time with a link

If you've ever watched a house being built, you've seen that the carpenters can't build the frame until after the foundation has been built. Just as construction tasks have to proceed in the proper order to ensure that the house is sound, your project's tasks have to be scheduled in the right order to ensure a successful outcome. This chapter teaches you how to use linking to specify the proper order for tasks, which in turn develops the overall schedule for the project plan. You'll learn how to create links, what link types are available and how to use them, and how to change or remove links. The chapter also teaches you about lead time and lag time, which are settings that work with links to provide greater scheduling accuracy.

Why Using Linking Works Best

While the tasks you list in your project represent discrete actions, each of those actions typically has some type of relationship with other activities in the project. For example, you will need to gather client specifications before designing a new backup storage system for the client. Without knowing how much backup space the client needs, you would likely create a system that's too small or too large, thus failing to meet the client's requirements even though you might have successfully completed the other step for creating the system project. Other tasks can be related in an even more tangible way. For example, you can't install network equipment until you first purchase the equipment.

Those relationships between tasks—called *dependencies* in project management lingo—determine the order in which tasks should occur. After you place tasks in the proper sequence, the order plus the durations of the tasks result in the overall project schedule. In OpenProj, you apply *links* to determine the dependencies between tasks, which also schedules or *sequences* the tasks. When you apply a link in OpenProj, you indicate that on or around the time one task finishes, the next task should start.

Apply links to schedule tasks rather than typing in dates. Typing dates automatically puts a Start No Earlier Than constraint on the task, which can interfere with schedule calculation and artificially hold a task to a date which no longer makes sense. The section called "Using a Task Constraint" in Chapter 9 explains how and when to apply constraints.

The last chapter emphasized that you should avoid typing dates for tasks when building your project plan. That's because instead of typing dates, you should apply links to determine the schedules for tasks and the project. Linking tasks rather than typing dates provides these benefits:

- **Linking saves time when you build the plan.** You don't have to work with a calendar to identify the start and finish date for each task. OpenProj calculates those dates for you based on the links you apply.

- **Linking focuses your attention on the flow of activities, not the dates.** Really scrutinizing the relationships and sequence of the project activities puts you in a better position to identify potential pressure points and bottlenecks in the schedule.

- **Linking works with the calendar to make the plan more accurate and realistic.** OpenProj will automatically skip nonworking days that you've specified in the custom calendar you created for your project. Your project plan won't be realistic from the start unless it adheres to the basic "ground rules" you've set up in the calendar.

- **Linking makes changing the schedule more manageable.** Rather than having to type in new dates for dozens of tasks, you simply change the schedule for one task; OpenProj recalculates the start and finish dates for all subsequent linked tasks.

- **Linking enables you to create reusable project plan files.** When all the tasks in a project plan are properly linked, you only need to change the project Start date in the Project Information dialog box to reschedule the entire project. If you often manage very similar types of projects, making a copy of a project plan file that you've already built will save you a tremendous amount of time.

Applying a Default Link

When you apply a link, you are indicating that one task's schedule is dependent on another task's. OpenProj calls the dependent task the *successor*, and the linked task that drives the successor's schedule is called the *predecessor*. Although the predecessor task usually precedes the successor task in terms of their schedules, that isn't always the case; these names identify the fact that the schedule for one task (the predecessor), *drives* or determines the schedule for another task (the successor), no matter when either task occurs.

By default, OpenProj assumes that the finish date of a predecessor task drives the start date of the successor task, making the default link type a *FS (finish-to-start)* link. This link by default schedules the successor task to start immediately after the predecessor task finishes. On the Gantt chart, the linked tasks look like Figure 6.1.

As you can see in Figure 6.1, OpenProj calculates the *Start* date for task 3, scheduling it to start immediately after task 2 finishes. If you changed the *Duration* for task 2, OpenProj would reschedule task 3 accordingly. Linking (rather than typing dates) preserves OpenProj's ability to recalculate the schedule as individual tasks change.

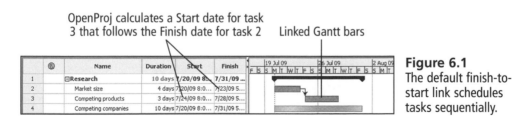

OpenProj calculates a Start date for task 3 that follows the Finish date for task 2   Linked Gantt bars

Figure 6.1
The default finish-to-start link schedules tasks sequentially.

Linking Two Tasks

When you link tasks, you select them first and then apply the link. The links you create should reflect the reality of how tasks must proceed in the schedule. If you have a list of six tasks, for example, task 1 might be linked to task 2, but it also might be linked to task 6. Create additional links as needed to reflect the schedule of work between dependent tasks.

On the other hand, don't create links that imply dependencies where none exist, because doing so creates a needlessly complex project plan that will be harder to manage and track later. Before you add each link, make sure you take a minute to think about whether a schedule dependency really exists between the tasks, or whether you're just tempted to add the link for cosmetic reasons (to make tasks look a certain way in the Gantt chart).

The steps for linking two tasks are simple:

1. Select the two tasks that you want to link. If the tasks are listed one after the other in the task spreadsheet, you can drag over the task ID (row) numbers. If the tasks are not on consecutive rows, click the first task and then **Ctrl+click** the second task.

 OpenProj makes the task you select first the predecessor. So, if you select a task lower in the list first when selecting tasks, OpenProj schedules the lower task earlier, which may be the opposite of your intent. Be sure to select tasks in the right order before linking them.

---

2. Click the **Link** button on the toolbar, or choose **Edit, Link**. The button has a picture of a linked chain on it. OpenProj applies the link and schedules the tasks, as shown in Figure 6.2.

As you apply links in this way, OpenProj builds the schedule for the project plan. Each Gantt bar illustrates the schedule for a particular task, laying it out along the timeline defined in the time axis along the top of the Gantt chart.

Link button

		®	Name	Duration	Start	Finish
	1		⊟**Research**	17 days	7/20/09 8:...	8/11/09
	2		Market size	4 days	7/20/09 8:0...	7/23/09 5.
	3		Competing products	3 days	7/24/09 8:0...	7/28/09 5.
	4		Competing companies	10 days	7/29/09 8:0...	8/11/09 5.
	5		⊟**Content**	10 days	7/20/09 8:...	7/31/09 .
	6		Develop outline	3 days	7/20/09 8:0...	7/22/09 5.
	7		Write narrative	10 days	7/20/09 8:0...	7/31/09 5.
	8		Consultations	5 days	7/20/09 8:0...	7/24/09 5.
	9		Revisions	3 days	7/20/09 8:0...	7/22/09 5.
	10		⊟**Financials**	5 days	7/20/09 8:...	7/24/09 .
	11		Develop financials	5 days	7/20/09 8:0...	7/24/09 5.
	12		Comprehensive review	3 days	7/20/09 8:0...	7/22/09 5.
	13		Corrections	1 day	7/20/09 8:0...	7/20/09 5.
	14		⊟**Completion**	2 days	7/20/09 8:...	7/21/09 .
	15		Finalize draft	2 days	7/20/09 0.0...	7/21/09 5.
	16		Submit to incubator	0 days	7/20/09 8:0...	7/20/09 8.

Figure 6.2 Tasks 3 and 4 also have been linked with an FS link.

Select the tasks to link and then click the **Link** button on the toolbar to apply the default link type, an FS (*finish-to-start*) link.

Understanding Timephased Information

Any schedule or OpenProj view like the Gantt view that plots work over time is called a *timephased diagram* or *view*. Note that if you move tasks around in a view that's not timephased, such as the Network view, keep in mind that making changes in such a view might change the applied links. So, you're better off applying links where you can see the impact, as in a timephased view like the Gantt view.

Linking Multiple Tasks

If linking two tasks saves you some time, just think how much time you'll save when you link even more tasks at one shot. By selecting and linking multiple tasks, you can build out a lengthy schedule in a matter of minutes.

To link multiple tasks, drag over the task ID numbers (or use Ctrl+click with the ID numbers or task names) to make your selections, and then click the **Link** button. For example, Figure 6.3 shows that finish-to-start links have been applied to tasks 4 and 6 through 9. Using Ctrl+click to select all of the tasks made it possible to skip the summary task, 5, which should not be linked.

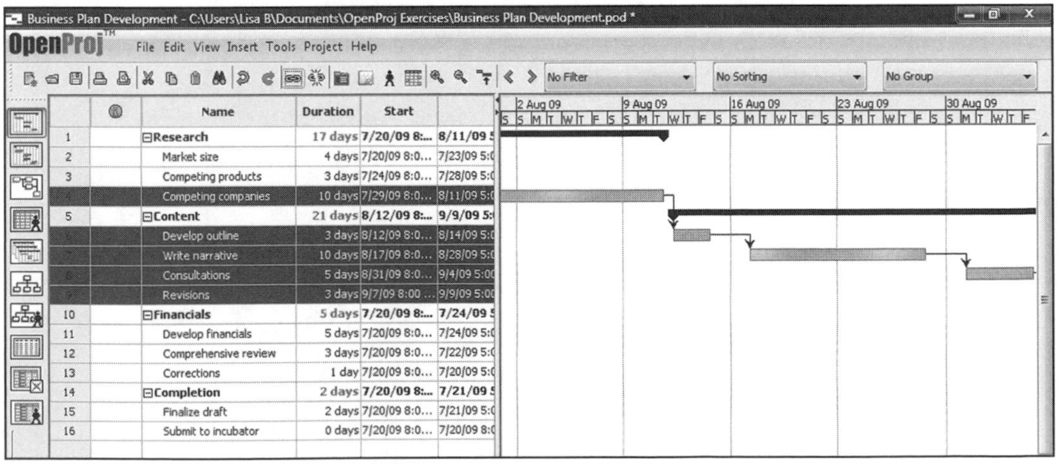

Figure 6.3 Save even more time by selecting and linking multiple tasks.

Unless you have specialized reasons for doing so, do not link summary tasks. You want to link the detail tasks that represent work and dates in the schedule, not the summary information. Recurring tasks also often do not drive any specific subsequent tasks, so they may not need to be linked to other tasks.

Working with the Task Information Dialog Box

The Task Information dialog box, which you saw in Chapter 5, offers several tabs where you can work with settings for a task. Some of these settings are available via the typically-used views in OpenProj as well.

To open the Task Information dialog box for any task, use either of these methods:

- Double-click any cell in the task.
- Click any cell in the task, and then click the **Task Information** button on the toolbar.

As shown in Figure 6.4, the Task Information dialog box offers several tabs of information pertaining to the task you double-clicked or selected to display the dialog box.

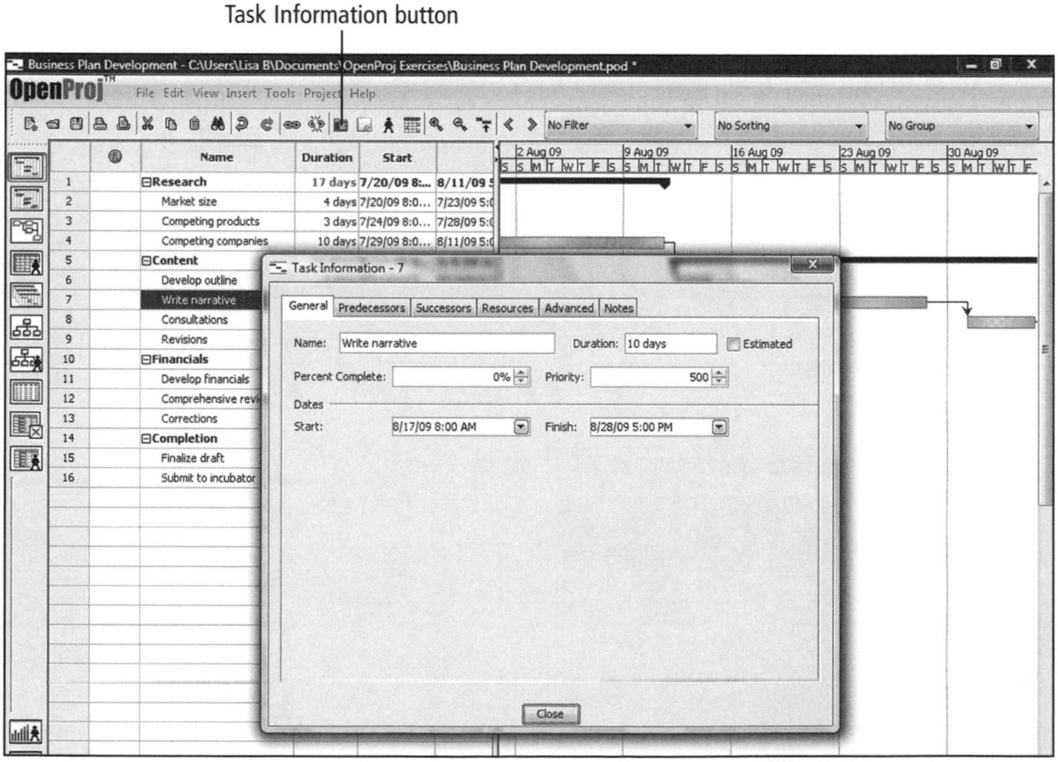

Task Information button

Figure 6.4 The Task Information dialog box offers a centralized location for finding the settings for adjusting a task.

You will see how to use settings on the available tabs as the book progresses. Click a tab to make its settings available, and then make the needed changes. In particular, you will see how to use the settings on the Predecessors tab in this chapter. No matter which tab you use, make the changes you want, and then click **Close** to close the dialog box when finished.

The Resource Information dialog box works much like the Task Information dialog box. You'll learn about Resource Information in the section titled "Opening the Resource Information Dialog Box" in Chapter 7.

 Double-click a task cell in the task spreadsheet portion of the Gantt view to open the Task Information dialog box. This dialog box offers a number of tabs where you can examine and change task settings.

Understanding and Using Other Link Types

You already know from life that events don't flow one after the other in a neat, convenient sequence. Nor will the tasks in the projects you manage. Some tasks kick off at the same time but finish at different times. Others need to finish at roughly the same time. OpenProj enables you to map out the reality of how your tasks will flow by using three additional link types in a project plan:

- **SS (Start-to-Start).** In this type of link, the successor task can start any time after the predecessor starts. By default, OpenProj schedules the predecessor and successor to start at the same time. You should use this type of link for tasks that run concurrently. For example, say you have three newsletter tasks named *Writing*, *Editing*, and *Design*. Workflow in your organization requires that a project design cannot start until the editing starts. So, you can apply an SS link between the *Editing* and *Design* tasks to reflect the stipulation that design may not begin until editing begins, but the tasks can run concurrently. Figure 6.5 shows example start-to-start links.

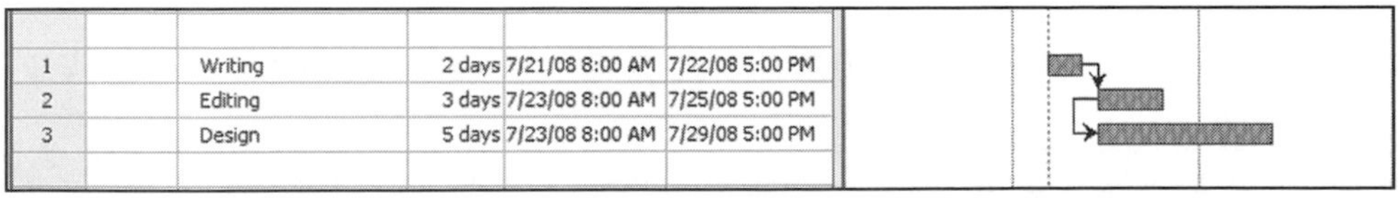

1		Writing	2 days	7/21/08 8:00 AM	7/22/08 5:00 PM
2		Editing	3 days	7/23/08 8:00 AM	7/25/08 5:00 PM
3		Design	5 days	7/23/08 8:00 AM	7/29/08 5:00 PM

Figure 6.5 SS (start-to-start) links enable OpenProj to schedule tasks to run concurrently, which means a successor can start after the predecessor starts.

- **FF (Finish-to-Finish).** When you apply this type of link, the successor task can finish any time after the predecessor finishes. By default, OpenProj schedules the predecessor and successor to finish at the same time. As with an SS link, the tasks joined by an FF link run roughly at the same time. Going back to the newsletter example, *Proofreading* and *Page Layout* tasks can run roughly concurrently, but the last round of proofreading must finish before final page layout corrections are made, as illustrated in Figure 6.6. (In the example in Figure 6.6, I made an additional scheduling adjustment—adding some lag time—because in the real world the example successor would have to finish after the predecessor. You'll learn about lag time shortly.)

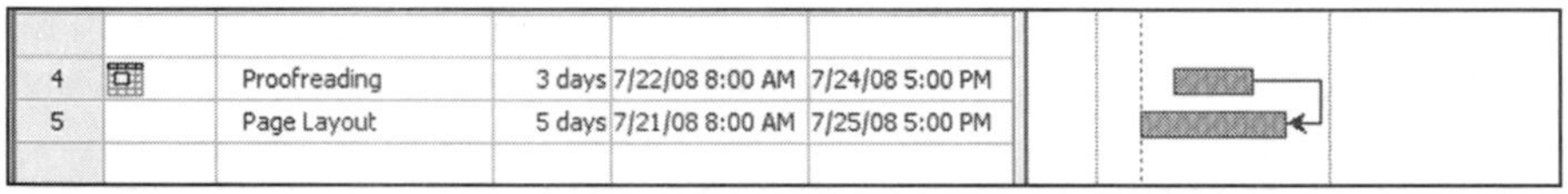

| 4 | | Proofreading | 3 days | 7/22/08 8:00 AM | 7/24/08 5:00 PM | |
| 5 | | Page Layout | 5 days | 7/21/08 8:00 AM | 7/25/08 5:00 PM | |

Figure 6.6 An FF (finish-to-finish) link means that the successor can finish after the predecessor finishes.

- **SF (Start-to-Finish).** This type of link tells OpenProj that the successor task can finish after the predecessor task begins. By default, OpenProj schedules the successor task to finish just before the predecessor starts, although in the example in Figure 6.7, adjustments again have been made to show how two tasks will overlap in the real world. For example, if you're scheduling the next issue of your newsletter, the successor task *Topic List* can finish any time after the *Next Issue Plan* task begins. As you might guess, this is an unusual link type that isn't used as often as the other link types. But other examples include situations where you need to order an item or materials in advance of the completion of a successor task. For example, if you need to order a kitchen sink two weeks ahead of finishing the install for the sink, you can create a SF link between the *Order Sink* task and the *Install Sink* task, and add two weeks of delay (lag time, discussed later) between them.

| 6 | | Next Issue Plan | 3 days | 7/23/08 8:00 AM | 7/25/08 5:00 PM | |
| 7 | | Topic List | 2 days | 7/23/08 8:00 AM | 7/24/08 5:00 PM | |

Figure 6.7 An SS (start-to-finish) link means that the successor can finish after the predecessor starts.

The *link lines* between the Gantt bars illustrate the link type. An FS link line joins the right end of the predecessor bar to the left end of the successor bar. An SS link line joins the left ends of both bars (Figure 6.5). An FF link line joins the right ends of both bars (Figure 6.6). And an SF link line joints the left end of the predecessor bar to the right end of the successor bar (Figure 6.7).

Changing a Link Type

When you want a task to use a link type that's not a default FS link, you have to change the link type after you apply the FS link. Changing the link type is a manual process, but it should be. As part of your diligent planning process, you need to consider how every two linked tasks should be scheduled and choose the link type that best reflects the desired schedule.

 Because the various link types enable you to capture a fairly realistic picture of how tasks will proceed in a project, adding the links is sometimes thought of as *mapping* or *modeling work-flow*.

When you work with links, you'll often work with the successor task to view or change link information. The predecessor task's Task ID number is used to identify the link. So, if tasks 9 and 10 are linked, the successor task 10 lists task 9 as a predecessor.

You can change the link type in one of three ways:

- Click the **link line** between the tasks. (The mouse pointer turns into a cross-hair when it's positioned on the link line.) Open the **Type** drop-down list in the Task Dependency dialog box that appears (see Figure 6.8), click the desired link type, and then click **OK**.

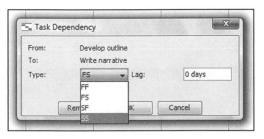

Figure 6.8
Double-click the **link line** to use the Task Dependency dialog box to change the link type.

- Double-click any cell in the successor task in the task spreadsheet to open its Task Information dialog box. (You also can click the task and click the **Task Information** button on the toolbar.) Click the *Predecessors* tab. Open the Type drop-down list for any listed predecessor, as shown in Figure 6.9, and click the desired link type. (If you need to work with more than one entry, press **Enter** after finishing each one.) Click **OK** to close the dialog box and apply the change.

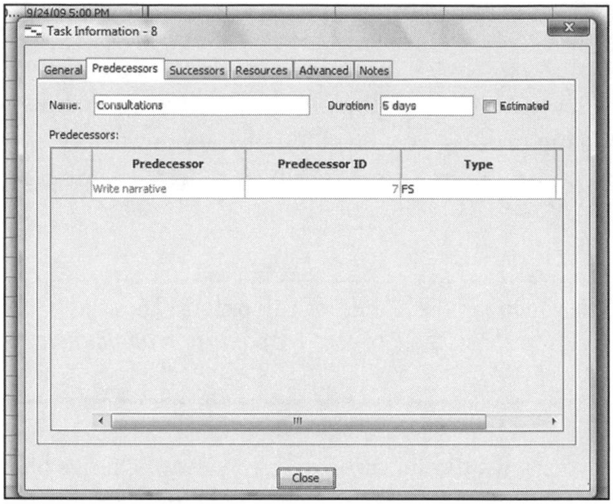

Figure 6.9
Double-click a
successor task cell in
the task spreadsheet
to use this dialog box
to change the link
type.

■ If you prefer to type rather than use the mouse, scroll the task spreadsheet part of
the view to the right so that you can see the *Predecessors* column. As shown in Figure 6.10, you can change the link to a type other than the default by adding the
abbreviation for an SS, FF, or SF link. Click the ***Predecessors*** cell, click again to
place the insertion point in the cell to the right of the predecessor task number,
type the desired link type abbreviation, and press **Enter**. Note that if a task has
multiple predecessors, OpenProj inserts a comma in between them.

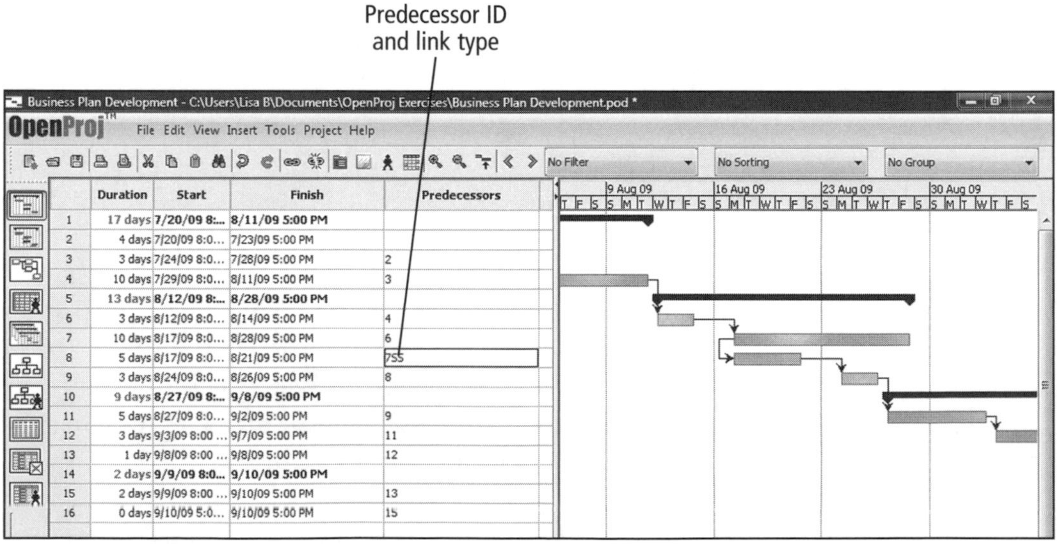

Figure 6.10 Including the link type abbreviation with the predecessor task's ID number in the
Predecessors field changes the link type.

After you change the link type, OpenProj recalculates the schedule for the successor task as required. `You need to review the impact of every change you make in your project plan to ensure that a minor change hasn't disrupted the schedule in any unexpected way. For example, look at the finish date for the final task in the project in either the *Finish* column or the Project Information dialog box to ensure that the change didn't push the project finish date beyond the date you want.

Removing a Link

There will be times when you end up with a link that's unwanted or otherwise no longer needed. For example, if you reassign a task to a resource from another team, the task's schedule may no longer be dependent on its previous predecessor.

You can select two linked tasks and then choose **Edit**, **Unlink** to remove the link. The toolbar offers an Unlink button, which looks like a broken chain, that you can click to remove a link between selected tasks.

As with applying and changing links, make sure that you examine the project plan carefully after you remove any link. You don't want any unwanted changes to come as a surprise to you later. In particular, note that unless the task has constraints applied to it, the unlinked successor task will be rescheduled to start on the project start date, as usual. You will need to adjust the schedule for the task in that case, preferably by linking it to another predecessor.

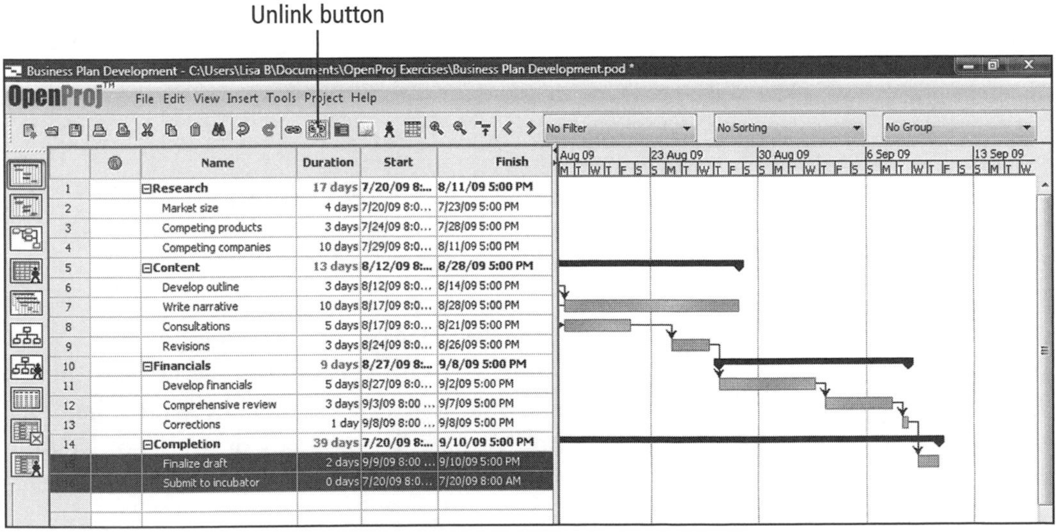

Figure 6.11 You can remove the link between selected tasks.

Understanding Lead Time and Lag Time

Even applying the right link types doesn't go far enough in reflecting reality because time and schedules are more fluid than a basic link can allow. Although tasks might seem to follow one after another, they really flow together more loosely, overlapping or occurring after a delay. In OpenProj, you schedule *lead time* or *lag time* along with a link to achieve more accuracy in representing how linked task schedules really compare.

With an FS link, *lead time* overlaps the task schedules, while *lag time* inserts a delay between the tasks. You enter lead or lag time in the Task Dependency dialog box or the *Predecessors* field.

When to Use Lead and Lag Time

With a default finish-to-start link, *lead time* represents a period during which the tasks overlap. For example, in a new home construction project, you break down the rough electrical work into three tasks called *Basement Electrical Rough*, *Floor 1 Electrical Rough*, and *Floor 2 Electrical Rough*, you assign two days of duration to each task, and you link them in sequence with FS links. However, you know that the *Floor 1 Electrical Rough* task can really start one day before *Basement Electrical Rough* finishes, meaning that the tasks overlap in time. Likewise, *Floor 2 Electrical Rough* can start a day before *Floor 1 Electrical Rough* finishes, so those two tasks overlap, as well. In this case, you would assign lead time to the links to set up the overlap so that the series of tasks which originally added up to six days of duration compresses down to four days of duration. Figure 6.12 illustrates this scenario.

8		Basement Electrical Rough	2 days	7/21/08 8:00 AM	7/22/08 5:00
9		Floor 1 Electrical Rough	2 days	7/22/08 8:00 AM	7/23/08 5:00
10		Floor 2 Electrical Rough	2 days	7/23/08 8:00 AM	7/24/08 5:00

Figure 6.12 Lead time overlaps tasks linked with FS links.

Lag time represents the opposite of lead time—a delay or non working period between two tasks. Building on the example shown in Figure 6.12, say you need to add *Finish Electrical Rough* as a task, but you know it should start a week after the last of the other three tasks finishes to allow for an inspection. Adding five days (a workweek) of lag time to the link between *Floor 2 Electrical Rough* and *Finish Electrical Rough* builds in the necessary break, as illustrated in Figure 6.13.

Whether you've added lag time or lead time, keep in mind that the Lag text box entries you make remain in place even when you change task durations. You need to change the Lag entry separately, if required.

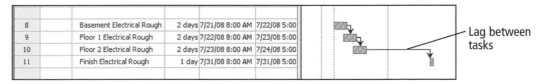

Figure 6.13 Lag time inserts a delay between tasks linked with FS links.

 If you will be using your project plan to get accurate tracking of actual person hours of work and accumulated costs, do *not* just extend task durations rather than taking the step of adding lag times. Extending a task's duration adds hours of work plus the costs associated with using the assigned resources to plan totals calculated by OpenProj. If no real work is occurring, the totals will be artificially high. Proper use of lag time eliminates this problem. If you will be sharing your file with other users or a version of the plan file will be reused over time, always add a task note to document how much lag or lead time you added and why you added it. Chapter 9 explains how to add a task note.

Of course, lead and lag times behave a little differently with other link types. For example, adding lag time to a start-to-start link delays the start of the successor task and impacts whether and by how much the two tasks continue to overlap. Lead time with a start-to-start link schedules the successor task to start before the predecessor.

When applying lead time and lag time to task links, always examine the impact of any change to make sure the resulting schedule reflects what you intended.

Specifying Lead or Lag Time

Specifying lead time and lag time can be a little more cryptic than specifying a link type because you enter it as a positive or negative duration value, like this:

- **Lead times are negative values.** For example, -2d represents two days of lead time, and -2h represents two hours of lead time.
- **Lag times are positive values.** For example, 2d (+2d) represents two days of lag time, while 2h (+2h) represents two hours of lag time.

If you do not enter a duration abbreviation with lead or lag time, OpenProj assumes that you mean days. Also note that you can enter lead and lag times as percentages in the task sheet, such as +25% to specify lag time equal to 25% of the predecessor task's duration. For example, as shown in Figure 6.14, if you have a one-day task that's a successor to a 4-day task and specify 25% lag time, the scheduled lag time is one day. (In this case, the lag time also spans two non working days over the weekend.)

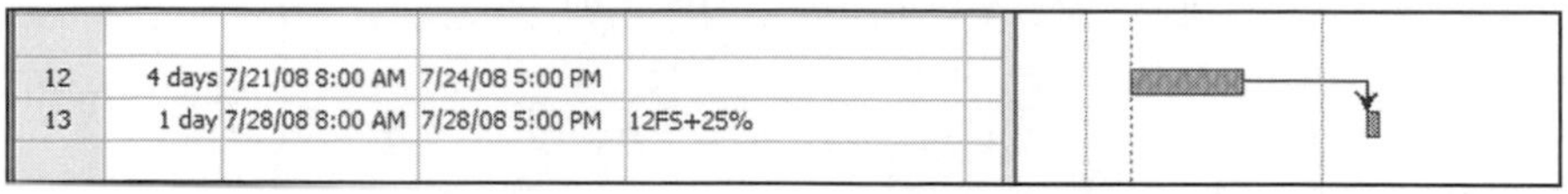
12
4 days 7/21/08 8:00 AM 7/24/08 5:00 PM
13
1 day 7/28/08 8:00 AM 7/28/08 5:00 PM 12FS+25%

Figure 6.14 Lag time can be entered as a percentage of the duration of the predecessor task.

You can add lead or lag time to a link in two of the three locations where you can change the link type:

- Click the **link line** between the tasks. Change the **Lag** entry in the Task Dependency dialog box (see Figure 6.15) by selecting and typing over the existing entry or clicking the spinner arrow buttons, and then click **OK**.

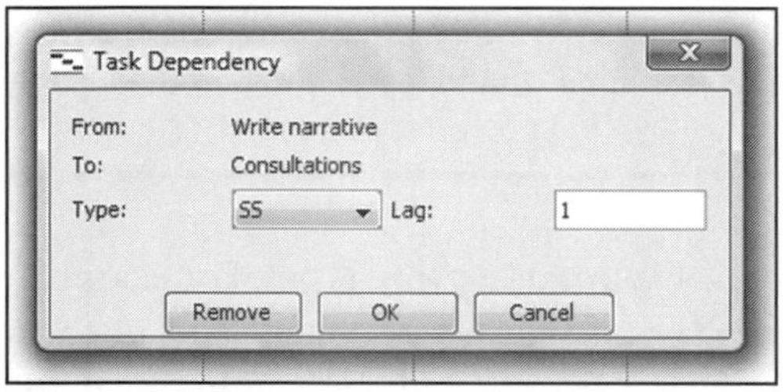
Task Dependency
From:
Write narrative
To:
Consultations
Type:
SS
Lag:
1
Remove
OK
Cancel

Figure 6.15 Specify lead or lag time in the Lag text box.

> **TIP** You don't have to type the + (plus sign) for a lag time entry in the Task Dependency dialog box. Just enter the desired value.

- Working on the task spreadsheet instead, scroll the sheet to the right so that you can see the *Predecessors* column. As shown in Figure 6.16, you can add the lead or lag time by typing a positive or negative value, plus a duration abbreviation. Click the ***Predecessors*** cell, click to place the insertion point in the cell to the right of the predecessor task number, type the desired lead or lag entry, and press **Enter**.

Lag Time and Buffers as Planning Tools

According to project management gurus, what you're about to read is not necessarily proper project planning advice. Professional project managers strive to make every project plan perfect—mapping out a schedule that will be as close to reality as possible.

However, when I've managed projects, I found it more prudent to always build in a cushion somewhere. You see, I accept the likelihood that something beyond my control might impact my project's schedule. And I also accept the reality that there is always some degree of a learning curve when planning and managing projects, so there's always the possibility that some task durations might be estimated incorrectly.

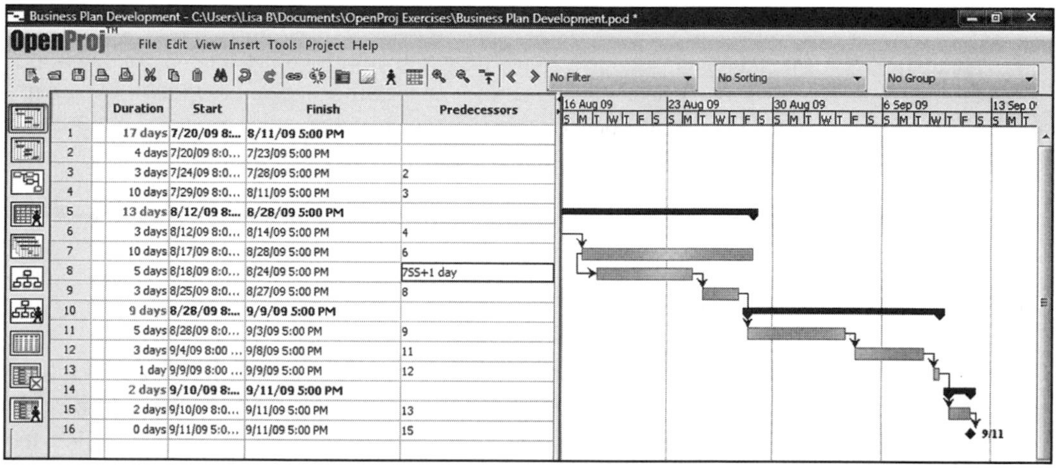

Figure 6.16 Add the lead or lag time in with the *Predecessors* field entry, as for task 8 shown here.

Although you can increase the length of a project plan overall by entering generous task durations, keep in mind that each duration will also represent hours of time and budgeted costs in your project plan once you assign resources. So, if you want to increase the project schedule without overly inflating the amount of work and costs scheduled, you build extra lag time in between tasks, instead.

You can add lag time by simply increasing the amount of lag time you would otherwise enter for some linked tasks. For example, if you are in the construction business and often order custom cabinetry that usually takes as little as three weeks to arrive but may take more, add four weeks of lag time rather than three between the task where you order the cabinets and the task where the cabinets are installed.

You also can add lag time between linked tasks where you wouldn't otherwise add lag time at all. For example, in a project that spans a few months, adding a day or so of lag time between two tasks per month can be a prudent way to allow for a margin of error in planning and execution.

If you need to have a cushion of extra time that's visible in the schedule and can be tracked, you can add in tasks that represent non working periods between tasks. As long as you don't assign resources to the tasks, OpenProj will not add in hours of work or costs for the tasks. With this method, the buffer of extra time is explicit and perhaps more visible. However, it should be clear to everyone involved in the project that the project manager retains ownership over deciding how and when to use the buffer, if needed. Achieving a theoretical idea of perfection is a great goal, but you should do what's right for your projects and your situation. It truly is better to "under-promise and over-deliver" if you want to keep your larger career moving in the real world.

> Some professional project managers would disagree with using lag time to create buffers. These project managers instead build in extra time for the schedule in the form of an extra task or tasks representing buffer time for the schedule. They then guard and dole out the buffer time as needed, decreasing the buffer task(s) duration by an amount equal to any increase in duration for "live" tasks in the plan.

Chapter Review

In Chapter 6, you saw how to move your list of tasks one step closer to a full-fledged project plan. You learned how to add basic finish-to-start links to tasks to sequence them in the schedule. You also learned about the other three link types—start-to-start, finish-to-finish, and start-to-finish—and how to change any link to another type. The chapter also taught you how to remove a link, and how to refine the schedule by using lead time and lag time with links. Finish up by working through the Review Questions and Projects now.

Review Questions

Write your answers to the following questions on a sheet of paper.

1. Why do you skip typing in *Start* and *Finish* dates for tasks?
2. How do you instead build the task schedules?
3. The _____ task drives the schedule of its _____ task.
4. Name the default task type and its abbreviation.
5. How do you link two tasks using the toolbar?
6. How do you display the Task Information dialog box?
7. What tab in the Task Information dialog box do you use to change the link type?
8. How do you open the Task Dependency dialog box?
9. Enter lead time as a _____ value and lag time as a _____ value.
10. Enter lead or lag time in the _____ text box in the Task Dependency dialog box.

Projects

> To see the solution files created by completing the projects in this chapter, go to www.courseptr.com, click the **Downloads** link in the navigation bar at the top, type **Open-Proj** or this book's ISBN-10 number in the search text box, and then click **Search Downloads**.

Project 1

1. Create a new, blank project file assigning the Project Name *Software Project*.
2. Use the Project Information dialog box (**Project, Project Information**) to set a project *Start* date of **6/14/10**. Leave **Standard** selected as the Calendar setting and click **OK**.
3. Save the file as *Software Project*.

 Create a folder named *OpenProj Exercises* in your *Documents* or *My Documents* folder and save your exercise practice files there.

---

4. Make the following entries in the *Name* and *Duration* fields:

Gather Client Requirements	4d
Write Specifications	2w
Client Review and Approval	2d
Launch Programming	0

5. Save your changes to the file and keep it open for the next project.

Project 2

1. Drag over the task ID numbers for all four tasks in the *Software Project* file.
2. Click the **Link** button to link them.
3. Leaving the tasks selected, click the **Unlink** button.
4. Choose **Edit, Link** to re-link the tasks.
5. Click the **link line** for the link between tasks 3 and 4. Select **FF** from the Type drop-down list in the Task Dependency dialog box, and then click **OK**.
6. Double-click any cell in task 2's row in the task spreadsheet.
7. Click the **Predecessors** tab, review the information about the predecessor task, and click **Close**.
8. Select the *Predecessors* cell for task 2, add a **-1** lag entry for the task 1 predecessor, and then press **Enter**.
9. Select the *Predecessors* cell for task 2, add a **+2** lag entry for the task 2 predecessor, and then press **Enter**.
10. Save your changes to the file and then close the file.

Project 3

1. Open the *Site Search* file you created during the Chapter 5 projects.
2. Save the file as *Site Search with Links.*
3. If the *WBS* field appears, right-click the **WBS** field column header and click **Hide Column**.
4. Select the following tasks and link them with FS links by clicking the **Link** button:

   2–6

   8–13

   15–21
5. Ctrl+click task ID numbers and then link the following pairs of tasks:

   6 and 8

   13 and 15
6. Change the links for tasks 3–5 to SS links by double-clicking each task, clicking the *Predecessors* tab in the Task Information dialog box, choosing **SS** from the Type drop-down list on the predecessor's row, and then clicking **OK**.
7. Click the link line between tasks 5 and 6, change the Lag entry to **-2d**, and then click **OK**.
8. Use the method of your choice to change the links as indicated for the following tasks:

   17   Change to SS link

   20   Add +2d lag

   21   Change to FF link
9. Save your changes to the file and close the file.

CHAPTER 7

LISTING THE RESOURCES YOU NEED

This Chapter Teaches You How To:

- Display Resources view
- Review resource information
- Add work and material resources
- Bring in resources from lists you already have
- Use generic or placeholder resources
- Understand and enter resource cost information
- Set up a resource's calendar

Each person has limited availability for getting work done. That's why most projects in organizations are tackled by teams of individuals. As the project manager, you bring the team together and guide decisions about which of the people involved will handle which tasks. You also are responsible for making sure that the team has the equipment and (in some cases) consumable materials needed to complete the assigned tasks. This chapter helps you shift your project planning in OpenProj from the "to do" perspective to the "who" perspective. You'll learn about the different types of resources you can use for a project and how to add different types of resources into the project plan. Most cost information also relates to resource usage, so the chapter explains how to add resource cost information. Finally, you'll see how to ensure proper scheduling by learning how to adjust a resource calendar.

Displaying Resources View

Until this point in your project planning, you've worked in the default Gantt view to add task information, organize tasks, and link them. To add the resources that you will assign to the tasks in your project plan, you have to switch to *Resources* view.

 Resources are the people, equipment, and consumable items used to complete project tasks. Enter resources in Resources view.

Opening Resources View

Resources view is another view you'll need to use for virtually every project plan file that you create. To open Resources view, click the **View** menu and then click **Resources** or click the **Resources** button, which is the fourth from the top in the view buttons along the left side of the screen. The Resources view immediately appears onscreen, as shown in Figure 7.1.

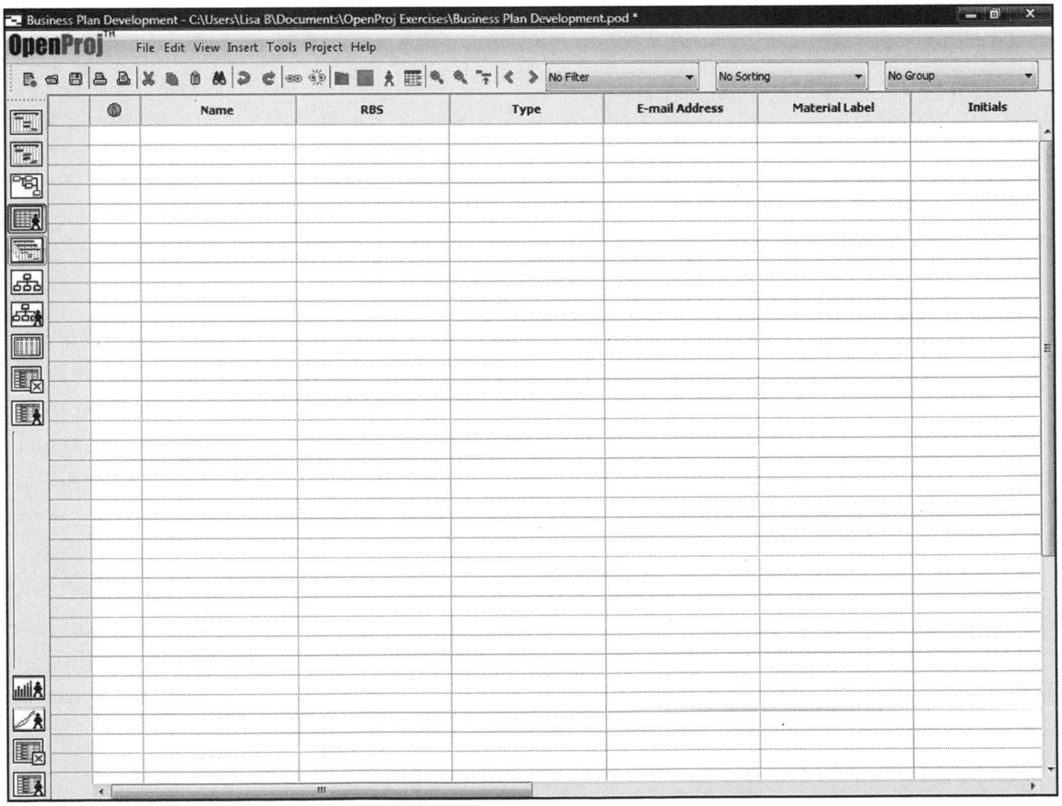

Figure 7.1 Use Resources view to add resources into the project plan.

Like the task spreadsheet portion of the Gantt view, the Resources view is a spreadsheet-like collection of rows and columns forming cells. After you make an entry in a cell, you can press the **right arrow** or **Tab** key to move to the next cell to the right, or press the **down arrow** or **Enter** to move down to the next row.

You can format and work with the Resources view using the same techniques as for the task spreadsheet. You'll learn about sheet formatting in Chapter 9.

 The buttons for resource-oriented views and for assigning resources have the silhouette of a smaller person. Want to work with resources? Click the button with the person on it!

Reviewing the Resources Fields

As in the task spreadsheet, each column in Resources view represents a field of information. And similarly, you don't have to use all of the fields in Resources view to set up a resource. For example, you have to enter information into the cost-related fields only if you plan to use OpenProj to track project cost information.

The first few fields enable you to specify some of the most essential resource information. In particular, you *must* use the *Name* and *Type* fields to set up each resource. These information-oriented fields include:

- **Indicators (i).** As in the task spreadsheet of the Gantt view, this column holds special icons that make you aware of certain conditions or notes pertaining to a resource. You'll learn more about the common resource indicators that appear in this column as needed in the book.

- **Name.** Enter the name that you want to use to identify the resource. You will see this name when you assign the resource to a task, and by default you will see this name on the Gantt graph beside the Gantt bar for any task to which the resource is assigned.

- **RBS.** Just as adding the WBS enables you to define the hierarchy of tasks in a project plan, you can use the *RBS* field in conjunction with the RBS view to define a hierarchy of resources for the project plan. See the later section called "Creating the Resource Hierarchy" to learn more.

- **Type.** This field offers a drop-down list that you use to specify the type of resource you are creating. You'll learn about the available resource types—work and material—shortly.

- **E-mail Address.** Use this field to enter the e-mail address for work resources, so you have that information at your fingertips.

- **Material Label.** If you choose Material in the *Type* field, you'll make an entry in this field to identify the quantity in which the material will be consumed. See "Entering a Material Resource" later in this chapter to learn more.

- **Initials.** You don't have to make an entry in this field at all. OpenProj will automatically fill it in for you. However, if think you might want to display initials on the Gantt chart, for example, you can make the entries that you want in this field.

- **Group.** You can make an entry in this field to identify whether a resource belongs to a particular department such as *Accounting* or *Engineering*, or if a resource can be identified by another category such as *Freelance* or *Consultant*.

The next field enables you to specify how much of the resource's time OpenProj should allocate to your schedule:

- **Max. Units.** If you press **Tab** to move on by this field, OpenProj will enter 100% by default. The percentage entry in this field indicates how much of the resource's daily scheduled work time will be allocated initially to each task to which you assign the resource. So, if a resource from another department can only work half-time for your project, enter 50% here. If the resource is a vendor sending three people for every assignment, enter 300%. Note that each time you assign the resource, you can either stick with the Max. Units entry you entered on Resources view or enter a new value to control the resource's units applied to that particular assignment.

If you will use OpenProj to track cost information for your project plan, you will need to use the next four cost-related fields. Most costs in business are related to hours of work or contracted usage amounts—that's why you specify most cost information on the Resources view:

- **Standard Rate.** You will make an entry in this field for most work and material resources. The amount you enter here tells OpenProj how much cost to add to the project for each hour of work assigned for the work resource or each quantity of usage assigned for a material resource. Think of this entry as the dollars per hour or cost per amount.

- **Overtime Rate.** You can make an entry in this field if you will need to account for overtime pay for a work resource. I have to caution you that OpenProj doesn't automatically kick in the overtime rate for you. You have to deploy a workaround to calculate costs correctly, a topic you'll learn more about in Chapter 11.

- **Cost Per Use.** You can make an entry in this field for any cost or material resource for which there is a flat charge every time you use the resource. For example, if the resource is a phone installer, it might charge a $30 fee for every installation, no matter how long it takes. That's a cost per use (Cost/Use).

Some resources might have both a Standard Rate and Cost Per Use. For example, a plumber might charge a flat service call fee of $50 (the Cost Per Use), plus an hourly rate of $60 (the Standard Rate).

- **Accrue At.** The entry in this field specifies how OpenProj accounts for the timing of resource costs in the budget for the project. The default entry, *Prorated*, means that OpenProj adds in costs at the time when work is scheduled (or scheduled work has been marked as completed). However, with some types of resources, the costs might apply at the *Start* or *End* of the assigned task. For example, if you only have to pay an external resource after the person finishes all work on assignments, select *End* as the *Accrue At* field choice for that resource.

The last field enables you to specify scheduling and identification information for each resource as needed:

- **Base Calendar.** If a work resource follows a calendar that's different from the base calendar that you've assigned to the project file in the Project Information dialog box, you need to choose the correct calendar for the resource from the drop-down list here. For example, you might have set a project to use the 24 Hours calendar, but human work resources work shorter hours, so you need to choose the Standard calendar or a custom calendar with fewer work hours.

Adding Resource Information

Now that you have a sense of the information that the fields in Resources view are set up to hold, you are ready to delve into the types of resources you can create in OpenProj, how to use each type of resource, and how to enter the right Resources view information for each type of resource. This section tells you what you need to know about creating Resources view entries for your project plan.

Understanding Resource Types

Assigning resources to tasks enables OpenProj to track two types of information: hours of work and costs. Sometimes the costs are associated with hours of work, but sometimes costs are associated with non-work-related situations such as usage of the resource (as in a *Cost/Use*), the amount of something consumed, or just a fee associated with the completion of a single task. To account for all of these various cost scenarios, OpenProj enables you to create two different types of resources.

Work resources have been available in OpenProj since the earliest versions. Use this type of resource for people contributing hours of work on a project. This includes people from your company; external resources like consultants, freelancers, temps, and contract employees; and persons from vendors that you hire such as a construction company. For each hour of work assigned to a work resource, OpenProj adds an hour's worth of cost for the resource to the project. Any time you assign a work resource to a task, hours of work will be added to the task, even if you only added a *Cost/Use* entry for the resource.

Material resources represent items or commodities consumed to complete tasks in the project. Think reams of paper, feet of wire, units of computers, cubic yards of concrete, and so on. These material resources are used for tasks and add costs to the project, but they don't add hours of work. This type of resource was added for more recent versions of OpenProj.

According to OpenProj's online help, a material resource also might include a piece of equipment used on a project. For practical purposes, it can be argued that some pieces of equipment for which you are charged on an hourly or daily basis, such as rented construction equipment, should be treated as a work resource so that OpenProj can account for costs automatically. Plus, the availability of a particular piece of equipment might affect the schedule of a task, more like a work resource than a material resource. So if you're more interested in the schedule and cost calculation and you pay an hourly rate to use a piece of equipment, treating the equipment as a work resource may be more appropriate. If, on the other hand, the schedule matters less and you don't want to add hours of work to the project when you assign the piece of equipment to a task and you pay a flat fee (cost per use) for the use of the equipment or your organization already owns the equipment, treating it as a material resource might be more appropriate.

Work resources typically represent people that add hours of work and have hourly costs. **Material resources** are consumables that you pay for by quantity, like quarts of oil, or pieces of equipment for which you pay a flat fee (or the equipment is already owned by the organization). For more accurate cost accounting, you may want to treat equipment for which you pay an hourly rate as a work resource, keeping in mind that this will inflate the overall work hours calculation.

Entering a Work Resource

Work resources typically require you to add information to the greatest number of fields in Resources view. You not only have to identify the resource, but you also have to enter the necessary cost and calendar information. Follow these steps to add a work resource to the list of resources in Resources view, entering only the most essential information at this point:

1. Click in the first blank *Name* cell in Resources view.
2. Type the work resource's name and then press **Tab** twice.

You can sort information in Resources view. If you think you might want to sort the resources in Resources view by last name, you need to enter the resource's last name first, as in *Smith Jane*. You also can add a separate last name column and sort by that, if needed. The section called "Filtering and Sorting Sheet Data" in Chapter 12 will cover sorting.

3. Leave **Work** selected in the *Type* field and press **Tab** three times to move past it, the *E-mail Address*, and the *Material Label* field. (OpenProj does not let you make an entry in the *Material Label* field for work resources.)

4. Type the ***Initials*** field entry that you'd like to use for the resource (you can include this field rather than the full resource name to identify the resource in a field set if desired) and then press **Tab**.

5. Type a ***Group*** field entry to categorize the resource and then press **Tab**. Remember that you can create any *Group* labels that you want, but typically you might enter a department, job description or class, or other type of identifier that your organization uses to group people.

6. Make a new percentage entry in the ***Max. Units*** field only if the resource is available part time for your project or if the resource represents multiple workers. Then press **Tab**.

If you leave the *Max. Units* entry set to 100%, you can override that entry when you make individual assignments. So, if a resource will be 100% available most of the time, you don't need to change the *Max. Units* field entry.

When entering resources, in some cases you may need to select and delete the placeholder contents in a cell before typing a new entry. This is particularly true with cells where you enter dollar values, especially if you clicked the cell rather than pressing Tab to move to it.

7. Type a ***Standard Rate*** field entry so that OpenProj can calculate the cost for the work the resource performs. If you just enter a number, such as **25**, OpenProj assumes you are entering the cost per hour, or $25/hr. If the costs have been provided in another way, such as an annual figure, you can use the appropriate abbreviation to make the entry. For example, 2000/w represents $2,000 per week, or 40000/y represents $40,000 per year. If you enter a figure other than an hourly figure, OpenProj will convert to the resulting hourly rate when calculating costs for the resource's work on the project. Press **Tab** to finish the *Standard Rate* entry.

8. If you will be authorizing and tracking overtime for the resource, make the appropriate value entry in the **Overtime Rate** field and then press **Tab**. As for the *Standard Rate,* you can enter this value as an hourly rate or another rate that OpenProj will convert for you as needed when making its calculations.

9. If the resource has an associate cost per use (that is, a fee OpenProj should add to the budget every time you assign the resource to a task), enter that amount into the **Cost Per Use** field and press **Tab**.

10. If you want to choose an **Accrue At** field entry other than *Prorated*, click the drop-down list arrow that appears when the field is selected, click either **Start** or **End**, and then press **Tab**.

11. By default, OpenProj assigns the Standard calendar as the *Base Calendar* field entry for each work resource. At a minimum, you need to change this entry to match the project base calendar assigned in the Project Information dialog box, so click the **Base Calenda**r field drop-down list arrow, click the desired calendar, and press **Tab**.

12. Enter the desired value in the **Code** field, if any.

13. You can then press **Enter** to finish the last resource entry, or repeat Steps 1 through 12 to add additional work resources. Figure 7.2 shows a completed work resource entered in Resources view. Note that a number of Resources view columns have been resized so that you can see more of the entries for the new resource.

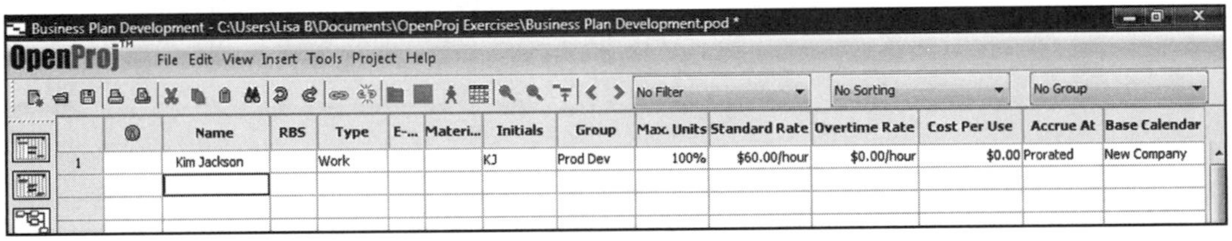

		ⓘ	Name	RBS	Type	E-...	Materi...	Initials	Group	Max. Units	Standard Rate	Overtime Rate	Cost Per Use	Accrue At	Base Calendar
	1		Kim Jackson		Work			KJ	Prod Dev	100%	$60.00/hour	$0.00/hour	$0.00	Prorated	New Company

Figure 7.2 Row 1 of Resources view now has a work resource entered.

You may wonder what to do about making entries in the cost columns, because in many organizations salary information is confidential. In such cases, an organization might enter an average cost for each resource who falls in a particular job category. Or, resources from some departments might be assigned specific allocated cost values. You as project manager need to understand the personnel costing policies used by your organization and work within those boundaries.

Cost information for equipment resources requires your prior investigation. Consult with vendors and get a written estimate, if needed. Dramatically underestimating costs for these types of resources can come back to bite you when your project goes over budget and you don't have additional project funding to draw on.

Entering a Material Resource

Material resources often involve fewer field entries because there are no associated hours of work and only one type of cost. However, when you create a material resource, you do have to quantify how cost will be measured and consumed by making an entry in the *Material Label* field. For example, for reams of paper, you would enter **Ream** in the *Material Label* field. For cubic yards of concrete, you would enter **Cu. Yd.** or something similar. These steps walk you through material resource entry:

1. Click in the first blank *Name* cell on the Resources view.

2. Type the material resource's name and then press **Tab** twice.

3. Click the drop-down list arrow for the *Type* field, click **Material**, and press **Tab** twice.

4. Type the desired quantity identifier into the *Material Label* field and press **Tab**.

5. Type the *Initials* field entry that you'd like to use for the resource and then press **Tab**.

6. Type a *Group* field entry to categorize the resource and then press **Tab** twice. OpenProj doesn't let you make an entry in the *Max. Units* field for a material resource, so you can **Tab** on past it.

7. Type a *Standard Rate* field entry. The value you enter should correspond to the entry you made in the *Material Label* field in Step 4. So, if you entered Cu. Yd. for cubic yard there, you should enter the price per cubic yard in this field. Then press **Tab** twice.

8. If the resource also has an associated cost per use, enter that amount into the *Cost Per Use* field and press **Tab**.

9. If you want to choose an *Accrue At* field entry other than Prorated, click the drop-down list arrow that appears when the field is selected, click either **Start** or **End**, and then press **Tab**. Because material resources don't have associated hours of work to schedule, you can skip the *Base Calendar* field.

10. You can then press **Enter** to finish the last resource entry, or repeat Steps 1 through 9 to add additional material resources. Figure 7.3 shows a completed material resource entered in the Resources view. The field widths again have been adjusted so you can see the pertinent information.

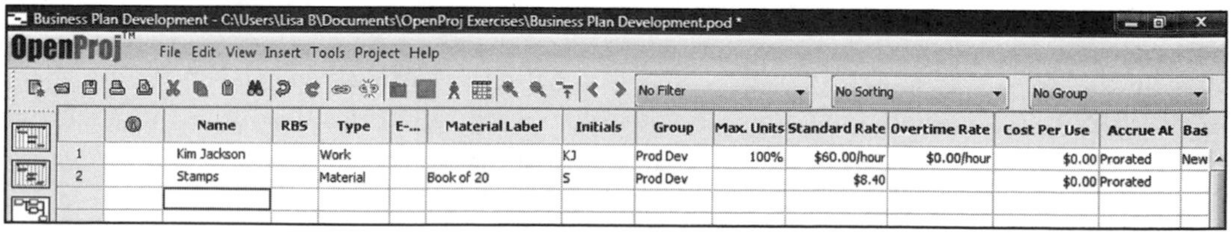

		@	Name	RBS	Type	E-...	Material Label	Initials	Group	Max. Units	Standard Rate	Overtime Rate	Cost Per Use	Accrue At	Bas
	1		Kim Jackson		Work			KJ	Prod Dev	100%	$60.00/hour	$0.00/hour	$0.00	Prorated	New
	2		Stamps		Material		Book of 20	S	Prod Dev		$8.40		$0.00	Prorated	

Figure 7.3 Row 2 of the Resources view now has a material resource entered.

Copying or Importing Information

If you already have a list of resources typed into a file in another application such as an Excel worksheet, or an Access database table, you do not need to type the information again to add it to Resources view.

If the resources are in a table in Word or Access or in a list on an Excel worksheet, you can drag to select the cells that hold the resource names to copy; right-click the selection and click the **Copy** command or press **Ctrl+C**; switch back to OpenProj and select the next blank cell in the *Name* field; and then right-click the cell and click **Paste** or press **Ctrl+V**. If you want to copy and paste additional information such as cost information into another field, you can do so. Just keep in mind that OpenProj requires you to paste the correct type of information into each field. If you try to paste copied text into a cost field in OpenProj, OpenProj will display an error message because a cost field requires a numeric value.

You can copy information from another application and paste it into Resources view to save work.

If the list of resources exists in another OpenProj file, you can use that file as a template on which to base a new project. Open the file and use the **File, Save As** command to save the file with a new name, and then delete the list of tasks, leaving the resources intact.

If the resource information exists in a Microsoft Project .mpp or .xml file, you can open the file to use its resources, as described in the section called "Importing a Microsoft Project or Other File" in Chapter 4. After opening the file, use **File, Save As** to save it with a new name. You can then delete the task information in the Gantt view, leaving the resource information in tact in Resources view.

After you paste or import resource information, always be sure to review the information in the Resources view. You may need to add information that wasn't present in the original file, such as specifying an alternate *Base Calendar* or typing a *Group* field entry. You also might need to correct information, for example making sure to add **/y** after imported *Standard Rate* field entries that represent annual salaries rather than hourly rates.

Opening the Resource Information Dialog Box

In Chapter 6, you learned to open and work with the Task Information dialog box. OpenProj offers an analogous dialog box for resources called the Resource Information dialog box. The Resource Information dialog box offers several tabs where you can work with settings for a resource.

To open the Resource Information dialog box, you have to be working in a resource-focused view like Resources view. For any resource, use either of these methods to open the dialog box:

- Double-click any cell in the resource.
- Click any cell in the resource, and then click the **Task Information** button on the toolbar. (The button name doesn't change for resources.)

As shown in Figure 7.4, the Resource Information dialog box offers several tabs of information pertaining to the resource you double-clicked or selected to display the dialog box.

You will see how to use settings on the available tabs as the book progresses. Click a tab to make its settings available, and then make the needed changes. Click **Close** to close the dialog box when finished.

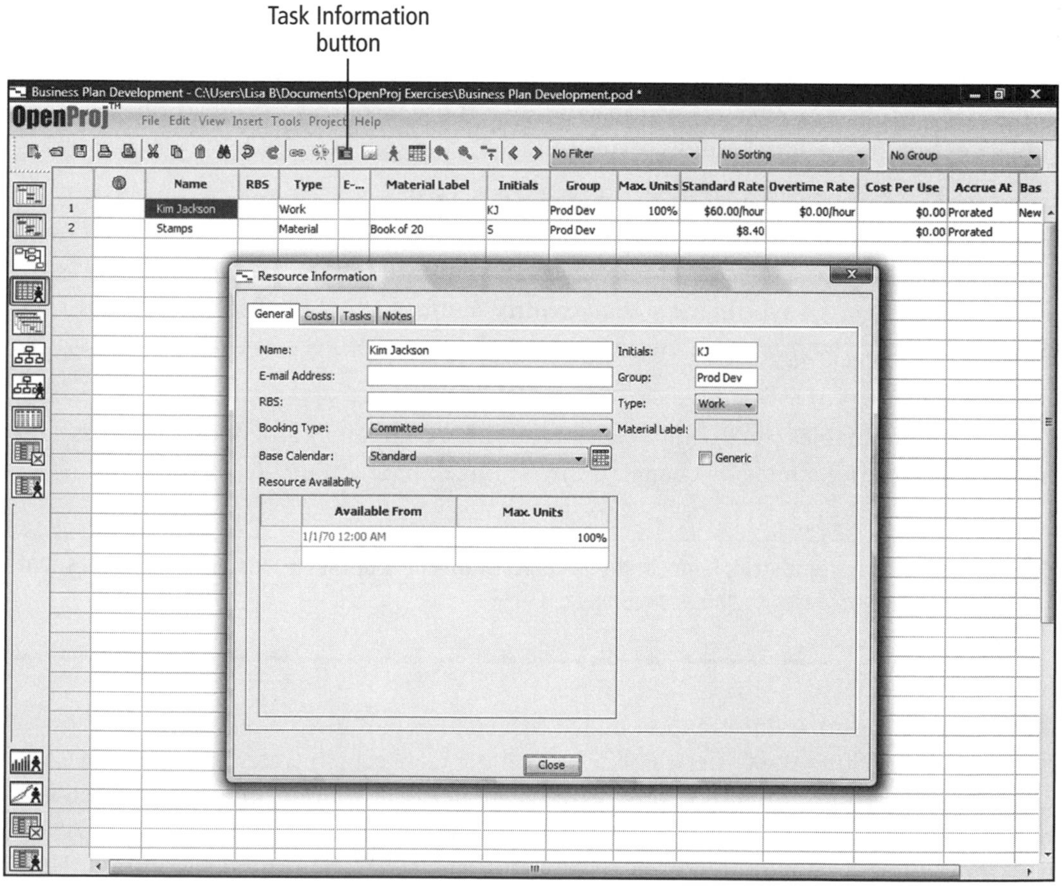

Figure 7.4 The Resource Information dialog box offers a centralized location for finding the settings for adjusting a resource.

Double-click a resource cell in Resources view to open the Resource Information dialog box. This dialog box offers a number of tabs where you can examine and change resource settings.

Generic or Placeholder Resources

Because you will be building your project plan in advance of getting approval for the plan within your organization, you may not have specific information about which persons will be available to you as resources for the execution of the project. In such a case, you can enter your resources as *generic* or *placeholder resources.*

Let's say you're putting together the project plan for a software programming project. You know you will need three programmers, but you don't yet know which of the programmers in your company will be made available for your project team. In this case, you can enter the resources as **Programmer 1**, **Programmer 2**, and **Programmer 3** in the *Resource Names* field of the Resources view. You can assign those resources to tasks throughout the project as you normally would.

Later, you find out the names of the three resources: *Jim Smith*, *Angela Case*, and *Laird Timmons*. To update the project plan to use the actual resource names, all you need to do is display the Resources view, select the *Name* cell for one of the placeholder resources (such as *Programmer 1*), and type in the actual resource name (such as *Jim Smith*). OpenProj will then replace the *Programmer 1* resource throughout the project with the new resource name, *Jim Smith*.

This technique enables you to build your project plan completely and update every assignment for a resource simply by changing the resource's name in the Resources view.

Changing a resource's name in the *Resource Name* field of the Resources view updates that resource name throughout the project.

Note that the Resource Information dialog box enables you to specify whether a resource is generic by clicking the Generic check box on the General tab (refer to Figure 7.4). You also can add a column to the Resources view spreadsheet to indicate visually whether a resource is marked as generic. Use the check boxes in this *Generic* field (see Figure 7.5) to turn the generic setting on and off for a resource. Refer to "Hiding and Reinserting a Field" in Chapter 9 to learn how to add a field.

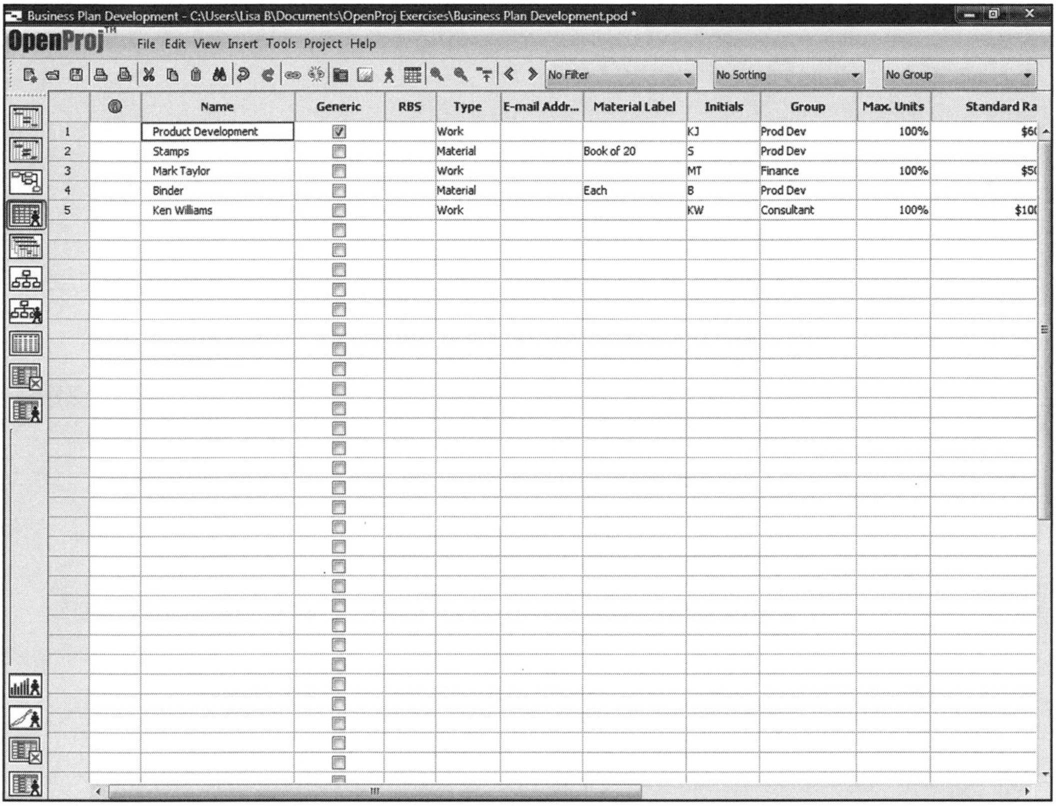

Figure 7.5 The Generic field offers check boxes for indicating which resources are generic.

Creating the Resource Hierarchy

If you want to organize resources in a hierarchy, you can do so in one of two ways:

- By using the *RBS* field in Resources view.
- By using outlining in conjunction with the RBS (or RBS chart) view.

You learned in Chapter 5 how to specify WBS codes for your tasks. You can similarly specify RBS codes for resources. While you aren't required to use any specific codes, it's typical to use an outline-like numbering scheme, as in: 1, 1.1, 1.2, 2, 2.1, 2.2, 2.3, and so on. You also can include text with your RBS codes if desired, as in the example in Figure 7.6.

If you want to illustrate the RBS more dramatically, you can use outlining and the RBS view to see the resource hierarchy. First, drag over the resource ID (row) numbers for resources that are "sub resources" in the hierarchy, and click the **Indent** button on the toolbar to indent them. Figure 7.7 shows resources that have been indented in this way.

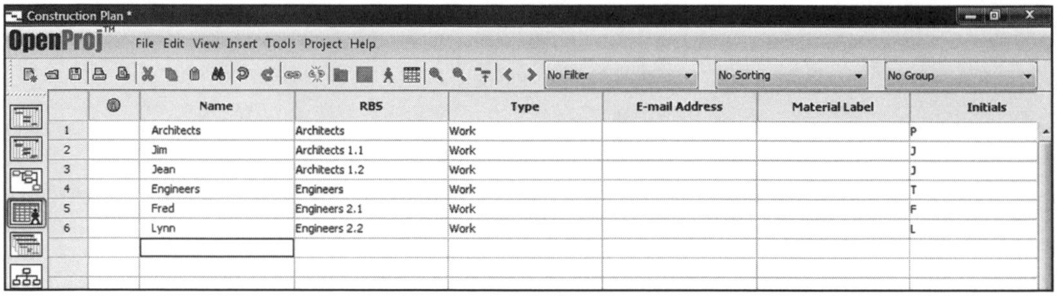

Figure 7.6 You can enter RBS codes as alphanumeric information.

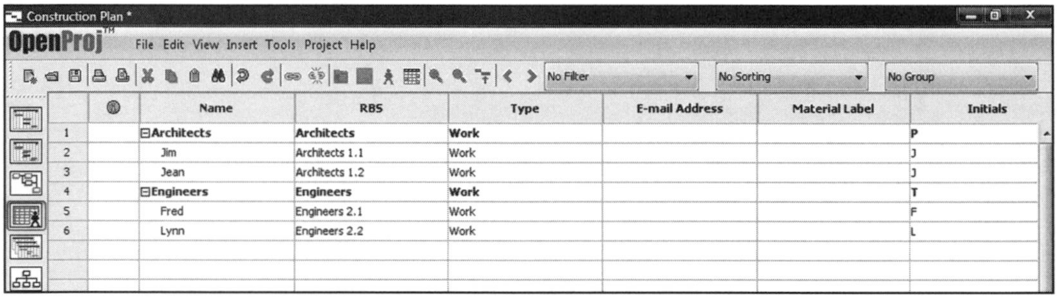

Figure 7.7 Indenting (outlining) resources also creates a hierarchy.

After applying the outlining, choose **View**, **RBS** or click the **RBS** button in the group of top view buttons at the left to see the resource hierarchy illustrated graphically, as shown in Figure 7.8. Choose **View**, **Resources** when you finish to return to Resources view.

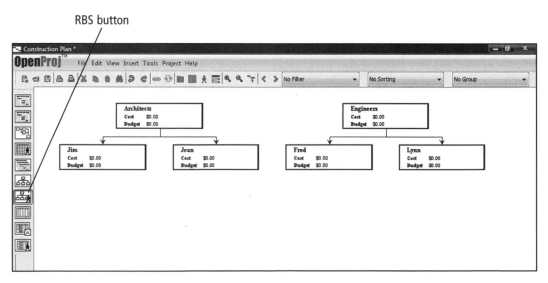

RBS button

Figure 7.8 The RBS view shows the graphical resource hierarchy.

Understanding Resource Costs

New OpenProj users often find all the resource cost information intimidating. I always tell them not to worry. You can implement OpenProj in stages if you wish. First, add task, outlining, and link information, and then track just that information for a project or two. For the next few projects, add resource names and types, assign the resources, and track work. Then, when you're ready to use OpenProj's cost tracking capabilities, add cost information to the Resources view.

Cost tracking in OpenProj is not always accurate to the penny like a real cost accounting system. OpenProj rounds off values, task durations may not always match reality, and resources may do work with associated costs outside what is assigned in the project. Due to these issues, OpenProj cost calculations and cost forecasts should always be viewed as approximate.

Updating Costs in Resources View

You've already seen in this chapter how to enter various resource costs on the Resources view. Each of these costs is used when you assign one or more resources to a task to calculate the *total cost* (*Cost* field) for the task. To find the total cost for each task, OpenProj adds together the following values:

- *(Standard Rate x hours of work assigned) + (Overtime Rate x hours of overtime authorized) + Cost Per Use* for each work resource assigned
- *Standard Rate x quantity assigned* for each material resource assigned
- *Fixed cost*, if any, assigned to the task in the Cost field set of the task spreadsheet

Ensuring that costs are tracked accurately means making sure you choose the right type of resource and enter the right cost information in Resources view. If you failed to enter information in a cost field previously or need to correct an earlier entry, click the desired cost field (*Standard Rate*, *Overtime Rate*, or *Cost Per Use*), type a new value, and then press **Enter**. OpenProj displays the updated information and automatically recalculates cost information throughout the project.

If you've already saved the baseline for the project plan, OpenProj does not recalculate baseline cost information when you change a cost value in Resources view. In such a case, you may want to clear and resave the baseline as described in the section "Working with the Baseline" in Chapter 11.

Creating Updating Rates and a Cost Rate Table

Resource cost rates may not necessarily remain static over the course of a project. For example, if company-wide salary increases take effect during the course of the project, the real costs for the assigned resources rise after that point in time. You need to tell the project to update the rate for a resource after an increase takes effect, in that instance.

To set up a resource so that its cost rates change at a specified date, follow these steps:

1. Double-click the **resource** in Resources view. The Resource Information dialog box for the resource opens.

> Double-clicking a resource in Resources view opens the Resource Information dialog box.

2. Click the **Costs** tab. The tab appears, displaying more detailed cost information, including five Cost Rate Table tabs (A through E).

3. Click in the next blank row of the *Effective Date* column, type the date when the resource's rate increase becomes effective, and press **Tab** to finish the entry.

4. On the same row as the Effective Date you just entered, click in the *Standard Rate, Overtime Rate, and Cost Per Use* cells and enter new rates as needed, as shown in Figure 7.9.

5. Click **Close** to close the dialog box. For any work assigned to the resource beyond the *Effective Date* specified in Step 3, OpenProj will use the new rate(s) in any cost calculations.

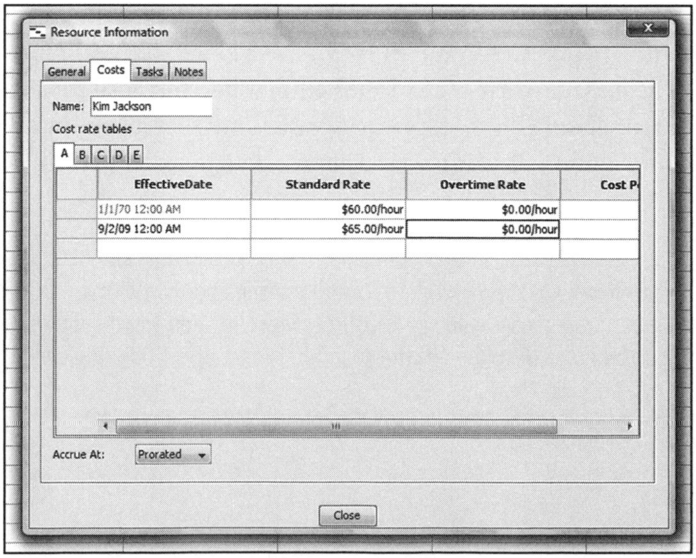

Figure 7.9
This resource's raise will be effective 9/2/09.

Rather than rates that change over time, other resources might have rates that vary depending on the nature of the task being performed or the specific person assigned from the external company. For example, a consulting firm might charge one rate for tasks handled by a senior consultant and another rate for tasks handled by a junior consultant. Or the consultant might charge one rate for writing a business plan for you but a lower rate for reviewing a business plan that you've already written.

When a resource works by different rates, you need to set up a *cost rate table* for the resource. As when specifying a rate change, use the Resource Information dialog box to create each cost table:

1. Double-click the **resource** in Resources view. The Resource Information dialog box for the resource opens.

2. Click the **Costs** tab. The tab appears, displaying more detailed cost information, including five Cost Rate Table tabs (A through E). The tab A (Default) task table is already set up based on the cost information entered for the resource in Resources view.

3. Click the next empty cost rate table tab. The tab should appear with zero values entered in each of the rate fields.

4. Click the *Standard Rate, Overtime Rate*, or *Cost Per Use*, as needed, make the desired rate entry, and press **Tab**. The resource shown in Figure 7.10 normally charges a $100/h Standard Rate, but for some tasks charges a lower $75/h Standard Rate, as indicated on its new cost table B.

5. Click **Close** to close the dialog box and finish creating the rate table.

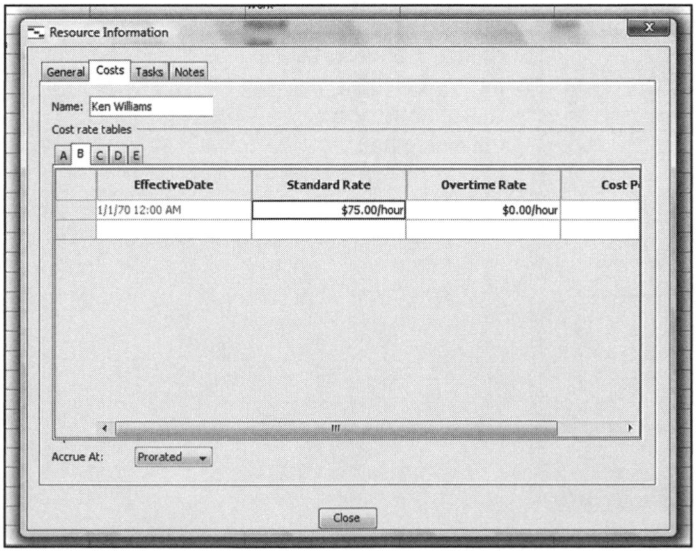

Figure 7.10
Cost table B gives a lower Standard Rate for this resource.

In the next chapter you will learn how to select specific cost rate information when you've assigned a resource to a task.

Adjusting a Resource's Calendar

Even if you've created a custom calendar for the project and a resource is following that calendar, not every resource has exactly the same working schedule. First, you might need to account for a resource's non working days like vacation days or days taken off for surgery or a maternity leave. Or, a resource might work a flexible schedule such as 7 a.m. to 2 p.m. rather than 8 a.m. to 5 p.m. In situations like these, you need to adjust the resource's calendar to reflect the resource's actual working schedule.

Whenever a resource's specific calendar differs from the project base calendar, the resource's calendar overrides the project base calendar. That is, OpenProj schedules any task to which you've assigned a resource according to the resource's calendar rather than the project base calendar.

Follow these steps to adjust a resource's calendar:

1. Click the resource in Resources view.

2. Click **Tools** and then click **Change Working Time**. The Change Working Time dialog box appears, with the selected resource's name appearing as the For choice to tell you that the changes you make will apply to that resource's calendar. Figure 7.11 shows an example.

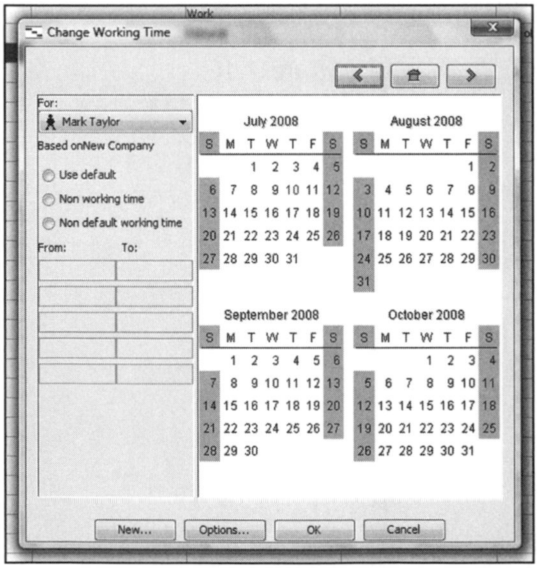

Figure 7.11
The resource whose calendar you are changing appears as the For Calendar choice at the top of the dialog box.

3. Change the calendar settings for the resource just as you did when setting up a custom calendar. The section called "Setting Up a New Calendar" in Chapter 4 explains how to make the types of changes required, such as marking a non working day or changing working hours.

4. Click **OK** to close the Change Working Time dialog box and save your changes to the Resource's calendar.

Specifying Resource Availability

Other resources may not be available to work on your project for the full duration of the project. For example, if you've "borrowed" a person from another department in your company, you might only be able to use that resource starting on a particular date. Or, if you have a limited budget available for resources from a temp service, you may only be able to hire temp workers part time for a week or two. In the case of outside vendors and consultants, other commitments might limit their work on your project to a very specific window of time.

In such a case, you can specify a resource's *availability*—the period or periods of time during which a resource is actually available to work on your project. Use these steps to indicate when a resource is available to work on your project:

1. Double-click the resource in Resources view. The Resource Information dialog box for the resource opens.

2. Click the **General** tab, if needed.

3. If the information that's present is correct for the beginning of the first availability period, skip to Step 4. Otherwise, on a row in the Resource Availability area, click the *Available From* cell, click the drop-down list arrow, and select the availability starting date using the calendar that appears. Also change the **Max. Units** setting as needed.

4. To specify the end of the availability period, click the next *Available From* cell and use its drop-down calendar to specify the end of the availability period. Change the **Units** entry to 0%. Figure 7.12 shows an example of an ending availability entry.

 If you make a mistake when specifying an availability period, right-click the box to the left of the row and click **Delete**.

5. Repeat Steps 3 and 4 to set up other availability periods for the resource as needed.

6. Click **Close** to close the dialog box and finish specifying availability.

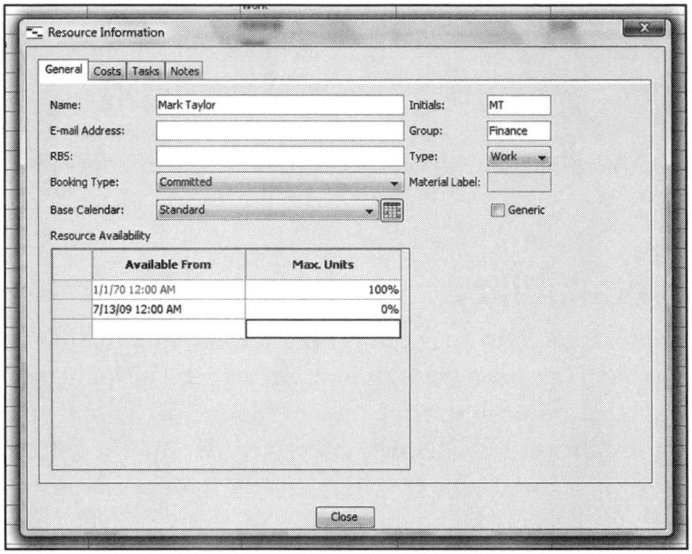

Figure 7.12
Set up availability periods in the Resource Availability area of the General tab.

> If you try to assign a resource with limited availability to a task scheduled during a period outside that availability, OpenProj will reschedule the task to match the resource's available period. So, make sure you keep a close watch on the changes that OpenProj makes when you assign a resource with limited availability specified.

Chapter Review

In this chapter, you shifted your emphasis to listing the people, equipment, and consumable materials you'll need to accomplish the tasks in the project, as well as the costs for using those resources and others. You learned how to display Resources view, where you enter Resource information, and how to create work and material resources there. You learned how you could add resources from other sources, and how to use a placeholder resource until you have concrete information about who will be working with you. Finally, you saw how to build in more specifics about a resource's costs and schedule, including how to set up a resource cost table, edit a resource's calendar, and identify a resource's availability for your project. Become even more familiar with these skills by completing the Review Questions and Projects now.

Review Questions

Write your answers to the following questions on a sheet of paper.

1. What menu and command do you choose to change to Resources view?

2. Name the two main types of resources.

3. A _____ resource represents a consumed quantity.

4. Make an entry in the _____ field of Resources view if the resource charges a fee every time you use or assign it.

5. The entry in the _____ field of Resources view indicates whether the resource will be working full time or part time on the project, or whether multiple persons will be used for each assignment.

6. How do you replace a resource throughout the project plan?

7. How do you display the Resource Information dialog box?

8. What tab in the Resource Information dialog box do you use to specify a rate increase or set up cost tables?

9. True or False: OpenProj always follows the project's base calendar, no matter when a resource actually works.

10. When a resource can only work on your project during a fixed time period, specify that resource's _____ in the Resource Information dialog box.

Projects

 To see the solution files created by completing the projects in this chapter, go to www.courseptr.com, click the **Downloads** link in the navigation bar at the top, type **Open-Proj** or this book's ISBN-10 number in the search text box, and then click **Search Downloads**.

Project 1

1. Create a new, blank project file, with *Resource Planning* as the Project Name.

2. Save the file as *Resource Planning*.

 Create a folder named *OpenProj Exercises* in your *Documents* or *My Documents* folder and save your exercise practice files there.

3. Click **Project** and then click **Project Information**. Choose **24 Hours** from the Calendar drop-down list and then click **Close**.

4. Click **View** and then click **Resources** to change to Resources view.

5. Make the following entries in the *Name, Type, Material Label,* and *Group* fields, skipping other fields for now:

John Swift	Work	blank	Accounting
Marc Welby	Work	blank	Engineering
Cat 5 Cable	Material	ft.	Expense
Folders	Material	box	Expense

6. Change the *Base Calendar* field entry for the two work resources to **Night Shift**.

7. Enter a *Standard Rate* of **50** for John Swift, a *Cost Per Use* of **300** for Marc Welby, a *Standard Rate* of **.50** for Cat 5 Cable, and a *Standard Rate* of **1.50** for Folders.

8. Double-click **John Swift** and click the **Costs** tab. On the next blank row of the A cost tab, specify **1/7/10** as the *Effective Date* cell entry. Click the **Standard Rate** cell, enter **55,** and press **Enter**. Click **Close** to apply the rate change.

9. Save your changes to the file and keep it open for the next project.

Project 2

1. Click the *Resource Name* cell for the **Marc Welby** resource.

2. Type **Grace Hopper** and press **Enter**.

3. Click the **Grace Hopper** resource.

4. Click **Tools** and then click **Change Working Time**. Use the arrow buttons at the top to display January 2010. Use Shift+click to select January 11-13. Click the **Non Working Time** option button,. Click **OK** to close the dialog boxes and change her calendar.

5. Enter a new work resource named **Ladder**.

6. Double-click the **Ladder** resource. On the General tab of the Resource Information dialog box, set its availability from **1/7/10** to **1/15/10**. (Hint: Set the **Max. Units** to 0% for the second entry.) Click **OK**.

7. Save your changes to the file and then close the file.

Project 3

1. Open the ***Site Search with Links*** file you created during the Chapter 6 projects.

2. Save the file as *Site Search with Resource List.*

3. Click **View** and then click **Resources** to change to Resources view.

4. Enter the following resource information in the *Name, Type, Material Label,* and *Group* fields, skipping other fields for now:

Jane Black	Work	blank	Planning
Smith Todd	Work	blank	Architect
Paper	Material	ream.	Planning
Realtor	Work	blank	External
Lynnette Taylor	Work	blank	Planning
Attorney	Work	blank	External
Realtor Fee	Cost	blank	Expense
Closing Costs	Cost	blank	Expense
Loan Costs	Cost	blank	Expense
Land Cost	Cost	blank	Expense

5. Enter *Standard Rates* of **75** for Jane Black and Lynette Taylor, and **70** for Smith Todd.

6. Enter a *Standard Rate* of **3.5** for the *Paper* resource.

7. Enter a *Cost/Use* of **500** for the *Attorney* resource.

8. Save your changes to the file and close the file.

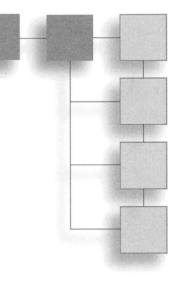

CHAPTER 8

ASSIGNING RESOURCES TO TASKS

This Chapter Teaches You How To:

- Understand the impact of effort-driven scheduling
- Assign single or multiple work resources to a task
- Assign a material resource to a task
- Remove or replace an assigned resource
- Assign a resource part time to a task
- Review resource assignments
- Apply another cost for a resource
- Override or turn off effort-driven scheduling

After you identify the tasks and the team required for your project, you need to bring the two together to specify "who" will do "what" in the plan. Your job now as project manager is to decide which individuals and materials are needed for specific tasks and to make those connections in the project plan. This vital step enables OpenProj to give you (and your project plan) a reality check: The ability to see whether you can realistically complete all the project deliverables on time with the team, materials, equipment, and financial resources that have been allocated. This chapter shows you how to apply resources to tasks to make assignments. You'll learn more about how OpenProj calculates task durations based on work resource assignments and how you can make those assignments. You'll see how to assign material and cost resources, as well as how to remove or replace any assigned resource. Managing resources in more detail requires other views, so the chapter explains how to view assignments and how to apply an alternate cost for a resource. The chapter concludes by explaining how you can turn off or work around effort-driven scheduling calculations.

Understanding Effort-Driven Scheduling

When you assign a resource to a task, you make what OpenProj calls an *assignment*. If you assign another resource to the same task, that creates a second assignment, even though it's a single task. Assign a third resource to the same task, and you've now got three assignments, but still one task.

OpenProj uses the resource assignments you make for a task, along with the duration you initially entered for the task, to calculate the task's ultimate schedule. By default, it follows the logic that project managers intuit in the real world: If you apply more resources to a job, you can get it done more quickly. In project management lingo, this is called *effort-driven scheduling*.

So how does OpenProj know how to recalculate the duration? It uses a simple equation for each task:

$$D = W / U$$

where

D = Duration (the length of time between the *Start* and *Finish* of the task)

W = Work (the number of person hours required to complete the task)

U = Units (the resource's assignment units for work on the task)

 OpenProj uses *effort-driven scheduling* by default, meaning that when you already have at least one resource assigned to a task and then you assign more resources, OpenProj will reduce the duration of the task to reflect the work contributed by the additional resource according to the formula D=W/U.

Until you make a first assignment for the task (assigning one or more resources at the same time), only the left side of the equation has any actual value, the duration.

As an example, consider a 1w task on a standard eight-hour per day calendar. If you assign one resource to that task on a full-time basis (100% or 1 unit), OpenProj can then complete the formula:

1w = 40h/100%

OpenProj schedules 8h of work per day over five days (the default workweek) for the resource.

It might seem that assigning the first resource part time would cause OpenProj to increase the duration, or that assigning more than one resource right off the bat would decrease the duration, but that's not the case! Instead, OpenProj completes the right side of the equation for the first time using the reduced or increased values indicated by the initial assignment of one or more resources. Consider the 1w task example again, but this time, assume you're assigning the first resource at 50% (half time):

1w = 20h/50%

When OpenProj fills in the equation in this instance, it uses the 50% unit value to calculate that it should only plug in 20h of work spread over the duration. The resource will be scheduled to work 4h per day (50% of an eight-hour work day) or each of the five days of the task's duration.

Think about the 1w task again, but this time, assume you are adding two resources to the task initially. In this case, OpenProj plugs the following values into the right side of the equation:

1w = 80h/200%

OpenProj schedules a full 8h of work per resource per day, for a total of 80h of work.

These examples illustrate that the first resource assignment you make for the task completes all the values in the D = W/U formula. Until that formula is complete, OpenProj cannot recalculate the duration for the task because it does not have enough information to do so.

When you make another resource assignment for the task, however, OpenProj can then adjust the duration by recalculating the formula result. If you add another resource to double the assigned units, the duration is recalculated to be half as long:

.5w = 40h/200% (40/2)

In terms of scheduling each resource's work, OpenProj plugs in 8h, 8h, and 4h of work over the shorter 2.5 day duration (half a default workweek).

Figure 8.1 illustrates how setting the D = W/U formula works, and how effort-driven scheduling adjusts a task based on assignments. For Task A, I added a single full-time resource. For Task B, I added two full-time resources at the same time, setting the initial values for the task at 1w = 80h/200%. For Task C, I first added one full-time resource, setting the task values at 1w = 40h/100%; this was the first assignment made. Then I added a second resource, making a second and separate assignment that changed the Units value to 200%; OpenProj recalculated the duration for the task accordingly (.5w = 40h/200%).

 OpenProj adjusts the duration by default because of the default task type for tasks—the fixed units task type. See the later section called "Changing the Task Type to Override Effort-Driven Scheduling" to learn how and when you might need to change the default task type.

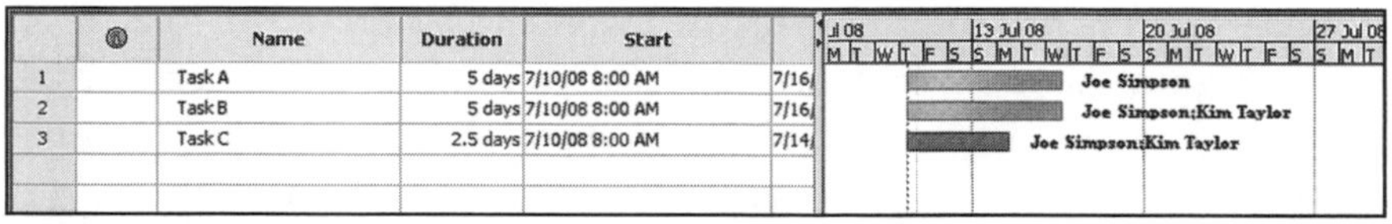

Name
Duration
Start
1 Task A 5 days 7/10/08 8:00 AM 7/16
2 Task B 5 days 7/10/08 8:00 AM 7/16
3 Task C 2.5 days 7/10/08 8:00 AM 7/14
13 Jul 08
20 Jul 08
27 Jul 08
Joe Simpson
Joe Simpson;Kim Taylor
Joe Simpson;Kim Taylor

Figure 8.1 Effort-driven scheduling reduced the duration when a second assignment was made for task C.

You don't have to remember the D = W/U formula as long as you remember these two guidelines when you assign resources in your project plan:

- OpenProj does not adjust the task duration when you make the initial assignment, no matter how many resources you add or how many units you specify.
- When you add additional resources (assignment units), OpenProj by default decreases the task duration.

MISSTEP

Now that you understand how effort-driven scheduling works in OpenProj, you need to consider real-world factors. For example, a substantial body of research demonstrates that two people working together don't necessarily finish a task in half the time it would take a single person, and in some cases two people may take just as long as a single person would! In practical terms, when two or more people work together, it takes time for them to communicate and coordinate their efforts. So, you as project manager have to decide how best to account for situations where adding more resources won't reduce a task duration by as much as OpenProj calculates. One option is to assign the additional resources, and then to increase the new duration by some amount to better anticipate the actual timeframe in which the resources will create the task. Another option is to work with the task type and effort-driven scheduling settings, as described later in the chapter.

Assigning Resources to Tasks

When you want to assign resources to tasks, you have to work in a view where you can see the tasks. Most users work in the default Gantt view. The task spreadsheet portion of the Gantt view contains a *Resource Names* field where you *could* type in resource names, separated by a semicolon, if you want to. However, as with entering task start and finish dates, there's a better way than typing.

You can use the Assign Resources dialog box to assign resources to tasks. To open the Assign Resources dialog box, click the **Assign Resources** button on the toolbar (see Figure 8.2), or click **Tools** and then click **Assign Resources** (shortcut: **Alt+F10**). Note that you need to have a task selected for the toolbar button to be active.

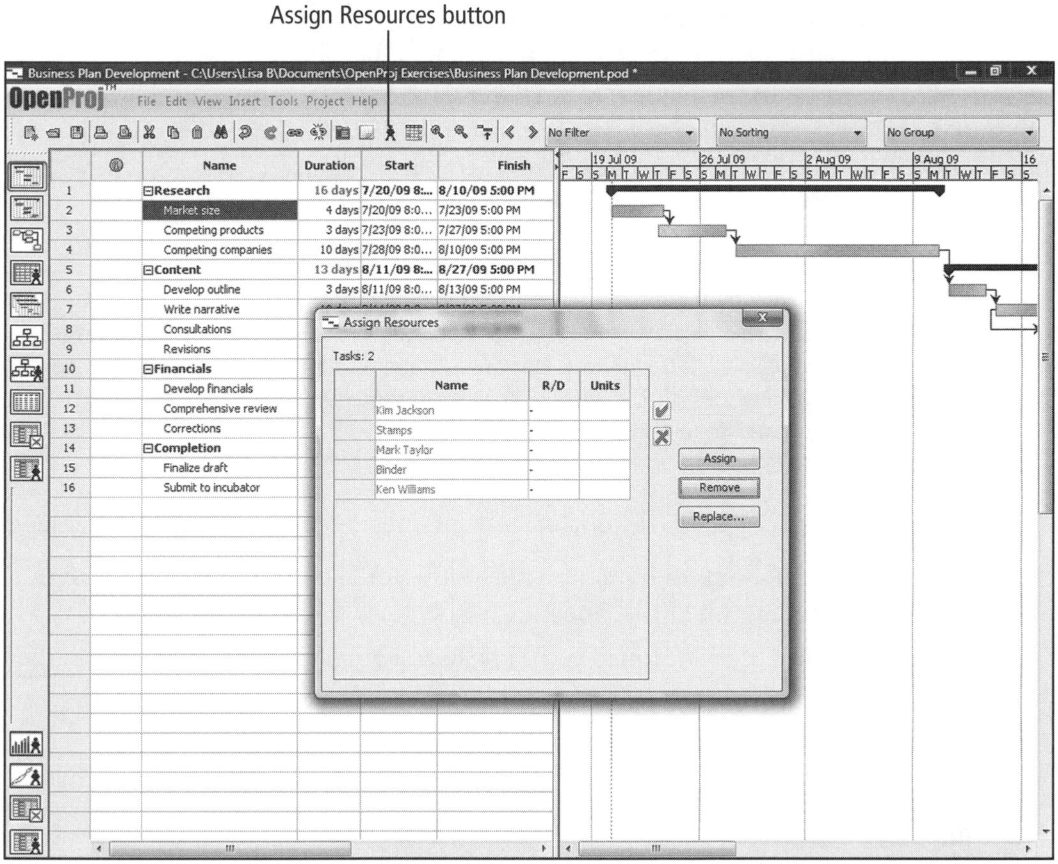

Assign Resources button

Figure 8.2 The Assign Resources dialog box provides the most convenient method for entering resources.

Click the **Assign Resources** button on the toolbar to open the **Assign Resources** dialog box for making assignments. The Assign Resources button has a picture of a resource (person) on it. Click a task in the task spreadsheet, click the desired resource in the Assign Resources dialog box, and then click **Assign**.

This dialog box can remain open onscreen while you work. After you make an assignment for one task, click on the task spreadsheet to select the next task for which you want to make an assignment. This ability to keep the dialog box open and available greatly speeds the resource assignment process.

Assigning the First Work Resource(s)

Assigning resources to tasks is the last major stage in building your project plan. Of course, you shouldn't make assignments for work resources randomly. As project manager, you should take a thoughtful approach toward choosing the right player to take on each position in the ballgame. If you assign a resource to a task that the person doesn't have the skills or the time to handle, your project plan will be unrealistic from the start.

Also keep in mind that the resource's calendar takes precedence over the project base calendar. If the resource has a non working day scheduled during the period when the task is scheduled, OpenProj might adjust the task start, finish, and/or duration to reflect the resource's schedule. If you don't like that change, remove the resource as described later in the chapter and then apply another resource.

When you're ready to make the first work assignment for a task or tasks, follow these steps:

1. Click the **Assign Resources** button on the toolbar, or click **Tools** and then **Assign Resources** (shortcut: **Alt+F10**). The Assign Resources dialog box appears.

2. Click any cell in the task to which you'd like to assign one or more resources in the task spreadsheet.

You also can select multiple tasks and apply the assignment to all of them. To do so, Shift+click or Ctrl+click to select the *Name* cell for multiple adjacent or nonadjacent tasks.

3. Select the resource(s) to assign in the Assign Resources dialog box. To select multiple resources, drag over adjacent resources in the *Name* column, or Ctrl+click to select resources that are non-adjacent.

When you first open the Assign Resources dialog box, *none* of the resources listed in the dialog box are selected. You must make sure you click on a specific resource to select it first, because if you click **Assign** without doing so, no resources will be assigned to the selected task.

4. Click the **Assign** button in the Assign Resources dialog box. As shown in Figure 8.3, the resource's name appears beside the Gantt bar for the task to which the resource has been assigned, and the Assign Resources dialog box both highlights the resource and displays 100% in the *Units* cell.

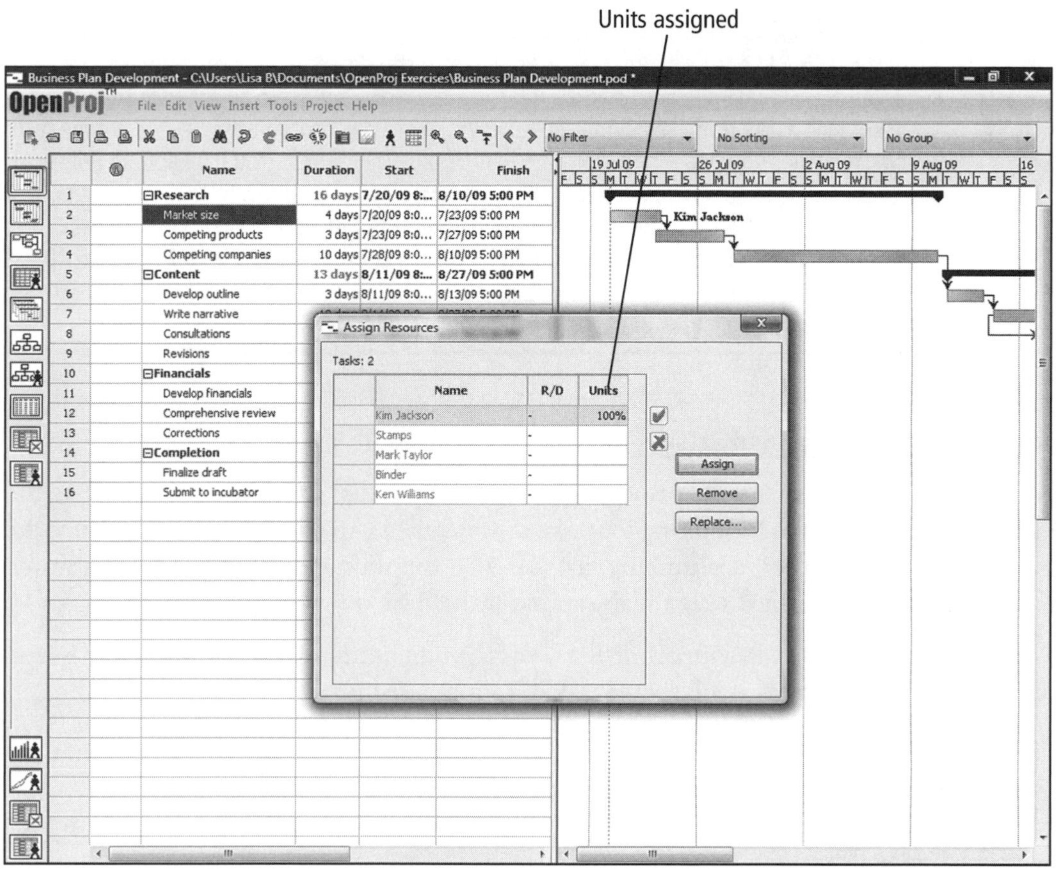

Units assigned

Figure 8.3 The assigned resource's name appears by the Gantt bar.

5. Repeat Steps 2 through 5 to make additional assignments, as needed.

6. Click the **Close** (X) button in the Assign Resources dialog box to close the dialog box.

If you fail to select all the initial resource(s) that you want to assign in Step 3 and instead assign the resources one at a time, OpenProj reduces the duration for the task. To fix this situation from the Assign Resources dialog box, first remove the resource as described later in the chapter, and then select and assign all the needed resources at the same time. Or, you can click the **Undo** button, to remove the assignment and reinstate the duration.

Just as you should not link summary tasks, you also should generally not assign resources to summary tasks. That's because summary tasks are already set up to summarize the work for the resources assigned to the subtasks. Assigning work resources at the lowest outline level possible will help you get a more accurate read of project progress. You'll be able to tell which resources are up to speed on which specific subtasks, so you'll know who to ping if a task falls behind schedule. The exception to this rule of thumb might occur when you are assigning resources that reflect ongoing overhead time and costs, or when you're not ready to "build out" the specific subtask detail later in a project plan. In the latter case, you can assign the resources to summary tasks until you create more detail below them.

Adding More Work Resources

When you are reviewing your project plan to identify areas where you can improve the schedule, you will often be looking for tasks to which you can add resources to reduce the schedule. For example, if a plumbing task has a 3d duration, adding two more full-time resources will by default reduce the duration for that task down to 1d.

You can use the Assign Resources dialog box to assign additional work resources to any task so that OpenProj recalculates the task duration based on effort-driven scheduling:

1. Click the **Assign Resources** button on the toolbar, or click **Tools** and then **Assign Resources** (shortcut: **Alt+F10**). The Assign Resources dialog box appears.
2. Click any cell in the task to which you'd like to assign an additional resource in the task spreadsheet.
3. Select the resource(s) to assign in the Assign Resources dialog box. To select multiple resources, drag over adjacent resources in the *Name* column, or Ctrl+click to select resources that are not adjacent.
4. Click the **Assign** button in the Assign Resources dialog box. As shown in Figure 8.4, the resource's name appears beside the Gantt bar for the task to which the resource has been assigned, and the Assign Resources dialog box now reflects the fact that multiple resources have been assigned. Assigning the additional resources shortened the duration for task 4.
5. Click the window **Close** (X) button in the Assign Resources dialog box to close the dialog box.

Sometimes, task schedules don't recalculate immediately when you make additional assignments to a task. If OpenProj seems "stuck" in this way, you can close the Assign Resources dialog box, save and close the file, and reopen it.

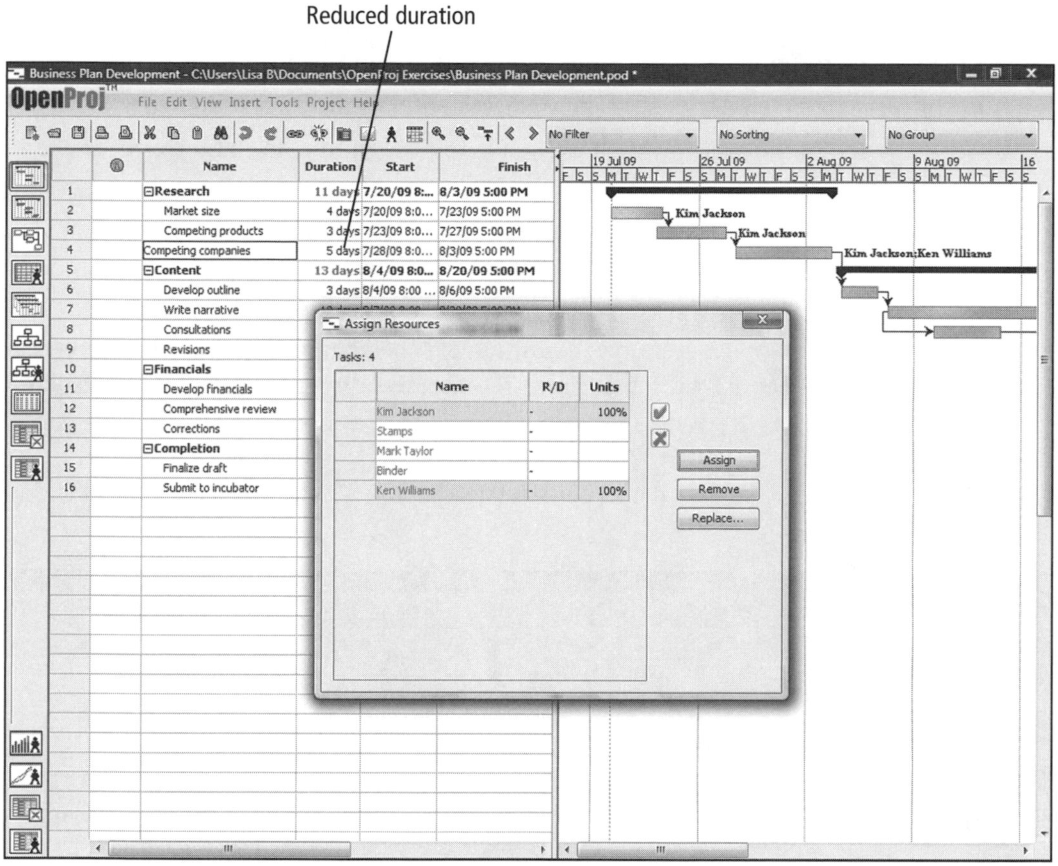

Reduced duration

Figure 8.4 Adding another work resource to a task reduces its duration.

Assigning a Material Resource

Assigning a material resource has no impact on the schedule at all. Assigning the material resource simply indicates how much of the resource will be consumed and adds the associated cost for that quantity of the resource to the project plan. Assigning a material resource works in a similar fashion to assigning a work resource, except that you specify the quantity of the resource to be used as the units. For example, if your material resource is *Binder* and the material label you entered is *Each*, then you would enter the number of binders to be used when assigning the *Binder* resource. OpenProj would then multiply the *Standard Rate* you entered for the *Binder* resource times the number of binders specified and add that cost to the budget.

To assign a material resource to a task, follow these steps:

1. Click the **Assign Resources** button on the toolbar, or click **Tools** and then **Assign Resources** (shortcut: **Alt+F10**). The Assign Resources dialog box appears.

2. Click any cell in the task to which you'd like to assign the material resource in the task spreadsheet.

3. Click the *Units* column cell for the material resource to assign in the Assign Resources dialog box and type the quantity of the material resource to be assigned.

4. Press **Enter** or click the **Assign** button in the Assign Resources dialog box. As shown in Figure 8.5, the resource's name appears beside the Gantt bar for the task along with the quantity assigned, and the Assign Resources dialog box also displays the assigned units.

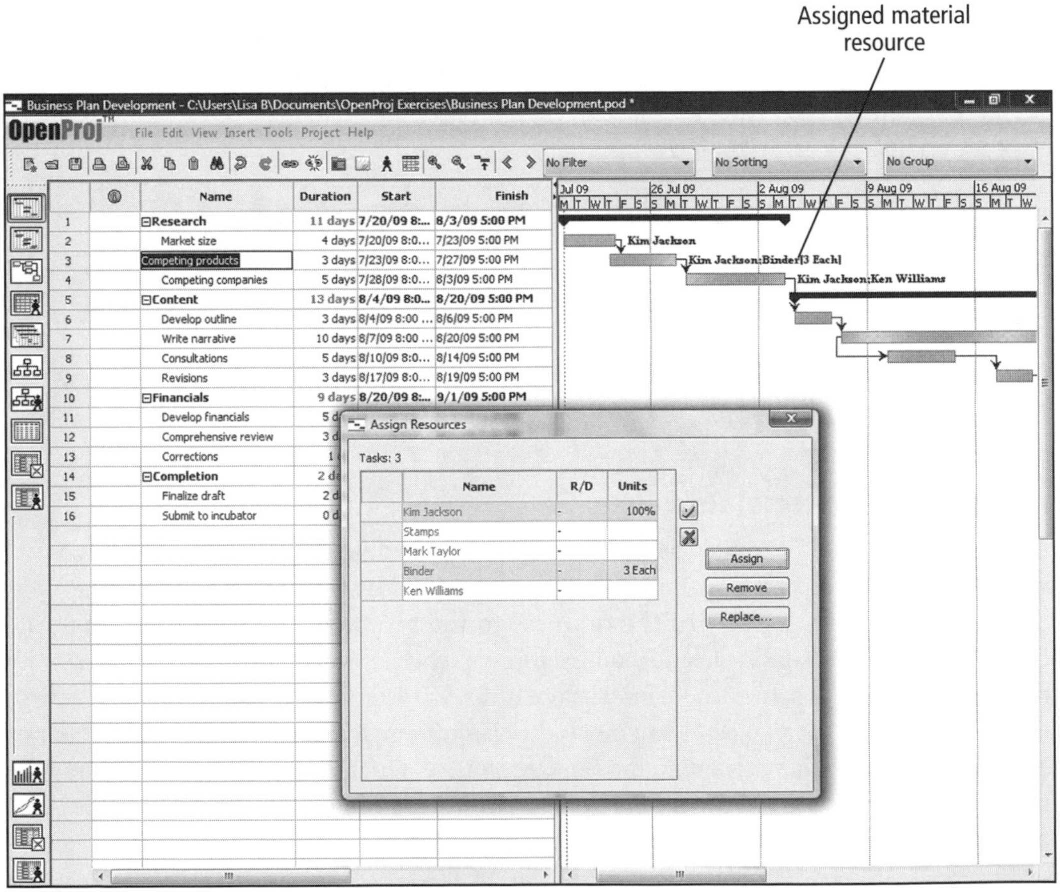

Figure 8.5 Assigning a material resource adds the specified quantity and cost to the plan.

5. Repeat Steps 2 through 5 to make additional material resource assignments as needed.

6. Click the **Close** (**X**) button in the Assign Resources dialog box to close the dialog box.

Removing a Resource

Removing a resource takes that resource off the task. For example, you might discover that someone from another department can no longer work on your project, or you might decide that you'd like to remove a work resource from one task so that you can assign that person to another task where she will make a greater impact.

If the resource being removed was not the first resource assigned, then OpenProj will reverse the duration change applied based on effort-driven scheduling when you assigned the resource.

To remove an assigned resource in the Gantt view, click the **Assign Resources** button. Click the task from which you want to remove the resource in the task spreadsheet, click the resource to remove in the Assign Resources dialog box, and then click the **Remove** button in the Assign Resources dialog box. Click the **Close** (**X**) button to close the dialog box.

If you right-click the resource's row number in the Resources view and then click **Delete**, keep in mind that OpenProj removes the resource's assignments, too. So, it's a good practice to review the assignments for any resource before deleting the resource.

Replacing a Resource

As you refine your project plan, you will be reviewing your decisions and choices to ensure you've properly staffed the project and have applied persons with the right skill set to each task. But suppose you assigned a resource to a task, only to have the task schedule move because the resource has non working time scheduled or the assignment is outside of the resource's availability for the project.

If you identify a task where you would like to change direction on an assignment or some external circumstance requires an assignment change, you can replace an assigned resource. Once again, the easiest way to do this is to use the Assign Resources dialog box. Click the **Assign Resources** button. Click the task for which you want to replace the resource in the task spreadsheet, click the resource to replace in the Assign Resources dialog box, and then click the **Replace** button in the Assign Resources dialog box. Select the desired new resource in the Replace Resource dialog box that appears (Figure 8.6) and then click **OK** to apply the change. Click the **Close (X)** button to close the Assign Resources dialog box.

Figure 8.6
The Replace Resource dialog box enables you to substitute one resource for another for a single assignment.

There may be times when you need to replace a resource throughout the entire project. For example, if the leader of another department who is making a resource available for your project decides to switch people, you will need to replace that person throughout the project plan. In other cases, if you don't know the name of a resource from another department during the planning phase, you may use a generic placeholder name (such as *Analyst*) and then later replace it with an actual person's name.

The fastest way to replace a resource throughout the entire project is to use the Resources view, as follows:

1. Click **View** and then click **Resources**.
2. Click on the *Name* field cell for the resource to replace. For example, if you used a placeholder resource such as *Analyst*, click that resource name.
3. Type the name of the replacement resource and press **Enter**. OpenProj immediately updates the resource assignments throughout the project.

You can choose **View**, **Gantt** to change back to the Gantt view after replacing the resource.

Understanding and Using Units Percentages for Assignments

The earlier steps for assigning a resource to a task didn't call for you to make any entry in the *Units* column of the Assign Resources dialog box. When you leave that column blank and then click **Assign**, OpenProj assumes that you want to use the *Max. Units* setting you specified for the resource on the Resources view for the assignment. If you specified an accurate *Units* setting on the Resources view, then for most assignments you won't have to enter a *Units* setting.

If you want to assign a resource to work part time on a task, then you have to make an entry in the *Units* cell for the resource in the Assign Resources dialog box when you make an assignment *before* you click the Assign button. If it's the first resource you assign to the task, the task duration won't change. After you've completed the assignment, however, any change to the *Units* setting for a single resource will cause the task duration to recalculate by default. You might change a resource to a part-time assignment after the fact, such as if a resource becomes less available for the assignment or if you believe the assignment will not require the resource's full attention. Or, if the resource is an external vendor who can provide additional staff members to help complete a task more quickly, you might want to increase the *Units* setting for an assignment.

To change the *Units* setting to reflect either scenario, open the Assign Resources dialog box by clicking **Assign Resources** on the toolbar. Click the task for which you want to make the units change in the task spreadsheet. Click the *Units* cell for the assigned resource in the Assign Resources dialog box, enter a new percentage, and press **Enter**. As shown in Figure 8.7, OpenProj displays the new *Units* setting for the resource. You can then click **Close** to close the dialog box.

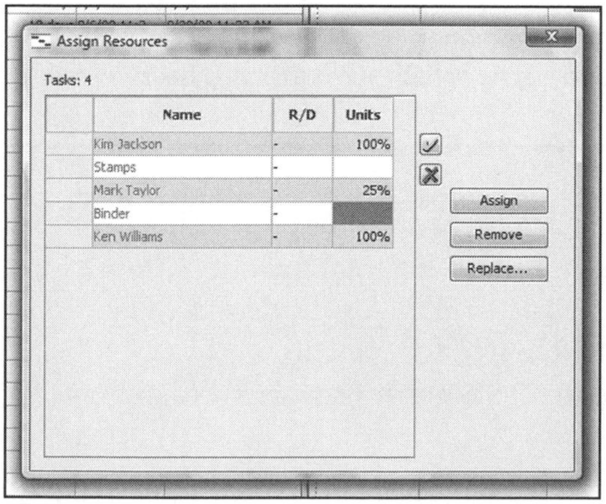

Figure 8.7
In this instance, Mark Taylor's assignment has been reduced to *25% Units* (quarter time).

When you make the entry in the *Units* column, type the value representing the percentage that you want. You don't need to include the percentage sign. So, for example:

■ An entry of **50** would represent 50%, or an assignment where the resource can work half of her scheduled working day on the task. In other words, any percentage less than 100% is less than the resource's full working day.

■ An entry of **300** would represent 300%. Change the *Units* entry to a value more than 100%, for example, when a vendor can send multiple staff members to work with you. 300% represents three full-time team members. In other words, any multiple of 100% represents multiple staff members handling the assignment.

What if you want to assign a part-time resource as the only person working on a task and you *do* want the task duration to increase accordingly? You can do this with little problem. When you first assign the resource, make sure you enter 100% in the *Units* column to override any lesser *Units* entry you made on the Resources view. After you click the **Assign** button to assign the resource, click the *Units* cell again, type a new part-time percentage, and press **Enter**. OpenProj will then recalculate the task duration.

Viewing and Changing Resource Assignment Information

As you prepare to finalize a project plan, which is the topic of Chapter 10, you as the project manager will be looking for potential bottlenecks and problems with your schedule. As part of that process, you may need to evaluate assignments and how they play out on a day-by-day basis.

The term *timescaled* simply means that the information is broken out or charted by time period. The Task Usage and Resource Usage views by default show assigned hours on a daily basis.

Two of the views in OpenProj provide a timescaled breakdown of each assignment that you can review when you're looking for issues or want to see what quantity of work for a task or resource is occurring during a given time period. Task Usage view (see Figure 8.8) lists each task in the project and then lists all the resource assignments for the task beneath it. Resource Usage view looks similar (see Figure 8.9), but it organizes assignments by resource.

To display one of these views, click the **View** menu. Then, click either **TaskUsageDetail** or **ResourceUsageDetail**, depending on the view that you want to display. You also can click either the **Task Usage** or **Resource Usage** button in the top view buttons at the left.

Task   Assignments

		Name	Work	Duration	Start		19 Jul 09							
							F	S	S	M	T	W	T	F	S
	1	⊟Research	136 hours	11 days	7/20/09 8:00 AM	Work				8h	8h	8h	16h	8h
	2	Market size	32 hours	4 days	7/20/09 8:00 AM	Work				8h	8h	8h	8h	
		Kim Jackson	32 hours	4 days	7/20/09 8:00 AM	Work				8h	8h	8h	8h	
	3	Competing products	24 hours	3 days	7/23/09 8:00 AM	Work							8h	8h
		Binder	3	3 days	7/23/09 8:00 AM	Work							1	1
		Kim Jackson	24 hours	3 days	7/23/09 8:00 AM	Work							8h	8h
	4	Competing companies	80 hours	5 days	7/28/09 8:00 AM	Work								
		Kim Jackson	40 hours	5 days	7/28/09 8:00 AM	Work								
		Ken Williams	40 hours	5 days	7/28/09 8:00 AM	Work								
	5	⊟Content	208 hours	13 days	8/4/09 8:00 AM	Work								
	6	Develop outline	24 hours	3 days	8/4/09 8:00 AM	Work								
		Kim Jackson	24 hours	3 days	8/4/09 8:00 AM	Work								
	7	Write narrative	80 hours	10 days	8/7/09 8:00 AM	Work								
	8	Consultations	80 hours	5 days	8/10/09 8:00 AM	Work								
		Kim Jackson	40 hours	5 days	8/10/09 8:00 AM	Work								
		Ken Williams	40 hours	5 days	8/10/09 8:00 AM	Work								
	9	Revisions	24 hours	3 days	8/17/09 8:00 AM	Work								
		Kim Jackson	24 hours	3 days	8/17/09 8:00 AM	Work								
	10	⊟Financials	72 hours	9 days	8/20/09 8:00 AM	Work								
	11	Develop financials	40 hours	5 days	8/20/09 8:00 AM	Work								
		Mark Taylor	40 hours	5 days	8/20/09 8:00 AM	Work								
	12	Comprehensive review	24 hours	3 days	8/27/09 8:00 AM	Work								
		Mark Taylor	24 hours	3 days	8/27/09 8:00 AM	Work								
	13	Corrections	8 hours	1 day	9/1/09 8:00 AM	Work								

Figure 8.8 View the assignments for each task in Task Usage view.

Resource   Assignments

		Name	Work	Work Contour	Assignmen...		19 Jul 09							
							F	S	S	M	T	W	T	F	S
	1	Kim Jackson	200 hours			Work	0h	0h	0h	8h	8h	8h	16h	8h
		Market size	32 hours	Flat	0 days	Work				8h	8h	8h	8h	
		Competing products	24 hours	Flat	0 days	Work							8h	8h
		Competing companies	40 hours	Flat	0 days	Work								
		Develop outline	24 hours	Flat	0 days	Work								
		Consultations	40 hours	Flat	0 days	Work								
		Revisions	24 hours	Flat	0 days	Work								
		Finalize draft	16 hours	Flat	0 days	Work								
		Submit to incubator	0 hours	Flat	0 days	Work								
	2	Stamps	0 hours			Work	0h	0h	0h	0h	0h	0h	0h	0h
	3	Mark Taylor	88 hours			Work	0h	0h	0h	0h	0h	0h	0h	0h
		Develop financials	40 hours	Flat	0 days	Work								
		Comprehensive review	24 hours	Flat	0 days	Work								
		Corrections	8 hours	Flat	0 days	Work								
		Finalize draft	16 hours	Flat	0 days	Work								
	4	Binder	0 hours			Work	0h	0h	0h	0h	0h	0h	0h	0h
		Competing products	3	Flat	0 days	Work							1	1
	5	Ken Williams	96 hours			Work	0h	0h	0h	0h	0h	0h	0h	0h
		Competing companies	40 hours	Flat	0 days	Work								
		Consultations	40 hours	Flat	0 days	Work								
		Finalize draft	16 hours	Flat	0 days	Work								
						Work								
						Work								
						Work								

Figure 8.9 View the assignments for each resource in Resource Usage view.

You can right-click the row ID for the task or resource, and then click **Collapse** or **Expand** to collapse or expand the assignments for the task or resource.

> In Resources view, a sprocket indicator appears to the left of any resource that you've assigned in the current project. The indicator tells you the resource is part of the project team.

If you need to modify the hours of work on a given day for any task or assignment, you can click the cell on the assignment row and enter a different value for the number of hours of work. Most likely, you will need to work with more overall details of the assignment, and for that you can use the fields at the left. (Scroll the spreadsheet portion of the view to the right to see the fields that you may not have viewed before.) Later chapters will cover some of the special fields there, such as the *Work Contour* field in the Resource Usage view.

Note that if you're working in Task Usage view and you double-click an assignment, the Task Information dialog box appears. If you're working in the Resource Usage view and double-click an assignment, the Resource Information dialog box appears. And as in the Gantt and Resources views, you can display an alternate field set in the left portion of the view by right-clicking the gray button where the row and column headings intersect and clicking the desired table in the context menu.

Using a Different Cost Rate Table for an Assignment

In Chapter 7, you learned how to create a cost table to indicate differing fee rates for a resource. You would typically encounter this situation when you're using an outside vendor such as a legal or consulting firm to handle work in your project. Such firms often charge different rates for different levels of service. For example, a consulting firm might charge one rate for planning and another for implementation, or an engineering firm might charge one rate for design and development and another rate for construction project management.

If you have an assignment for which you need to apply a different cost rate table to ensure that OpenProj accurately calculates the planned costs for the assignment, you can use one of two methods. In the first method, you use the Task Information dialog box:

1. Create the cost table for the resource as described in the section "Creating Updating Rates and a Cost Rate Table" in Chapter 7.

2. In the **Gantt** view, double-click the task to which you want to apply another cost rate table. In Task Usage view, double-click the assignment to which you want to apply another cost rate table to open the Task Information dialog box.

3. Click the **Resources** tab.

4. Click the **Cost Rate Table** cell (scroll the list of resources right) for the resource for which you want to change the cost rate table. In the drop-down list that appears, click the letter representing the cost rate table to apply to the assignment. In the example in Figure 8.10, the cost rate table B has a lower *Standard Rate* for the assignment.

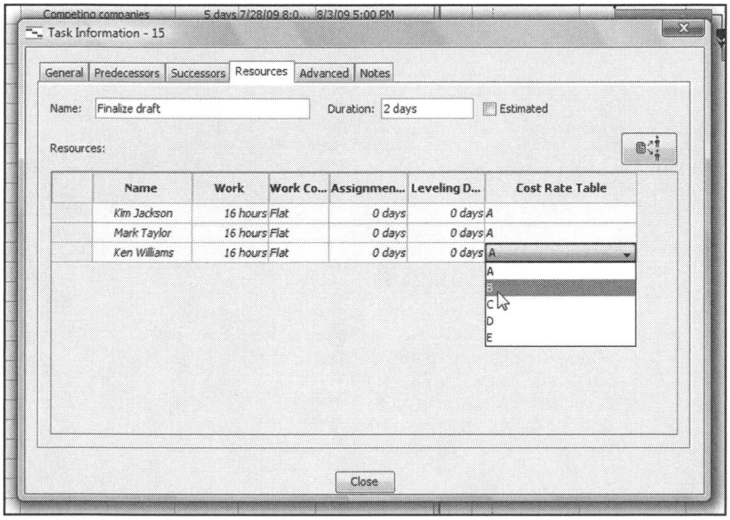

Figure 8.10 Use the Task Information dialog box to apply another cost rate table.

OpenProj enables you to resize the Task Information dialog box by dragging a border of the dialog box. You also can resize the columns on the Resources tab by dragging the right border of any gray column heading. In Figure 8.10, I both increased the size of the dialog box and made some Resources tab columns more narrow so you could see more of the resource information.

5. Click **Close** to close the Task Information dialog box and apply the change. Open-Proj immediately recalculates the costs for the assignment.

You also can assign an alternate cost rate table in the Resource Usage view. Change to Resource Usage view, and if needed, resize columns and drag the divider between panes so that you can see the *Cost Rate Table* field. Click the **Cost Rate Table** cell for the assignment for which you want to change the rate table, and then click the letter for the rate table to use, as shown in Figure 8.11.

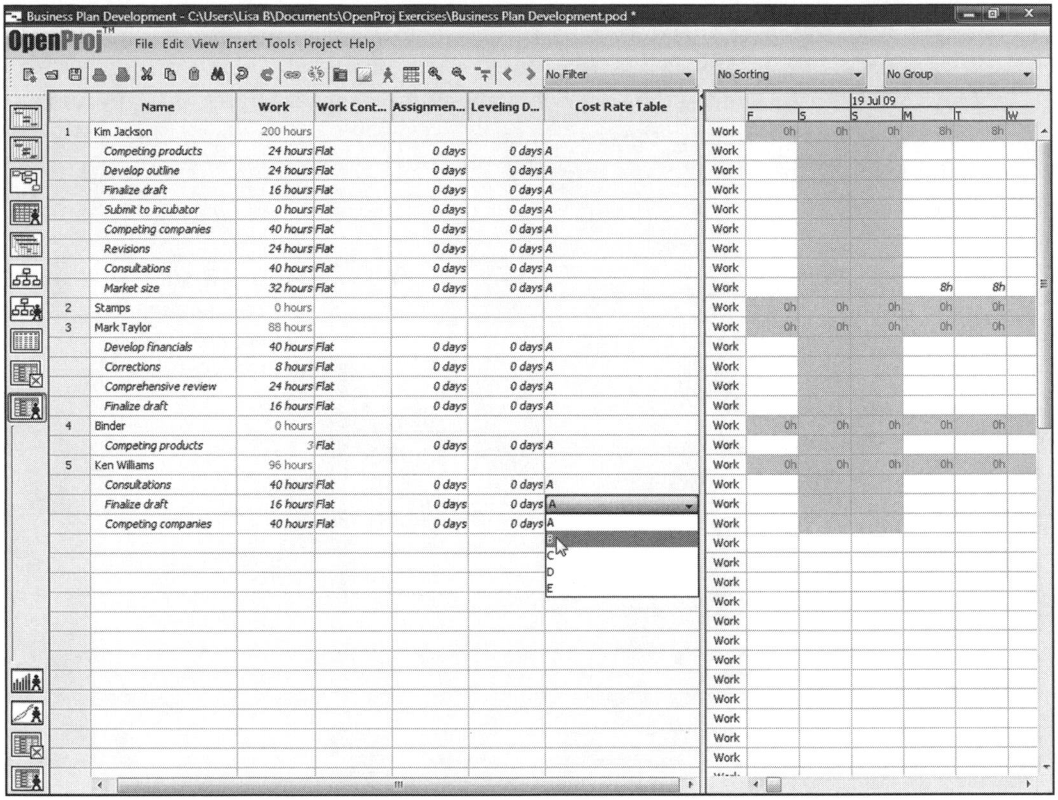

Figure 8.11 You also can apply another cost rate table in Resource Usage view.

Changing the Task Type to Override Effort-Driven Scheduling

This chapter has noted repeatedly that under OpenProj's default effort-driven method of scheduling tasks, adding more work resources to a task generally causes OpenProj to decrease the task's duration. By default, the total number of hours allocated to the task (called the work) remains constant as you add more resources (units), with OpenProj adjusting the duration accordingly. For example, say a four-day task has the Standard eight-hour calendar. You assign the first resource, which also uses the Standard eight-hour calendar at 100% Units. Then, you assign a second full-time resource to the task (so now two people will be working full time on the task); applying that second resource to the task causes OpenProj to recalculate the task duration and reduce its duration to two days.

You can stop OpenProj from making duration, work, or units changes for selected tasks, if you want, by changing the *Type* setting for the task on the Advanced tab of the Task Information dialog box:

- **Fixed Units.** This is the default task type when effort-driven scheduling is enabled. After the initial work resource assignment has been made, adding more resources makes the duration shorter; removing resources increases the duration. OpenProj will not adjust the assignment units for added resources, but it will adjust the duration.

- **Fixed Duration.** This setting keeps the duration constant when you apply resources to the task. For example, if your project requires filing accounting information by a particular federal filing deadline, you'll want the duration and schedule for the task to remain fixed. With effort-driven scheduling enabled, adding resources to this task decreases the amount of work each resource contributes on each day. For example, if you apply two full-time resources to a four-day task, OpenProj doesn't cut the duration in half; it cuts the number of hours (work) each resource supplies each day in half. If you turn off effort-driven scheduling for a *Fixed Duration* task, OpenProj sets the duration for the task when you assign the initial resource(s), does not change the units setting for any resource assignments, and does change the total hours of work for the task, adding more work as you assign more work resources.

- **Fixed Work.** This task type disables effort-driven scheduling, and in most cases has the same effect as working with a *Fixed Units* task: adding resources shortens the duration and removing resources increases the duration. Making the first resource assignment sets the hours of work for the task. So, if you have a 1w task (on a Standard calendar) but assign the initial resource at 200%, the task will have 80h of work rather than 40h. From there, adding more resources decreases the duration (by dividing the hours of work between the resources), but not the total hours of work or the units settings for the resource assignments.

Figure 8.12 shows how OpenProj adjusts duration, work, and units when you've made multiple assignments to various types of tasks.

	Name	Work	Duration			M	T	W	T	F	S	S	M
												20 Jul 08	
1	Fixed Units with Two Resources	40 hours	2.5 days	7	Work	16h	16h	8h					
	Jim Freemont	20 hours	2.5 days	7	Work	8h	8h	4h					
	Andrea Larson	20 hours	2.5 days	7	Work	8h	8h	4h					
2	Fixed Work with Two Resources	40 hours	2.5 days	7	Work	16h	16h	8h					
	Jim Freemont	20 hours	2.5 days	7	Work	8h	8h	4h					
	Andrea Larson	20 hours	2.5 days	7	Work	8h	8h	4h					
3	Fixed Duration, Effort-Driven On	40 hours	5 days	7	Work	8h	8h	8h	8h	8h			
	Jim Freemont	20 hours	5 days	7	Work	4h	4h	4h	4h	4h			
	Andrea Larson	20 hours	5 days	7	Work	4h	4h	4h	4h	4h			
4	Fixed Duration, Effort-Driven Off	80 hours	5 days	7	Work	16h	16h	16h	16h	16h			
	Jim Freemont	40 hours	5 days	7	Work	8h	8h	8h	8h	8h			
	Andrea Larson	40 hours	5 days	7	Work	8h	8h	8h	8h	8h			
					Work								
					Work								

Figure 8.12 The assignments here illustrate the impact of changing the task type and working with effort-driven scheduling.

You can specify the task type for a task in the Task Information dialog box. Double-click the task you want to change in the task sheet in Gantt view. The Task Information dialog box appears. Click the **Advanced** tab. Open the **Task Type** drop-down list (see Figure 8.13) and then click on the task type you want. Click **OK** to close the dialog box.

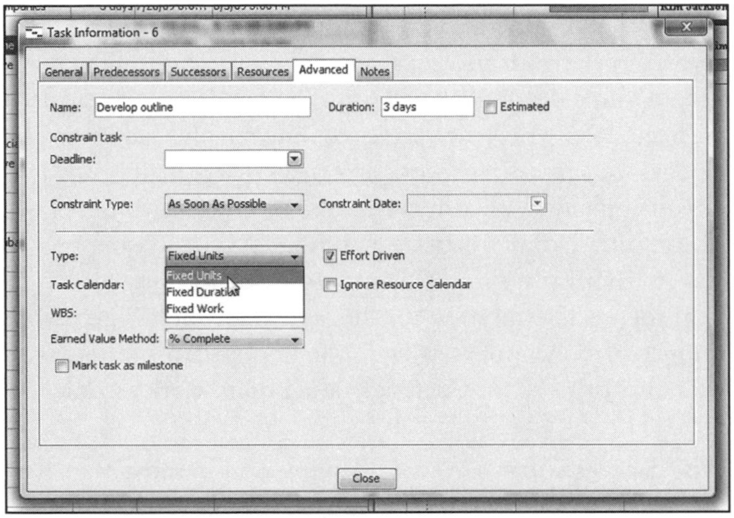

Figure 8.13
Use the drop-down list shown in this dialog box to control whether OpenProj adjusts the task's schedule.

Turning Off Effort-Driven Scheduling for a Task

You also can turn off the effort-driven scheduling feature for a task to disable the Duration = Work/Units equation so that adding more resources doesn't automatically decrease the duration, but instead adds more units and work. On the Advanced tab of the Task Information dialog box, clear the check mark beside **Effort Driven**. Then, to fix the task duration, choose *Fixed Duration* as the task type using the Task Type drop-down list.

Changing the Task Type for All Tasks

OpenProj doesn't offer an Options dialog box where you can set defaults like changing the default task type. There is a workaround for this issue that doesn't require much work, but you need to perform this process right when you create a new project plan file:

1. Enter the task names in the *Name* field of the Gantt view. Do NOT enter durations. Also apply any outlining as needed.

2. Right-click a field column heading in the task spreadsheet, and click **Insert Column**.

3. Open the **Field** drop-down list in the Insert Column dialog box, type **ty** to scroll down, click **Type**, and click **OK**.

4. Open the **Type** drop-down list for the first task, and click the desired task type (Figure 8.14).

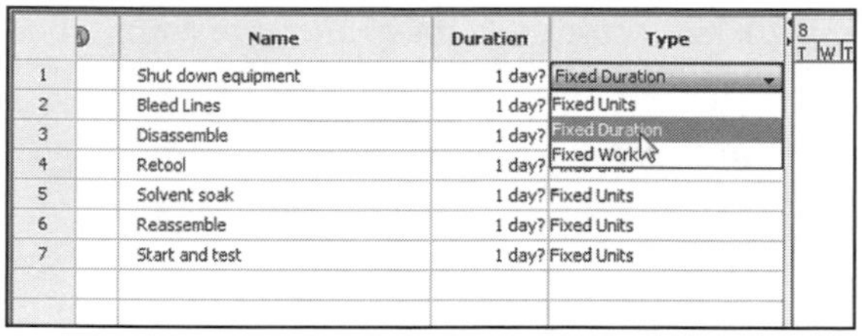

Figure 8.14
Add the *Type* field and use it to change the task type.

5. Click the **Type** cell for the first task, and press **Ctrl+C** to copy it.

6. Select each of the successive Type cells, and press **Ctrl+V** to paste the new task type.

7. Right-click the **Type** field column heading in the task spreadsheet, and click **Hide Column** to remove it from view. You can then proceed with entering durations and building the project plan as usual.

While this method isn't elegant, it's faster than opening the Task Information dialog box for every task in the schedule in order to make a task type change.

Chapter Review

You've now seen how as the project manager, you apply the resources from the Resources view to the tasks in your project plan to make assignments by using the Assign Resources dialog box. The chapter taught you the impact of making the first work resource assignment on a task versus assigning additional work resources, in which case effort-driven scheduling reduces the duration of the task. You also learned how to assign material and cost resources, how to remove and replace resources, how to work with assignment units settings and cost tables, how to view more information about assignments, and how to work around effort-driven scheduling when you don't want to use that scheduling method. Stop now and review what you've learned before continuing on to Chapter 9.

Review Questions

Write your answers to the following questions on a sheet of paper.

1. What button on the toolbar do you use to open the Assign Resources dialog box?

2. Briefly describe how to make an assignment for a work resource once the Assign Resource dialog box is open.

3. Briefly describe how to make an assignment for a material resource once the Assign Resource dialog box is open.

4. To take off a resource assigned to a selected task, use the _____ button in the Assign Resources dialog box.

5. To replace a resource throughout the entire project, type a new Resource Name in the _____ view.

6. True or False: An assignment with a 50% units setting is a full-time assignment.

7. If a resource such as an outside vendor or another department will be supplying two people full time for an assignment, what should the units setting for that assignment be?

8. The _____ and _____ views list project assignments.

9. If a resource charges different rates and you need to specify which rate to use, choose another _____ in the Assignment Information dialog box.

10. The default task type is _____ with _____ turned on.

Projects

To see the solution files created by completing the projects in this chapter, go to www.courseptr.com, click the **Downloads** link in the navigation bar at the top, type **Open-Proj** or this book's ISBN-10 number in the search text box, and then click **Search Downloads**.

Project 1

1. Create a new, blank project file with *Quick Assignments* as the Project Name.

2. Save the file as *Quick Assignments*.

Create a folder named *OpenProj Exercises* in your *Documents* or *My Documents* folder and save your exercise practice files there.

3. Click **Project** and then click **Project Information**. Set the **Start Date** to a Monday a few weeks in the future and then click **OK**.

4. Enter the following task information in the *Name* and *Duration* fields of the task sheet of the Gantt view:

Planning	1w
Writing	2w
Layout	1w
Proof and Print	1w

5. Link the tasks with default finish-to-start (FS) links.

6. Click **View** and then click **Resources** to change to the Resources view.

7. Make the following entries in the *Name, Type, Material Label,* and *Standard Rate* fields, skipping other fields for now:

Lynne C	Work	blank	45
Tim L	Work	blank	35
Proof	Material	page	7.50
Newsletters		copies	0.75

8. Click **View** and then click **Gantt** to switch back to the Gantt view in the *Quick Assignments* file.

9. Save your changes to the file and keep it open for the next project.

Project 2

1. With a task selected, click the **Assign Resources** button on the toolbar, or choose **Tools, Assign Resources**.

2. Click the **Planning** task in the task spreadsheet, if needed, click the **Tim L** resource in the Assign Resources dialog box, and then click **Assign**. This assigns the Tim L resource to the task.

3. Click the **Writing** task in the task spreadsheet.

4. Click the **Tim L** resource in the Assign Resources dialog box and then click **Assign**. This assigns the Tim L resource to the task.

5. With the Writing task still selected, click the **Lynne C** resource in the Assign Resources dialog box, type **25** in the Units column, and press **Enter**. This adds Lynne C as a second part-time work resource, reducing the task duration to 8 days.

6. Click the **Layout** task in the task spreadsheet. Click the **Lynne C** resource in the Assign Resources dialog box, Ctrl+click the **Tim L** resource to select it as well, and then click **Assign**. This assigns both resources to the task. Because both were assigned simultaneously, the duration does not change.

7. Click the **Proof and Print** task in the task spreadsheet.

8. Click the **Proof** resource in the Assign Resources dialog box, type **32** in the *Units* column, and press **Enter**. This adds *Proof* as a material resource, adding $240 in expenses (32 × the $7.50 Standard Rate for the material resource) to the project.

9. With the Proof and Print task still selected, click the **Newsletters** resource in the Assign Resources dialog box, type 2500 in the *Units* column, and press **Enter**. This adds the second material resource and calculates its cost information.

10. Click the **Close (X)** button to close the Assign Resources dialog box.

11. Right-click the select all button (gray box) where the row and column headings of the task spreadsheet intersect, and click **Cost**.

12. Scroll the left pane to the right until you see the *Remaining Cost* field. This field shows the total cost that OpenProj has calculated for each task.

13. Right-click the **select all** button (gray box) where the row and column headings of the task spreadsheet intersect, and click **Entry** to return to the default field set for Gantt view.

14. Save your changes to the file and then close it.

Project 3

1. Open the *Site Search with Resource List* file you created during the Chapter 7 projects.

2. Save the file as *Site Search with Assignments*.

3. Click **View** and then click **Gantt** to change to the Gantt view, if needed.

4. If the Gantt bars aren't visible onscreen, click **task 2**, and then click the **Scroll To Task** button on the toolbar.

5. Click the **Assign Resources** button on the toolbar to open the Assign Resources dialog box.

6. Make the following assignments. If multiple resources are listed for a task, use Ctrl+click to select them both before assigning them. If no *Units* are specified, you need not make a *Units* entry:

Task	Resource	Units
2	Jane Black	
	Smith Todd	
3	Jane Black	
	Smith Todd	
4	Jane Black	
	Smith Todd	
5	Jane Black	
	Smith Todd	
6	Jane Black	
	Smith Todd	
	Lynnette Taylor	
8	Lynette Taylor	25
9	Lynette Taylor	25

Task	Resource	Units
10	Lynette Taylor Realtor	
11	Lynette Taylor Realtor	
12	Lynette Taylor Realtor	
13	Jane Black Smith Todd Lynnette Taylor Realtor	
15	Jane Black Realtor	
16	Jane Black Realtor	
17	Jane Black Realtor	
18	Jane Black Realtor	
19	Smith Todd	
20	Lynette Taylor Realtor Attorney	

7. Select **task 6** in the task sheet, click the **Paper** resource in the Assign Resources dialog box, type **4** as the *Units*, and press **Enter**.

8. Click the **Close (X)** button to close the Assign Resources dialog box.

9. Click the *Duration* cell for task 10 (*Identify Site*), type **6w**, and press **Enter**.

10. Click **View** and then click **TaskUsageDetail**.

11. Scroll the right pane to review the assignments made.

12. Click **View** and then click **Gantt** to change to the Gantt view.

13. Click **Project** and then click **Project Information**.

14. Click the **Statistics** tab. Review the calculated *Duration*, *Work*, and *Cost* values along the left side of the tab.

15. Click **Close** to close the Project Information dialog box.

16. Save your changes to the file and close it.

CHAPTER 9

ENHANCING TASK AND
RESOURCE INFORMATION

T his Chapter Teaches You How To:

- Add a task or resource note
- Apply an alternate calendar to a task
- Constrain a task
- Apply a work contour
- Add a deadline for a task
- Work with fields in the spreadsheet
- Find information

Now that you've been through the major steps for setting up a project plan in OpenProj, you might be wondering how you can achieve a greater level of detail about your plans. Perhaps you need to track additional information about a task or resource, or you want to work with the specific schedule for an assignment, or compare the scheduled finish date for a task versus an alternate deadline. OpenProj enables you to nail down this type of information and more with regard to the tasks and resources in your project plan. While the available settings exceed the space available to cover them in this book, this chapter will introduce you to some of the most obvious and essential changes you might want to make in your project plan. You will learn how to work with task information and resource information, including adding notes. You will also learn how to change a task's calendar or apply a constraint or deadline for the task, in addition to learning how to account for a fluctuating work schedule for a particular assignment. Finally, you'll learn how to change the fields in a sheet or find information.

Adding a Note about a Task or Resource

Moving your project forward on the right course will require you to have a handle on many details surrounding tasks, resources, and assignments—why a task was scheduled at a particular time, what feedback a resource has given about how to handle a task, or why an assignment was switched from one resource to another, for example.

The Task Information and Resource Information dialog boxes each contain a Notes tab. You can click that tab and type in the note text, as shown in the example in Figure 9.1. When you finish creating the note, click **OK** to close the dialog box.

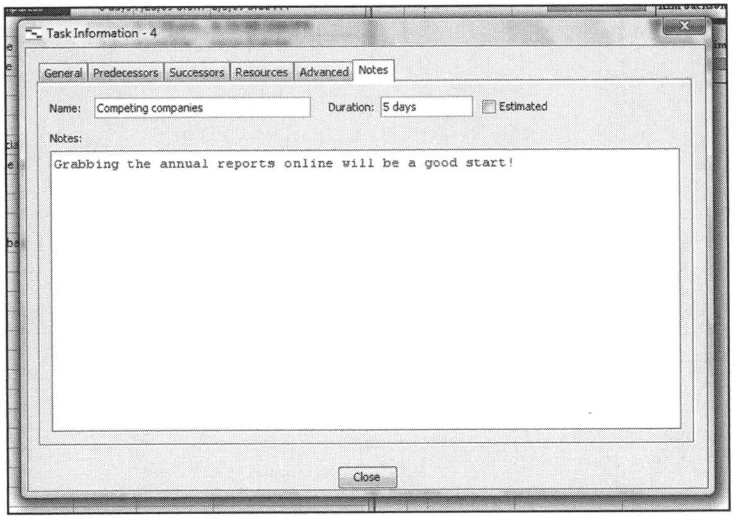

Figure 9.1
Use the Notes tab to track details about a task or resource.

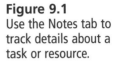

As you can see in Figure 9.1, the top of each tab in the Task Information dialog box includes the same basic information about the task: *Name*, *Duration*, and *Estimated*. You can edit the *Name* and *Duration* information on any of the tabs as needed, or click the *Estimated* check box to indicate that the duration is an estimated value.

An indicator for the note appears in the *Indicators* field to the left of the task, resource, or assignment name. To view the note, move the mouse pointer over that indicator. The note pops up, as shown in Figure 9.2.

Notes do not print by default. If you have to print notes, you can add the *Notes* field to the spreadsheet in either Gantt or Resources view. However, if your notes are very long, then they will be too long to display in the cell and print. In such a case, you can copy and paste the *Notes* field entries into another application, such as Word or Excel, where you'll have options for formatting and printing them. See "Hiding and Reinserting a Field" later in the chapter for a refresher on adding and removing fields.

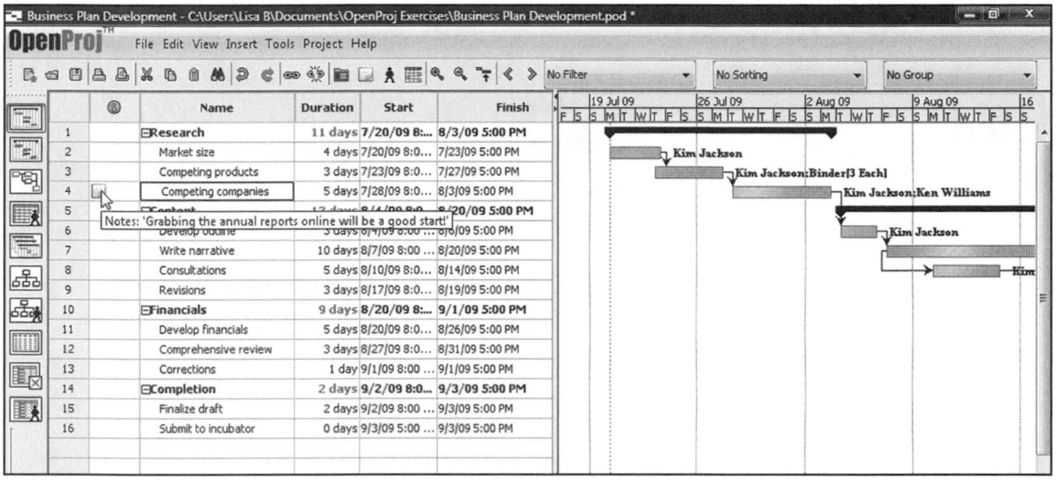

Figure 9.2 Point to the note indicator to view the note contents.

Assigning a Task Calendar

When you created resources in the Resources view in Chapter 7, you saw where you can assign the calendar that a resource will follow and learned how to update a resource's calendar to reflect vacation days. When the resource's calendar differs from the project base calendar and you assign the resource, OpenProj will move or partially reschedule the task so that it falls within the resource's allowable working times.

Similarly, you can assign an alternate calendar to a task; like a resource's calendar, a task's calendar will override the project base calendar and cause the task to be scheduled differently. For example, if your project calendar follows a calendar similar to the default Standard calendar and you have a task that you want OpenProj to schedule after hours, such as backing up information stored on the network, you can assign a custom calendar with evening hours to the task. This forces OpenProj to schedule the task during evening hours.

To assign a calendar to a task, use these steps:

1. Create the alternate calendar to apply to the task, if needed.
2. Change to a view that lists tasks, such as Gantt view.
3. Double-click a cell in the task spreadsheet to open the Task Information dialog box.
4. Click the **Advanced** tab.
5. Click the **Task Calendar** drop-down list arrow and then click the calendar to apply, as shown in Figure 9.3.
6. If you want the task calendar to override any calendars for resources assigned to the task, click the **Ignore Resource Calendar** check box to check it.

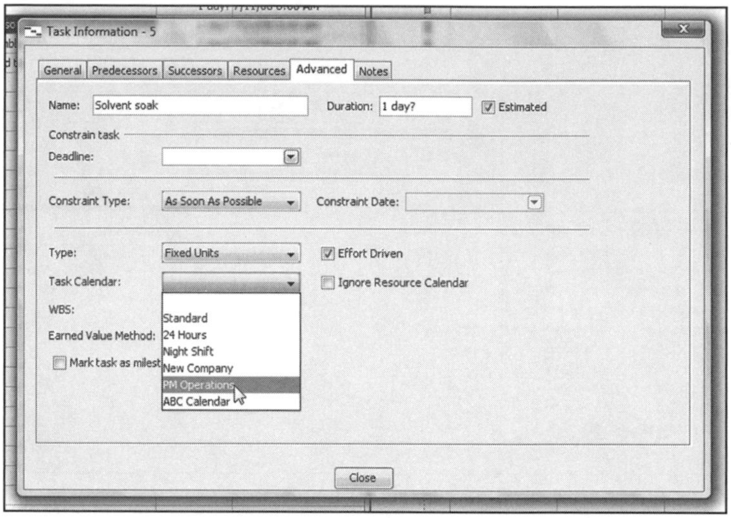

Figure 9.3
Applying a calendar
to a task.

7. Click **OK**. OpenProj applies the calendar to the task and reschedules the task if needed. An indicator appears in the *Indicators* column to let you know that the task has a special calendar applied. If you move the mouse pointer over the indicator, a tip pops up to identify that a special calendar has been applied, as shown in Figure 9.4.

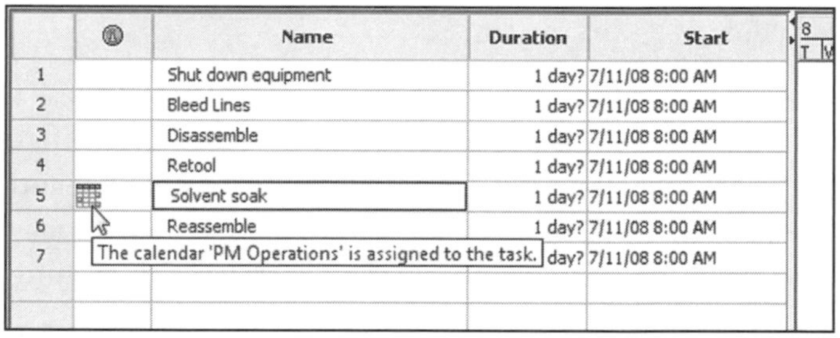

Figure 9.4
Viewing the indicator
for a task with its
own calendar applied.

Task and Resource Calendar Conflicts

When both an assigned resource and the task itself follow calendars that are different from the project base calendar, OpenProj attempts to schedule the task during any time period that's in common for both the task and resource calendars. If the task and resource calendars don't overlap at all, an error message appears telling you that there's Not Enough Common Working Time, as shown in Figure 9.5. The message informs you that you either need to change the task or resource calendar or check the **Ignore Resource Calendars** check box covered in step 6, above. Click **OK** to close the message box, and then take the appropriate action to ensure the task can be scheduled.

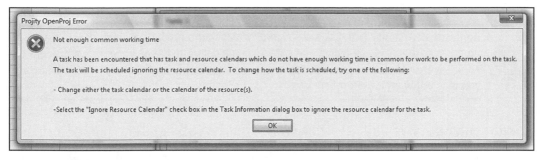

Figure 9.5 If the task and resource calendars don't have common working time, OpenProj can't schedule the task.

Using a Task Constraint

Normally, OpenProj is free to calculate and recalculate a task's schedule as needed based on the link to one or more predecessor tasks, the project base calendar, or alternate resource and task calendars, if applied. A *constraint* further limits OpenProj's ability to recalculate a task's schedule by tying the task's schedule, either loosely or more specifically, to a particular date called the *constraint date*.

By default, all tasks in a project scheduled from the project start date have an As Soon As Possible constraint applied. With that constraint, OpenProj will always schedule the task as early as possible given all other scheduling factors. A similar constraint, As Late As Possible, applies when scheduling from the finish date. You also can apply this constraint, for example, when you want to put off the work and expense associated with a task to the latest point possible in the schedule. These two constraints also are considered the most flexible, because they do not tie the task to a particular start or finish date.

Some constraints reduce OpenProj's scheduling capability but still enable OpenProj to change a task's schedule as long as the new schedule does not violate the constraint date you specify. Choose the Start No Earlier Than or Start No Later Than constraint and enter a constraint date to limit the timeframe for the task start date. Choose the Finish No Earlier Than or Finish No Later Than constraint and enter a constraint date to limit the timeframe for the task finish date.

The final two constraint types are the least flexible. When you choose Must Finish On and enter a constraint date, OpenProj can recalculate the task start date as needed, but the finish date must match the constraint date entered. Similarly, the Must Start On constraint locks the task to the designated start date, no matter what the finish date.

Applying a constraint to a task limits OpenProj's ability to reschedule the task and may even tie the task to a particular constraint date. Typing a date into the *Start* field for a task always applies a Start No Earlier Than constraint (when scheduling from the project start date), which you may not want in your schedule.

As with many other task settings, use the Task Information dialog box to apply a constraint:

1. Double-click a cell in the task in the task spreadsheet portion of the Gantt view to open the Task Information dialog box.

2. Click the **Advanced** tab.

3. Click the **Constraint Type** drop-down list arrow and then click the constraint to apply.

4. If the constraint requires that you specify a constraint date (as for all constraints except As Soon As Possible or As Late As Possible), use the **Constraint Date** drop-down calendar to select the date.

5. Click **OK**. OpenProj applies the constraint to the task. An indicator appears in the *Indicators* column to let you know that the task has a constraint applied. Move the mouse pointer over the indicator to get information about the constraint type and constraint date, like the example shown in Figure 9.6.

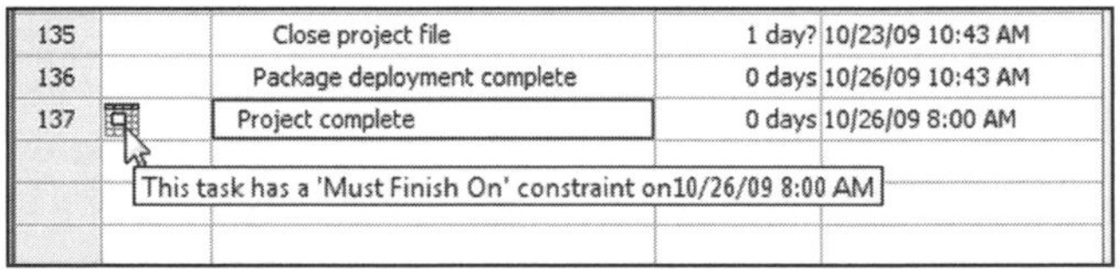

135		Close project file	1 day?	10/23/09 10:43 AM
136		Package deployment complete	0 days	10/26/09 10:43 AM
137		Project complete	0 days	10/26/09 8:00 AM

This task has a 'Must Finish On' constraint on 10/26/09 8:00 AM

Figure 9.6
Move the mouse pointer over a constraint indicator to see information about the constraint type and date.

You can apply a Must Finish On constraint to the final task. Then the task will not move on the project plan, and you'll have a visual indication that the schedule has gone awry. In other words, because the final task won't move, the Gantt bars for other tasks will move to the right in the graph and will have later finish dates than the final task, which highlights that the project plan is in reality running late.

In this book, I've intentionally avoided talking about another way to create and work with task schedules—by dragging on the graph portion of Gantt view to create and move Gantt bars. Dragging around Gantt bars is another inadvertent way to add unwanted constraints. Dragging a Gantt bar right on the graph adds a Start No Earlier Than constraint, and dragging a Gantt bar left on the graph adds a Start No Later Than constraint. So I advise against using this method until you're very proficient in OpenProj and have a good sense of which changes will create constraints to look out for.

Using a Work Contour

By default, OpenProj assumes an assigned resource will put in the same number of hours of work per day for each day of an assignment. However, for lengthy tasks or part-time assignments, the number of hours per day the resource puts in may fluctuate. The resource might put in more work at the beginning or end of the task, or more during the middle. This distribution of the hours of work for the assignment is called the *contour* or *work contour*.

The default work contour, which distributes hours equally through each day of the assignment, is called the Flat work contour. OpenProj also offers these additional contour types that you can apply to any assignment:

- **Back Loaded.** Schedules most of the hours of work at the end of the assignment.
- **Front Loaded.** Schedules most of the hours of work at the beginning of the assignment.
- **Double Peak.** Schedules the hours of work to reach a maximum twice during the duration of the assignment.
- **Early Peak.** Schedules the hours of work to reach a maximum near the start date of the assignment and then decline through the end.
- **Late Peak.** Schedules the hours of work to build up to the maximum near the end of the assignment and then decline.
- **Bell.** Schedules the work to increase quickly to a maximum amount, sustain that amount for a period, and then decline.
- **Turtle.** Schedules the assignment like the Bell contour, but increases and decreases the hours of work at a slower rate.

 OpenProj can't schedule more hours of work per day than the resource's calendar allows, no matter what contour you apply.

You might apply a contour to an assignment for practical reasons, such as if you know a resource has a lot of other work going on during the starting timeframe for the assignment or if you know that more work needs to be completed on another task before work can really take off on the current assignment. You also can add a constraint for financial reasons, such as to delay the accrual of costs associated with the assignment.

Follow these steps to apply a work contour to an assignment:

1. Choose **View, TaskUsageDetail** to display the Task Usage view, where you can see assignments. (You also could change to the Resource Usage view.)

2. Click the ***Work Countour*** field cell for the assignment to contour in the spread-sheet portion of the view at the left.

3. Click the desired contour. Figure 9.7 shows this drop-down list.

	Name	Work	Duration	Start	Finish	Work Contour	Assignmen...	Le
1	New Finance and Accounting	0 hours	0 days	6/15/09 8:00 AM	6/15/09 8:00 AM			
2	⊟Implementation Require	746.64 hou...	41.33 days?	6/15/09 8:00 AM	8/11/09 10:38...			
3	⊟Package Architecture V	320 hours	19 days	6/15/09 8:00 AM	7/9/09 5:00 PM			
4	Review technical architec	16 hours	2 days	6/15/09 8:00 AM	6/16/09 5:00 PM			
	Tim Grimes	*16 hours*	*2 days*	*6/15/09 8:00 AM*	*6/16/09 5:00 PM*	*Flat*	*0 days*	
5	Determine package impler	24 hours	3 days	6/17/09 8:00 AM	6/19/09 5:00 PM			
	Tim Grimes	*24 hours*	*3 days*	*6/17/09 8:00 AM*	*6/19/09 5:00 PM*	*Flat*	*0 days*	
6	Provide initial training	96 hours	12 days	6/17/09 8:00 AM	7/2/09 5:00 PM			
	Tim Grimes	*96 hours*	*12 days*	*6/17/09 8:00 AM*	*7/2/09 5:00 PM*	*Flat*	*0 days*	
7	Install the package	16 hours	2 days	6/22/09 8:00 AM	6/23/09 5:00 PM			
	Tim Grimes	*16 hours*	*2 days*	*6/22/09 8:00 AM*	*6/23/09 5:00 PM*	*Flat*	*0 days*	
8	Estimate usage volumes a	96 hours	12 days	6/24/09 8:00 AM	7/9/09 5:00 PM			
	Tim Grimes	*96 hours*	*12 days*	*6/24/09 8:00 AM*	*7/9/09 5:00 PM*	Flat ▾	*0 days*	
9	Ensure that installation is	32 hours	4 days	6/24/09 8:00 AM	6/29/09 5:00 PM	Flat		
	Tim Grimes	*32 hours*	*4 days*	*6/24/09 8:00 AM*	*6/29/09 5:00 PM*	Back Loaded	*0 days*	
10	Review and baseline tech	24 hours	3 days	6/30/09 8:00 AM	7/2/09 5:00 PM	Front Loaded		
	Tim Grimes	*24 hours*	*3 days*	*6/30/09 8:00 AM*	*7/2/09 5:00 PM*	Double Peak	*0 days*	
11	Package architecture vali	16 hours	2 days	7/3/09 8:00 AM	7/6/09 5:00 PM	Early Peak		
						Late Peak		
12	⊟Package and Requirem	152 hours	9.5 days	6/24/09 8:00 AM	7/7/09 1:00 PM	Bell		
13	Explore the package	8 hours	0.5 days	6/24/09 8:00 AM	6/24/09 1:00 PM	Turtle		
	Pam Champion	*4 hours*	*0.5 days*	*6/24/09 8:00 AM*	*6/24/09 1:00 PM*	*Flat*	*0 days*	
	Tim Grimes	*4 hours*	*0.5 days*	*6/24/09 8:00 AM*	*6/24/09 1:00 PM*	*Flat*	*0 days*	

Figure 9.7 Applying a contour to an assignment.

4. Press **Enter** to apply the contour. If you scroll the right pane until you see the assignment hours, you'll be able to see how the applied contour altered the assignment's day by day schedule.

	Tim Grimes	*16 hours*	*2 days*	Work											
8	Estimate usage volumes a	48 hours	12 days	Work	2.56h	0h	0h	4.48h	6.72h	8h	8h	6.72h	0h	0h	4.48h
	Tim Grimes	48 hours	12 days	Work	2.56h	0h	0h	4.48h	6.72h	8h	8h	6.72h	0h	0h	4.48h
9	Ensure that installation is	32 hours	4 days	Work	8h	0h	0h	8h							
	Tim Grimes	*32 hours*	*4 days*	Work	8h	0h	0h	8h							

Figure 9.8 Review the assignment schedule to see the impact of the contour.

If you look across the assignment row shown in Figure 9.8, you'll see that the daily hours of work applied often seem like nonsensical amounts. (Does anyone track whether they worked 1.28 hours on a task versus 1.25, for example?) To some degree, you'll be able to ignore slight scheduling issues introduced by applying a contour. On the other hand, applying a contour can cause OpenProj to reschedule the duration of the task. For example, applying the Turtle contour might change the duration of a 12-day task to 17 or so days to reflect that the 96 hours of work originally assigned to the resource handling the task now have been stretched over a longer time frame. Make sure that you check the impact a work contour assignment has on the duration of a task to which that assignment applies.

> **NOTE** You also can apply a work contour on the Resources tab of the Task Information dialog box.

Adding a Task Deadline

Assigning a *deadline* to a task provides OpenProj with another way to flag your attention if the task runs late based on work you mark as complete and other changes you make to the schedule. Figure 9.9 shows the marker for a deadline on a task's Gantt bar, as well as the indicator that appears when the task's finish date moves beyond the deadline.

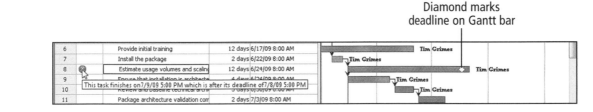

Figure 9.9 Apply a deadline to tell OpenProj to display additional information about when a task misses its due date.

Adding a task deadline only requires a few brief steps:

1. Double-click a cell in the task spreadsheet portion of the Gantt view to open the Task Information dialog box.

2. Click the **Advanced** tab.

3. Click the **Deadline** drop-down list arrow and then use the calendar that appears to choose the deadline date.

4. Click **Close**. OpenProj applies the deadline to the task, and an arrow for the deadline appears on the task's Gantt bar.

Adding a Fixed Cost to a Task

Chapter 7 talked about the various types of cost information that OpenProj tracks with regard to an assigned resource: the Standard Rate (which is multiplied by the hours of work assigned to a work resource or the quantity assigned of a material resource), as well as any Overtime Rate or Cost Per Use. In some cases, you may want to assign a cost to the task rather than the resource. For example, say you're working directly with a consulting firm that will program certain parts of an overall project for you. Your contract with the firm might specify a set fee for each completed deliverable. When you enter each deliverable into the project plan, you would then assign the contract cost to the task (and leave off cost information for the vendor's resource entry in the Resources view). A cost assigned directly to a task in this way is called a ***fixed cost***. If a resource is charging you both hourly or Cost Per Use rates and per-task costs, then OpenProj uses them all to calculate the **total cost** or sometimes just called the **cost** for the task.

To find the **total cost** for a task, OpenProj adds (hours of work or quantity consumed times Standard Rate) + (hours of authorized overtime work times Overtime Rate) + Cost Per Use + Fixed Cost (for the task).

To enter a fixed cost for a task, you need to use field set (collection of fields) for the task spreadsheet portion of the Gantt view. These steps explain how:

1. Choose **View, Gantt** to change to the Gantt view, if needed.
2. Right-click the **select all** button (gray box) where the row and column headings intersect and click **Cost** in the context menu that appears. (See Figure 9.10.)

		Name	Duration	Start
1		New Finance and Accounting System ch	0 days	6/15/09 8:00 AM
2		Baseline	41.33 days?	6/15/09 8:00 AM
3		Business Plan Development	19 days	6/15/09 8:00 AM
4		Constraint Dates	2 days	6/15/09 8:00 AM
5		Cost	3 days	6/17/09 8:00 AM
6		Delay	12 days	6/17/09 8:00 AM
7			2 days	6/22/09 8:00 AM
8	⊗	Earned Value	12 days	6/24/09 8:00 AM
9		Earned Value Cost Indicators	4 days	6/24/09 8:00 AM
10		Earned Value Schedule Indicators	3 days	6/30/09 8:00 AM
11		Entry (Click to rename)	2 days	7/3/09 8:00 AM
12		Entry*	9.5 days	6/24/09 8:00 AM
13		Export	0.5 days	6/24/09 8:00 AM
14		Name	2 days	6/24/09 1:00 PM
15		Rollup Table	4 days	6/26/09 1:00 PM
16		Schedule	3 days	7/2/09 1:00 PM
17		Site Search	0 days	7/7/09 1:00 PM
18		Summary	13.5 days	7/7/09 1:00 PM
19		Tracking	2 days	7/7/09 1:00 PM
20		Usage	4 days	7/9/09 1:00 PM
21		Variance	3 days	7/9/09 1:00 PM
22			2 days	7/9/09 1:00 PM
23			1 day	7/9/09 1:00 PM
24		Document implementation options	4 days	7/15/09 1:00 PM
25		Select implementation option	2 days	7/21/09 1:00 PM

Figure 9.10
Selecting the *Cost* field set.

3. Click the ***Fixed Cost*** field cell for the task, type the cost amount, and press **Enter**. OpenProj enters the new *Fixed Cost* value (Figure 9.11) and adds it to the amount for the task calculated in the total *Cost* field. Note that the *Cost* field does not appear in the *Cost* field set, but you can scroll the left pane right to see the calculated amount in the *Remaining Cost* field, shown in Figure 9.11.

	Name	Fixed Cost	Fixed Cost Accrual	Baseline Cost	Actual Cost	Remaining Cost
1	New Finance and Accoun	$0.00	End		$0.00	$0.00
2	⊟Implementation Requ	$0.00	End		$0.00	$23287.20
3	⊟Package Architectu	$0.00	End		$0.00	$8960.00
4	Review technical arch	$0.00	End		$0.00	$560.00
5	Determine package in	$0.00	End		$0.00	$840.00
6	Provide initial training	$0.00	End		$0.00	$3360.00
7	Install the package	$250.00	End		$0.00	$810.00
8	Estimate usage volum	$0.00	End		$0.00	$1680.00
9	Ensure that installatio	$0.00	End		$0.00	$1120.00
10	Review and baseline	$0.00	End		$0.00	$840.00
11	Package architecture	$0.00	End		$0.00	$0.00

Figure 9.11 The amount entered in the *Fixed Cost* field for task 7 has been added into the total *Cost* field entry for that task, a value also shown in the *Remaining Cost* field.

4. To change back to the default *Entry* field set, right-click the **select all** button (gray box) where the row and column headings intersect and click **Entry** in the context menu that appears.

A *field set* in OpenProj is the collection of fields shown in a sheet view or the sheet portion of a view. The default table for every sheet is called the *Entry* field set.

Modifying the Task or Resource Sheet

Even many novice OpenProj users learn quickly that they need to tweak the information that appears in the common views to meet their own project planning and reporting needs. For example, why include the *Predecessors* field in the Gantt view when the chart portion of the view shows the link lines? And why not change the widths of columns so that information displays properly? In this section, you'll learn about a few basic changes you can make to the field set shown in any sheet view or sheet portion of a view.

Many of the changes you make to a field set onscreen aren't necessarily saved when you save the file. For example, when you change the width of a field in a table, the field will typically revert to its default width the next time you open the file. And a field that you've hidden may reappear the next time you open the file. So make sure you check the widths of fields before printing to ensure all fields use the widths you want. If you add and remove fields to customize the field set but don't save it with a custom name, the edited field set will be given the same name as the file name when you save the file. The best practice when adding and removing fields is to save the field set with a custom name, as described later in this chapter.

Changing Field (Column) Width

Often, OpenProj gives you an onscreen clue that you need to change the width for the column in a sheet. Namely, long entries won't fully display in the column. OpenProj offers one method to change the width for a field. Move the mouse pointer over the right border of the column header until the mouse pointer changes to a double-headed arrow, then drag until the field reaches the desired width. Figure 9.12 shows this technique in action.

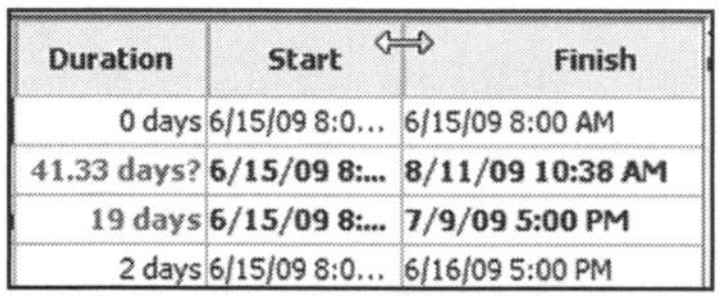

Duration	Start	Finish
0 days	6/15/09 8:0...	6/15/09 8:00 AM
41.33 days?	6/15/09 8:...	8/11/09 10:38 AM
19 days	6/15/09 8:...	7/9/09 5:00 PM
2 days	6/15/09 8:0...	6/16/09 5:00 PM

Figure 9.12
Drag the divider at the right side of the column header to resize the field.

Hiding and Reinserting a Field

When you no longer want to see a field within a view, you can *hide* it. Hiding a field does not delete it or the data it holds in OpenProj. Hiding the field merely removes the field from the current field set (and therefore the current view). To hide a field in any sheet, right-click the field column header and click **Hide Column** in the context menu that appears, as in the example shown in Figure 9.13.

Start	Finish
6/15/09 8:0...	6/15/09 8:00 AM
6/1!	Insert Column...	AM
6/1!	Hide Column	M
6/15,	Find	
6/17,		
6/17/09 8:0...	7/2/09 5:00 PM

Figure 9.13
Right-click a column heading and click Hide Column to remove the column from the current table.

To redisplay the column, right-click the header of the column to the left of where you want to reinsert the field and click **Insert Column**. Choose the field to reinsert from the **Field** drop-down list of the Insert Column dialog box and then click **OK**.

Clicking a column header selects the entire field (column). Clicking a row header selects the entire row (task or resource).

Adding a Basic Custom Field

OpenProj by default includes a number of fields that are empty placeholders for you to customize and use for your own purposes. You can use any of the numbered fields whose names start with *Text* (*Text1*, *Text2*, *Text3*, and so on) as a custom text field in your project plan. There are placeholder cost fields (*Cost1*, *Cost2*, and so on), placeholder number fields (*Number1*, *Number2*, and so on), and more. For example, you could add one of the number fields to the Resources view to hold a quality rating assigned to each resource.

The empty placeholder fields available for customization include the:

> Cost1-10 fields
>
> Date1-10 fields
>
> Duration1-10 fields
>
> Finish1-10 fields
>
> Flag1-20 fields
>
> Number1-20 fields
>
> Start1-10 fields
>
> Text1-30 fields

Follow these steps to add a basic custom field to a sheet:

1. Right-click the column header of the field to the left of where you want to insert the custom field and then click **Insert Column**.

2. Click the **Field** drop-down list arrow and then scroll to and click the placeholder field to customize. It appears in the dialog box, as shown in Figure 9.14.

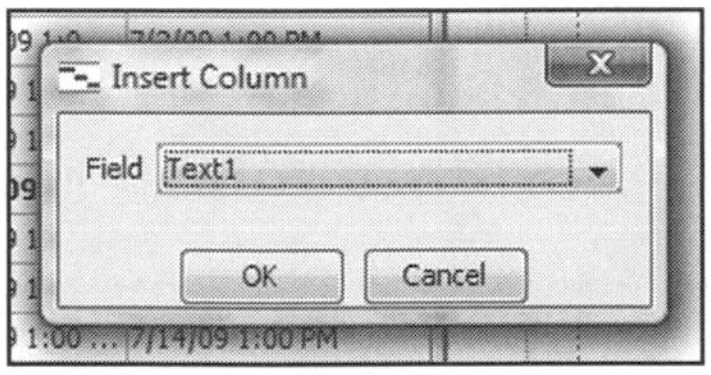

Figure 9.14
The selected field will appear.

To scroll the fields in the drop-down list more quickly, press the first letter in the field name. For example, press the **t** on the keyboard to jump down to the fields whose names begin with *T*.

---

3. Click **OK**. The new field appears in the sheet, ready for you to type entries.

When you insert a custom field in this way, you also can rename it. Right-click the placeholder field name in the field's column header, and then click **Rename**. In the Rename text box that appears, edit the field name in the New Name text box, and click **OK**.

Finding Information in a Column

One last trick that can help you as you finesse all the details in your project plan is to use Find to find information in a column so that you can update it more quickly. Find works much as it does in other leading applications, so the process should be familiar to you. In most instances, you'll start these steps with the Gantt view displayed, where you would typically make changes:

1. Click **Edit** and then click **Find** or click the **Find** button on the toolbar. (Shortcut: **Ctrl+F**.)

2. Type the words or phrase to find and replace in the **Find** text box.

3. Click the **Field** drop-down list and select the field in which you want to find and replace data. Figure 9.15 shows example Find settings.

Figure 9.15
Use Find to find entries in a specific field.

 When you're working in a view that shows tasks, the *Name* field in a list of fields refers to the *Task Name* field. When you're working with a view that shows resources, the *Name* field in a list of fields refers to the *Resource Name* field.

4. You can click the left **Find** button (with the down arrow) to search down through the list or the right **Find** button (with the up arrow) to search up through the list. When Find stops on an entry, you can click it in the spreadsheet and edit it, and then restart the Find by clicking one of the Find buttons.

5. When a final message box informs you that the search is finished, click **OK** and then click the **Close (X)** button to close the Find dialog box.

Chapter Review

This chapter taught you about a wide range of skills all used for a particular purpose: making the tasks, resources, and assignments in your project plan more detailed and accurate to further flesh out the project plan. In the chapter, you learned how to add a note for a task or resource. The chapter further showed you how to add an alternate calendar to a task, as well as how to apply a constraint or a deadline. You also learned how to contour the work on an assignment to account for a resource's real-world daily schedule or other conflicts between tasks. Finally, you learned how to work with the fields shown in a sheet and how to find information. In the next chapter, you'll learn about the important items in the plan that you must review as project manager before kicking off the work on the project.

Review Questions

Write your answers to the following questions on a sheet of paper.

1. Type in extra information on the _____ tab of the Task Information or Resource Information dialog box.

2. True or False: Notes print by default.

3. Do this to see what an indicator means.

4. When a task follows a different schedule than the overall project, assign a _____ to the task.

5. A _____ reduces OpenProj's flexibility in rescheduling a task.

6. If you add a _____ to a task, a yellow diamond on the task's Gantt bar appears and an indicator appears when the task runs late.

7. Do this to display another field set.

8. Unlike other costs associated with resources, you enter a _____ for a task.

9. Do this to a column header to begin the process for hiding or inserting a field.

10. True or False: OpenProj offers placeholder fields that you can use for custom information.

Projects

To see the solution files created by completing the projects in this chapter, go to www.courseptr.com, click the **Downloads** link in the navigation bar at the top, type **Open-Proj** or this book's ISBN-10 number in the search text box, and then click **Search Downloads**.

Project 1

1. Open the file named *Quick Assignments* that you created in the projects for Chapter 8.

2. Save the file as *Quick Assignments Adjustments*.

NOTE   Create a folder named *OpenProj Exercises* in your *Documents* or *My Documents* folder and save your exercise practice files there.

3. Drag the right border of the **Name** column header to resize the column to a size that's more appropriate to its contents.

4. Do the same for the **Start** and **Finish** columns, resizing them as desired.

5. Scroll the task spreadsheet portion of the view to the right until you can see the *Predecessors* field. Right-click the **Predecessors** field column header and then click **Hide Column**. Scroll the sheet portion of the view back to the left.

NOTE   Remember, changes you make to a field set onscreen aren't necessarily saved when you save the file. For example, when you change the width of a field in a table, the field will typically revert to its default width the next time you open the file. And a field that you've hidden may reappear the next time you open the file.

6. Right-click the **select all** button and click **Entry** to redisplay the unedited **Entry** field set.

7. Double-click a task sheet cell in task 4, *Proof and Print*.

8. Click the **Notes** tab, type **Check on proof type issued** in the Notes text box, and then click **Close**.

9. Move your mouse pointer over the note indicator to view its contents.

10. Save your changes to the file and keep it open for the next project.

Project 2

1. Double-click a task spreadsheet cell in task 2, *Writing*.

2. Click the **Advanced** tab in the Task Information dialog box, specify **8/17/09** as the task's Deadline entry, and then click **Close**.

3. Double-click a task spreadsheet cell in task 4, *Proof and Print*.

4. Click the **Advanced** tab, choose **Finish No Later Than** from the Constraint Type drop-down list, and then enter or specify **8/28/09** as the Constraint Date. Click **Close**.

5. Click **View** and then click **TaskUsageDetail** to change to the Task Usage view.

6. Double-click a task sheet cell in the **Tim L** assignment under task 2, *Writing*.

7. On the Resources tab, open the Work Contour drop-down list for Tim L in the Resources list, and click **Turtle**. Click **Close**.

8. Observe the impact of the assignment scheduling created by the contour you just added.

9. Click **View** and then **Gantt** to change to Gantt view.

10. Save your changes to the file and then close the file.

 Sometimes if you have multiple files open in OpenProj, you will see field sets from both files in the select all context menu. So, when working with fields and field sets, it's a good practice to work with one file at a time and to close and reopen OpenProj between files.

Project 3

1. Open the *Site Search with Assignments* file you worked on during the Chapter 8 projects.

2. Save the file as *Site Search with Ratings*.

3. In the left task spreadsheet portion of the Gantt view, resize the ***Duration*** field as desired.

4. Right-click the ***Start*** field column header and click **Insert Column**.

5. Open the **Field** drop-down list, type a **T** to scroll, and then click **Text1**. Click **OK**.

 The field you add here may not necessarily redisplay by default when you reopen the file. This is because you're not saving a custom field set. To learn more about that, see "Creating a Custom Field Set" in Chapter 12. To redisplay the *Text1* rating field, redisplay the Site Search (or Site Search with Ratings) field set. (Right-click the **select all** button and click the desired table.) If that doesn't work, display the Entry field set. Right-click the *Start* field column header and click **Insert Column**. Open the **Field** drop-down list, type a **T** to scroll, and then click **Text1**. Click **OK**.

6. Make the following entries in the new *Text1* field for the listed tasks only:

Task	Rating entry
2	Top
3	Middle
4	Top
5	Middle
6	Low

7. Click the upper-left cell in the task spreadsheet.

8. Click **Edit** and then click **Find**. Type **Middle** in the Find text box. Select **Text1** from the **Field** drop-down list, and then click the left **Find** button.

9. Click the left **Find** button again to find the next match.

10. Click the **Close (X)** button in the Find dialog box to finish using it.

11. Click **View** and then click **Resources**.

12. Right-click the *Initials* column header and then click **Hide Column**.

13. Right-click the *Group* column header and then click **Insert Column**.

14. Choose **Initials** from the Field drop-down list and then click **OK**.

15. Click **View** and then click **Gantt** to change to the Gantt view.

16. Right-click the **select all** button (gray button where the row and column headings intersect) and then click **Cost**. The *Cost* field set appears in the sheet part of the view.

17. Click the **Fixed Cost** cell for task 15, *Write Offer Contract*.

18. Type **250** and then press **Enter** to reflect an added attorney review flat fee. Note the new value calculated in the *Remaining Cost* field.

19. Right-click the **select all** button, and then click **Entry**. The Entry table reappears in the spreadsheet part of the view.

20. Save your changes to the file and close the file.

PART THREE

Finalizing and Launching a Project

CHAPTER 10

REVIEWING AND ADJUSTING THE PLAN

T his Chapter Teaches You How To:

- Perform a thorough review of your plan
- Review overall project statistics
- Understand the critical path
- Remove negative slack
- Adjust a task duration
- Find an overbooked resource and adjust assignments
- Manually edit an assignment
- Split a task

Before your plan achieves lift off, a key project management step is to make one last reality check. This chapter shows you the tools in OpenProj that enable you to identify specific problems and pressure points in the schedule so that you can adjust the plan accordingly. You will learn how to view statistics about the project plan, how to identify tasks that are critical, and how to improve the schedule by working with critical tasks. You'll see how to uncover factors like the amount of slack to check for and correct issues. Corrections you'll learn about include changing task durations and splitting tasks and finding overbooked resources and changing their assignments.

The Need to Ensure a Realistic Plan

OpenProj does a good job of scheduling a project based on the information you supply, but it cannot provide you with a judgment as to whether the plan meets the project objectives. OpenProj also can't tell you if the plan is realistic. However, if the plan fails to meet either of those tests, then the project will not finish on time and it will not deliver what it needs to deliver. When a project demands too much work in too little time with too few resources, the plan is likely to fail.

You as the project manager need to be as objective as possible in reviewing the project to ensure that it measures up. In finalizing the project plan before work begins, you need to ask and answer the following questions using the OpenProj tools described in this chapter to help you find the answers and take corrective action, when appropriate:

Is the project scheduled to finish at the right time?

Are the task durations accurate and based on the best information I have at this time?

Does the sequence of the tasks make sense and provide the quickest route to project completion?

Are there any risks that I haven't anticipated and planned for?

Is the budget adequate for the planned work and deliverables?

Are the resources adequate for the amount of work scheduled?

Is too much work scheduled for any one resource?

Viewing Overall Project Stats

When you want to see information about the overall project for review and decision-making purposes, you can view the project statistics through the Project Information dialog box using the following steps:

1. Choose **Project, Project Information**.
2. Click the **Statistics** tab. The statistics appear, as shown in Figure 10.1.
3. When you finish reviewing the statistics, click **Close**.

The Statistics tab of the Project Information dialog box shows you overall project start, finish, and duration information calculated for you by OpenProj. (The fact that the values are grayed out signals that they are calculated values.) In addition, it shows the total hours of work scheduled for the project and the budgeted cost. If the duration, finish date, and budget don't meet your needs, you can change your plan before the work begins.

As you later use OpenProj to track completed work for the project, the Statistics tab of the Project Information dialog box calculates even more information for you, such as actual duration, work, and cost, as well as completion percentages for duration and work. You

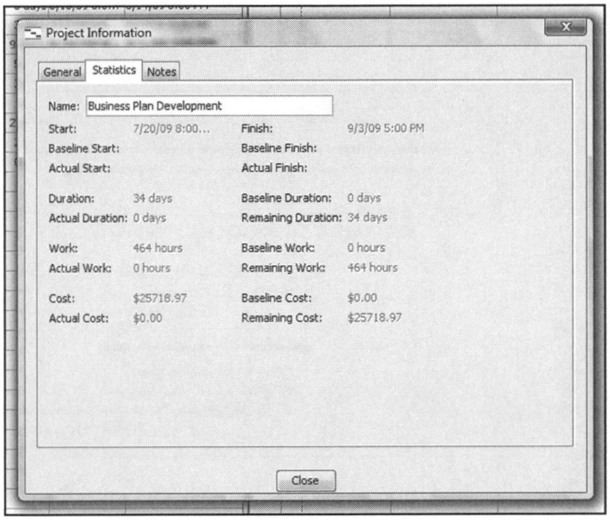

Figure 10.1
Project statistics provide additional information about the project status.

can check this tab at any time to see how "on track" the project is relative to your original plan. Chapter 11 will provide more details about what the evolving project statistics mean.

> **NOTE!** OpenProj also offers a report that conveys the overall project statistics. To learn how to view and print reports, see Chapter 13.

Understanding the Critical Path

Not every activity in a project has the same impact on the project's schedule and outcome. Project managers often need to focus on the tasks that are critical, but in this instance, "critical" has a specific meaning. In a project plan, the ***critical path*** is the sequence of tasks in the project that must finish on time for the project to finish on time.

A project might have several paths or linked sequences of tasks. The longest such path is the critical path and often runs all the way through the final tasks in the project. The critical path, therefore, defines the overall duration for the project. If the critical path becomes longer, the overall project duration increases, and vice versa. So, the ability to see the critical path enables you to make better decisions about planning and schedule changes.

OpenProj automatically identifies the critical path by formatting the Gantt bars for critical tasks in red. The Gantt bars for tasks that are not critical are blue on the Gantt graph. Although you may not be able to see the colors well because this is a black and white book, in Figure 10.2, tasks 6 and 8 through 10 have blue Gantt bars and are therefore not critical. They are not critical because tasks 6 and 8 have no successors, and the sequence of tasks

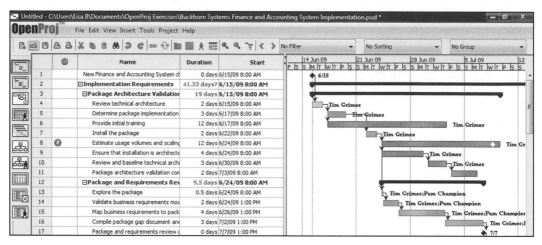

Figure 10.2 Tasks not on the critical path often fall in their own sequence that ends before the project ends.

9 through 11 also has no ultimate successors and ends long before the subsequent sequences of tasks in the plan.

OpenProj uses a calculated value called *slack* to determine whether or not a task is critical and should have a red Gantt bar. If a task can slip (happen later) without affecting the schedule of another task or the project finish, then the task has slack. So, for example, if a task in the schedule can happen two days later than scheduled without delaying another task or the project finish, the task has two days of slack.

Critical tasks have zero or negative *slack* time. Slack identifies the amount of time by which a task can slip or be delayed without affecting another task or the project finish. While all tasks on the critical path are critical, some tasks not on the critical path also might be marked as critical based on their calculated slack time.

As project manager, you typically don't need to see the amount of slack calculated for a task. The exception may be in cases of negative slack. See the later section called "Eliminating Negative Slack" to learn more about slack as a factor in fine-tuning the project plan.

If you assign a Must Finish On constraint to the final task in the critical path that is *after* the calculated finish date for the task, OpenProj may show tasks in the critical path as noncritical (blue Gantt bars), even though they have zero or negative slack time. This is bad, because as project manager, you need to know which tasks really are critical for planning purposes. If removing the Must Finish On constraint isn't an option, set the constraint date exactly at or slightly (say 0.5h) before the final task's calculated finish date.

Improving the Critical Path Schedule

Now that you can identify which tasks are critical, you can make better decisions about the project schedule. If you see that the calculated finish date for the project is too late based on the previously defined parameters for the project (such as a drop-dead project completion date handed down by your boss), then you need to make changes to the plan to improve or pull in the finish date. Or, if you've already started the project and it's running behind, you need to make adjustments to catch back up. In either case, you should focus on the tasks in the critical path, because shortening the critical path will shorten the project's overall duration.

The *critical path* identifies tasks that need to finish on time for your project to finish on time. When you want to improve the project's overall schedule, focus on shortening the critical path. As you change the plan to improve the schedule, check to make sure your changes haven't resulted in another area of the schedule becoming the critical path, at which point you'll need to shift your attention there.

You can make one of or any combination of the following changes to the project plan to shorten the critical path and project duration:

- **Move resources from non-critical to critical tasks.** If a resource has the appropriate skill set and schedule for a task on the critical path, shifting the resource from a non-critical task to the critical one can improve the schedule.

- **Move non-critical tasks so that you can redeploy their resources.** If you can't shift a resource from one task to another without making another schedule change, see if you can move a non-critical task earlier or later in the schedule to free up an assigned resource to work on a critical task, instead.

- **Make sure that you've assigned resources to all tasks.** Believe it or not, it is possible to fail to assign any resources to a task, thus preventing your schedule from taking advantage of the benefits of effort-driven scheduling.

- **Secure more resources for the project.** If budget and other factors allow, you can bring more resources to the team, with an eye toward making reassignments that shorten the critical path. For example, adding a temporary or freelance resource for a non-critical task might free up all or some of another resource's time to work on a critical task.

Throwing more resources at a project is sometimes called *crashing* or *expediting* the project. A project manager has to balance the costs for securing and using the added resources or for paying an external resource to work more aggressively versus the time gained in the project plan.

- **Use more of a resource's time, if available, for a critical task.** If you assigned a resource to work part time (less than 100% units) on a task, you may be able to secure more of the resource's time.

- **See if any work can be done simultaneously.** If some tasks can be rescheduled to occur at the same time, change links to adjust the schedule accordingly (that is, apply start-to-start links rather than finish-to-start links).

- **Examine critical tasks to see if they are all truly critical.** For example, you might be able to break down a task with a longer duration into multiple shorter tasks and move some of those tasks off the critical path. Or, you may have assumed that a certain task needed to be linked to a predecessor, when in reality the predecessor's schedule doesn't drive the task.

If you've done your best to bring the project plan in within the needed duration and you just can't get there, then you need to communicate about that reality with project stakeholders. If you're asked to continue with the plan, you will be doing so with full disclosure about the risk of the project being late. Otherwise, there may be an opportunity to adjust expectations by reducing the deliverables for the project, allowing more time, or completing only part of the project in the near term.

Eliminating Negative Slack

Sometimes, despite your best efforts, little inconsistencies will crop up in the project plan. One type of inconsistency or error that occurs is negative slack. If you keep in mind that slack represents time by which a task can be delayed before delaying other work, then negative slack means that the task is effectively already delaying other tasks or the project completion—even before the work begins!

There are a few situations in which negative slack occurs: when a successor task linked via an FS link has a Must Start On constraint date earlier than the finish date for the predecessor task; when a task's finish date is after any deadline date assigned to the task; or when a Must Finish On constraint date is before the current calculated finish date for the task. To view slack to find negative slack, you display the *Schedule* field set in the task spreadsheet of the Gantt view or Tracking Gantt view. To display the *Schedule* field set, right-click the **select all** button (gray box) where the sheet row and column headings intersect at upper-left, and then click **Schedule** in the context menu. Scroll the left spreadsheet portion of the view to the right to show the *Free Slack* and *Total Slack* fields (as shown in Figure 10.3) that you want to check for negative values. *Free slack* is the amount of time a task can slip without delaying other tasks, while *total slack* is the amount of time it can slip without delaying the project finish date.

Although it may seem counterintuitive, in some cases you need to look at the latest task with a negative slack entry and fix that task first. For example, if you add a Must Finish On

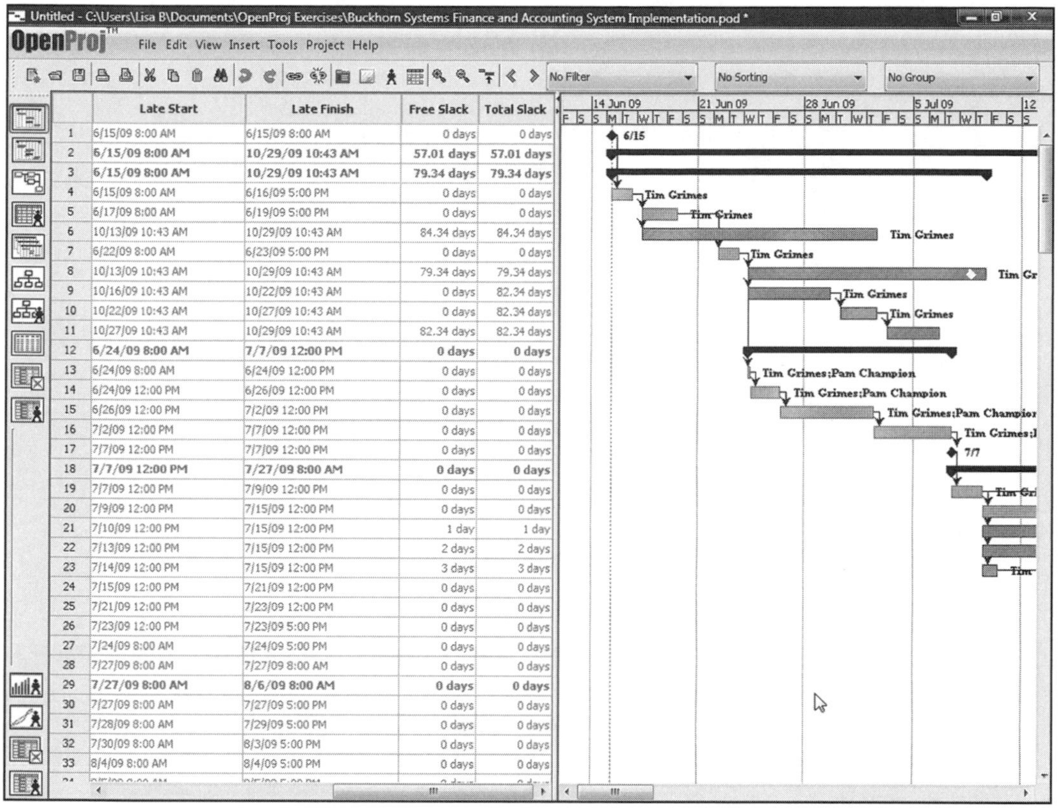

Figure 10.3 The *Schedule* field set shows slack values in the *Free Slack* and *Total Slack* fields.

Constraint to the final task in the project and assign a constraint date that's before the calculated finish date for the task, it will cause negative slack to appear throughout the critical path, as in the example in Figure 10.4. In this case, you need to decide whether you've built a schedule that's too tight (and therefore unrealistic), or whether the amount of negative slack is so minor that you want to run with the schedule as is. This is another case where "-.34 days" is not worth retooling the whole schedule for.

When you've finished checking slack values to look for negative slack, change back to the default *Entry* field set.

You also can display a graphical representation of slack with the Gantt bars in Gantt view. To do so, right-click on the graph at the right side of Gantt view, point to **Bar Styles** in the context menu, and click **Total Slack** in the submenu that appears. As shown in Figure 10.5, hatched extensions appear to the right of any Gantt bar for a task with slack to graphically chart the amount of slack. To hide those bars, right-click on the graph at the right side of Gantt view, point to **Bar Styles** in the context menu, and click **Total Slack** again.

	Late Start	Late Finish	Free Slack	Total Slack
1	6/12/09 2:16 PM	6/12/09 2:16 PM	-0.34 days	-0.34 days
2	6/12/09 2:16 PM	10/29/09 8:00 AM	56.67 days	56.67 days
3	6/12/09 2:16 PM	10/29/09 8:00 AM	79 days	79 days
4	6/12/09 2:16 PM	6/16/09 2:16 PM	-0.34 days	-0.34 days
5	6/12/09 2:16 PM	6/19/09 2:16 PM	-0.34 days	-0.34 days
6	10/13/09 8:00 AM	10/29/09 8:00 AM	84 days	84 days
7	6/19/09 2:16 PM	6/23/09 2:16 PM	-0.34 days	-0.34 days
8	10/13/09 8:00 AM	10/29/09 8:00 AM	79 days	79 days
9	10/16/09 8:00 AM	10/21/09 5:00 PM	0 days	82 days
10	10/22/09 8:00 AM	10/26/09 5:00 PM	0 days	82 days
11	10/27/09 8:00 AM	10/29/09 8:00 AM	82 days	82 days
12	6/23/09 2:16 PM	7/7/09 9:16 AM	-0.34 days	-0.34 days
13	6/23/09 2:16 PM	6/24/09 9:16 AM	-0.34 days	-0.34 days
14	6/24/09 9:16 AM	6/26/09 9:16 AM	-0.34 days	-0.34 days
15	6/26/09 9:16 AM	7/2/09 9:16 AM	-0.34 days	-0.34 days
16	7/2/09 9:16 AM	7/7/09 9:16 AM	-0.34 days	-0.34 days
17	7/7/09 9:16 AM	7/7/09 9:16 AM	-0.34 days	-0.34 days
18	7/7/09 9:16 AM	7/24/09 2:16 PM	-0.34 days	-0.34 days
19	7/7/09 9:16 AM	7/9/09 9:16 AM	-0.34 days	-0.34 days
20	7/9/09 9:16 AM	7/15/09 9:16 AM	-0.34 days	-0.34 days
21	7/10/09 9:16 AM	7/15/09 9:16 AM	0.66 days	0.66 days
22	7/13/09 9:16 AM	7/15/09 9:16 AM	1.66 days	1.66 days
23	7/14/09 9:16 AM	7/15/09 9:16 AM	2.66 days	2.66 days
24	7/15/09 9:16 AM	7/21/09 9:16 AM	-0.34 days	-0.34 days
25	7/21/09 9:16 AM	7/23/09 9:16 AM	-0.34 days	-0.34 days
26	7/23/09 9:16 AM	7/23/09 2:16 PM	-0.34 days	-0.34 days
27	7/23/09 2:16 PM	7/24/09 2:16 PM	-0.34 days	-0.34 days
28	7/24/09 2:16 PM	7/24/09 2:16 PM	-0.34 days	-0.34 days

Figure 10.4
A too-early Must Finish On constraint for the last task in a sequence or the critical path can cause negative slack throughout the schedule.

Negative slack appears for most of the tasks

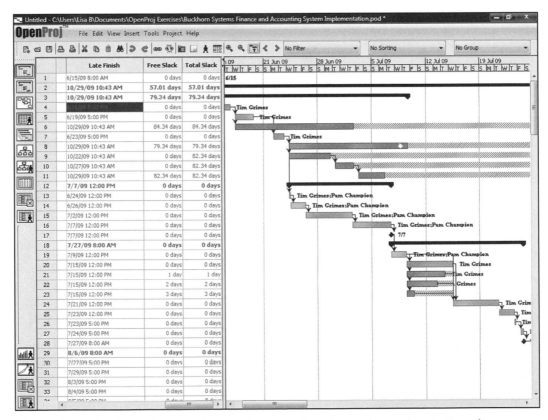

Figure 10.5 The Gantt chart can show slack graphically as hatched extensions to Gantt bars.

Slack can be a good thing. It gives you some wiggle room to move resources and tasks around as you execute the project plan. Although excessive amounts of slack might indicate a schedule that's too generous, in general you don't need to spend your time trying to eliminate all slack from the schedule.

Changing Durations

One simple adjustment you can make to a project plan is to change the duration for a task. You might need to change the duration based on feedback from an assigned resource that the task will take more or less time, for example. Or, if you entered an estimated duration (by including a question mark) because you were waiting for the data needed to finalize the task schedule, you can replace the estimated duration when the data is available.

To change the duration for a task, click its *Duration* field cell in the Gantt view, type a new duration (including any duration abbreviation needed), and press **Enter**. OpenProj will recalculate all dates affected by the duration change. You should review those carefully, as well as reviewing Project Statistics as described earlier in the chapter, to ensure that the change doesn't have an unexpected negative impact elsewhere in the plan.

When you're later tracking actual work completed on a task, OpenProj will automatically recalculate the duration as needed based on the actual start and actual finish information that you specify.

Avoid the temptation to just extend a task duration to pad the schedule. Remember, that will add more hours of work and costs to the project totals. If you want to build in a schedule cushion, add some lag time to linked tasks on the critical path, instead. If you don't mind adding extra hours of planned work into the schedule, then you also could add a task that represents a time contingency buffer. On the other hand, if a task's duration does need to increase and you get push back about it, call it as you see it. By presenting a well-developed, thoughtful plan in OpenProj, you're demonstrating that you take the project and the need for it to succeed seriously.

Finding Overbooked Resources

One planning mistake almost certainly will cause your project to run longer than expected: assigning too much work to a work resource. Such a resource is said to be *overallocated* or *overbooked* in OpenProj lingo. A resource is considered overallocated any time the hours of work assigned on a day exceed the resource's daily working hours per the calendar assigned to the resource.

The most obvious ramification of overbooking a resource is that it can make your project plan unrealistic. If you've assigned a resource 24 hours of work on a single day, all those tasks aren't going to happen. Even if you're working with salaried resources who you assume will put in the hours needed to "Git 'er done," your organization will eventually pay the price in terms of lower productivity and lower morale, and that's assuming none of your resources burn out during the course of your project and thus slow it down.

On the other hand, very small overallocations may occur depending on how you've created assignments. Even if a resource is only overallocated by .06 hours on a particular day, the resource is technically overallocated. It's a valid decision to just "live with" some small overallocations in the plan rather than wasting your time making changes that aren't really meaningful in the plan.

If you look carefully in Resource Usage view (**View, ResourceUsageDetail**), you can see when a resource has been overallocated. Whenever the total hours of work per day for a resource exceeds what you know to be its assigned calendar, then the resource is overallocated. For example, as you can see in Figure 10.6, the Tim Grimes resource has been assigned 16h of work per day for several consecutive days. You as project manager would need to evaluate whether Tim could really handle that.

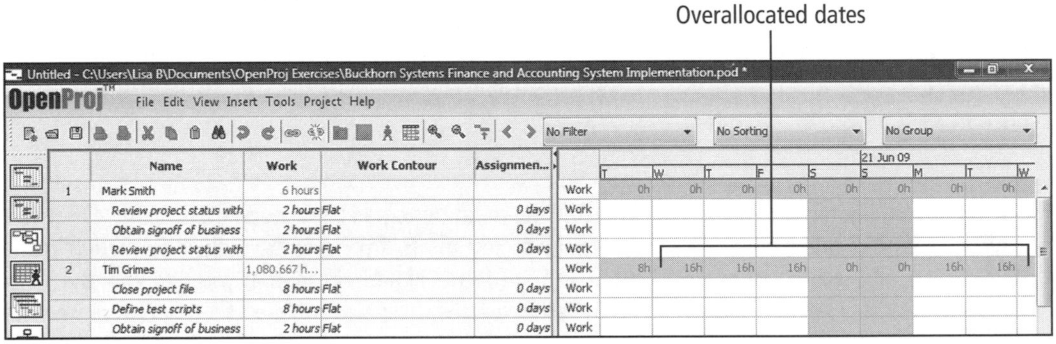

Overallocated dates

Figure 10.6 The Tim Grimes resource is overallocated based on the hours of work assigned per day.

Take the time to review and fix *overallocations* as needed before work on the project kicks off. Otherwise, you might be moving forward with a highly unrealistic plan.

You also can see a graphical view of resource overallocations in OpenProj. In this case, you will display a pane with one of the bottom views in OpenProj. Follow these steps to use the Histogram bottom view to find overallocated resources:

1. Display the view you want to appear at top, such as Gantt view or Resource Usage view.

2. Choose **View, Histogram** or click the **Histogram** bottom view button. The view appears in a bottom pane onscreen.

3. If your resource list is very lengthy, you can filter the list by clicking the **Resource Filter** drop-down list and then clicking the filter to apply. For example, you can filter to show only work resources or only those with unstarted assignments (although the latter choice would be more useful once work is underway on the project).

4. In the left side of the bottom pane, click the name of the resource for whom you want to view work information. As shown in Figure 10.7, a histogram graph of the assigned work for the resource appears at the right. The heavy black outline that follows the 100% gridline for working days indicates the resource's availability according to its calendar. Any time the histogram column goes over that mark, the resource is overallocated. For example, in Figure 10.7, Tim Grimes has a 200% level of work assigned for W, T, and F of the week shown.

5. When you finish using the Histogram view, choose **View, Histogram** or click the **Histogram** bottom view button to toggle the pane off.

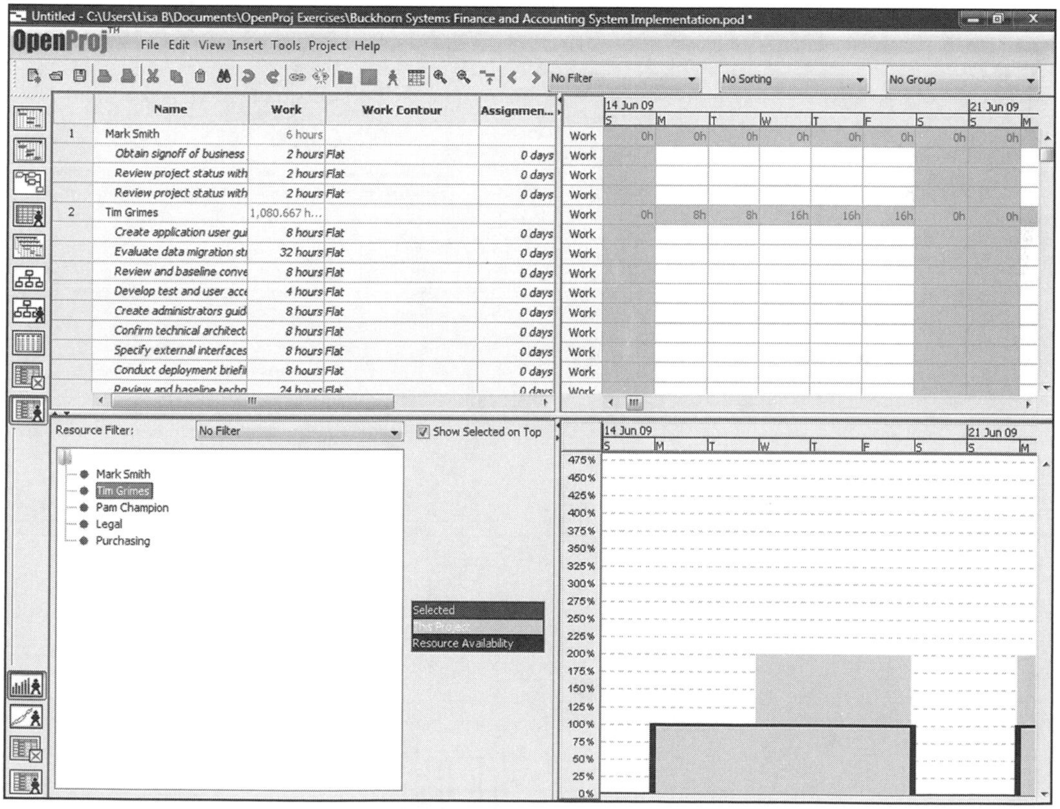

Figure 10.7 The Histogram bottom view shows a column chart of overallocations.

The appearance of the Histogram changes depending on which view you have selected in the top pane. (Just click in the top pane and use the View menu or the top view buttons to change that view.) For example, when the top pane has Gantt view displayed and you click a task there, the Histogram shows Resource Availability (black line), assigned hours for This Project (green) for each working day, and assigned hours for the selected task (blue portion of columns) for each working day. Figure 10.8 shows this view combo.

The rule of thumb varies, but many professional project managers never assume that a resource will give even a full 8 hours per day of task-related work. For example, I know of one project manager who only counts on 6 or 7 hours per day of actual work per person, with the remaining time being used for activities not specific to a particular project, such as e-mail, phone calls, and administrative tasks. You, too, should take a realistic look at how much actual "work time" occurs on a daily basis in your organization and adjust for it in your planning. This may mean adjusting each resource's calendar to account for a shorter workday. Or, take real conditions into account during your planning, making sure that task durations allow for the "overhead" of other ongoing activities.

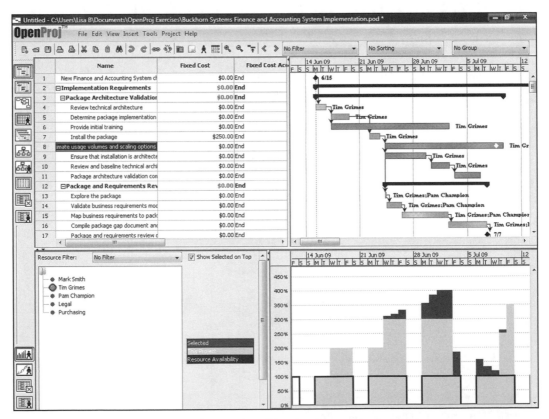

Figure 10.8 The Histogram view changes based on the view selected at the top.

Changing Assignments

After you've taken a look at the nature of the resource overallocation(s), you can decide how to address them to make sure that your plan only calls for a realistic amount of work for each resource. Note that the proper course might mean doing *nothing*. If a resource is only overbooked a few hours over the duration of the project and that resource is a salaried person, you can probably safely assume that the resource will absorb the extra time without delaying tasks or the project.

On the other hand, if a resource has consistently been assigned multiple extra hours of work per day over the entire course of the project or if there's a single day with an unreasonable amount of work assigned (such as 18 hours), you need to take action to impose sanity on the plan.

Generally speaking, you can use one of two methods to fix an overallocation:

- Remove the overallocated resource from a task and assign a different resource.
- Edit the assignment details in Resource Usage view, as described in the next section, "Editing Assignments Manually."

To substitute one resource for another, use the Assign Resources dialog box just as you learned in Chapter 8, "Assigning Resources to Tasks." In the Gantt view, click the **Assign Resources** button on the toolbar. Click the name of the task for which you want to change an assignment. Click the name of the resource to remove and then click the **Remove** button. Next, click the name of the replacement resource and click **Assign**. Click the dialog box **Close (X)** button when you finish making the reassignments.

> Of course, you should make sure that the replacement resource has time available to take on the new assignment. One way to do this is to view the resource's availability in the Histogram bottom view, as described earlier.

Editing Assignments Manually

If you need to track hours of work and costs associated for resources in greater detail, you can edit assignments on a day-by-day basis as needed. While you can perform this action in the Task Usage view, using the Resource Usage view (**View, ResourceUsageDetail**) works better because you can see the resource's total daily hours of work, so you'll know whether a change you make corrects the overallocation. After changing to the Resource Usage view, simply change the hours of work entered on the cell at the right that holds the data for the assignment date you want to edit.

On the other hand, if you want to split a task between two resources, for example having the first resource work on it solo the first day and the second resource work on it solo the second day, the view to work in is Task Usage (**View, TaskUsageDetail**), where you can see all the assignments for a task together. As in the Resource Usage view, edit the values in the cells at the right to update assignments. In the example shown in Figure 10.9, the assignments have been edited so that the work by the Tim Grimes resource follows the work by the Pam Champion resource.

14	Validate business require	36 hours	5.5 days	6/24/09 8:00 AM	Work	4h	8h	4h	0h	0h	8h	8h	
	Tim Grimes	20 hours	2.5 days	6/29/09 8:00 AM	Work						8h	8h	4h
	Pam Champion	16 hours	2.5 days	6/24/09 1:00 PM	Work	4h	8h	4h					

Figure 10.9 Edit assignments in the Task Usage view, in this case to schedule one resource's work after another's.

You can change the hours of work on any day for any assignment. You can delete the hours of work from the cell for one day and type that same amount into the cell for another day; just make sure you make the entry on the same row as the entry you deleted. You can even split an assignment between resources by deleting the hours of work for a particular date from one resource and adding those hours for another resource assigned to the task.

When you make an entry in a cell in the right side of the Resource Usage or Task Usage view, OpenProj assumes you are entering hourly values, so you don't need to type the **h**. Keep in mind that depending on the task type and whether or not effort-driven scheduling is turned on, changes made to an assignment's hours on a given day might cause OpenProj to recalculate assignment hours on other days. Be sure to check the impact of any change you make, and make further changes and/or change the task type if needed.

If you want to use this method to take a "what if" look at your project plan, you should consider making a copy of the file and then editing the copy so that you can view the Gantt view for each file to review the difference your changes made. You also can alter the Gantt view to illustrate assignments graphically when you review them. Right-click the graph side of the view at the right, and click **Show Assignments** in the context menu. As shown in Figure 10.10, each assignment appears as a separate row in the task spreadsheet, and a thin gold bar appears for each assignment on the Gantt graph. If you look closely at Figure 10.10, you can see how the assignment changes depicted in Figure 10.9 look when depicted graphically.

If you've applied a work contour to a resource, OpenProj might assign a tiny amount of work (such as .06 hour) to a resource at the beginning or end of the contour. You might simply choose to ignore such an overallocation because it's not really measurable or meaningful.

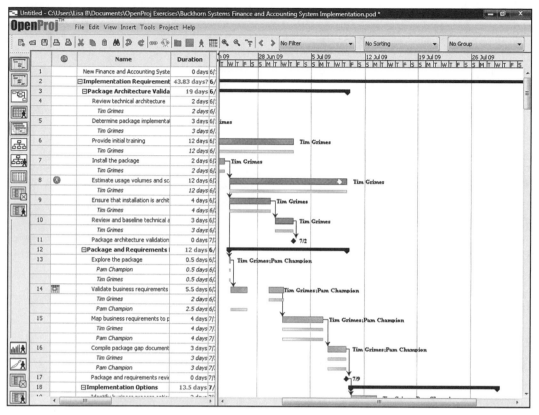

Figure 10.10 You can display assignments graphically in Gantt view.

Splitting a Task

Splitting a task inserts a non working period within the task so that the task is scheduled to start, stop for a period of time, and then resume and finish. You can split a task manually to correct a resource overallocation rather than leveling the project plan. One way to split a task manually is to manually edit assignments so different resources do their work on the task at different times; if there are days with no work assigned between the two assignments, the task will be split. You also can split a task without changing individual assignments to insert a non working period within a task—another option for resolving an overallocation. This means that you as project manager are evaluating which task to split and how to schedule the split.

Follow these steps to split a task:

1. Right-click the **Gantt** bar for the task to split on the Gantt graph. The mouse pointer changes to a special split pointer: double vertical lines with a right arrow.

2. Move the mouse pointer over the bar to the date on which you want the split to begin, and then click the left mouse button.

3. Move the mouse over the new segment of the bar on the right until you see the four-headed arrow pointer, and then drag right until the right segment of the bar spans the desired dates for the resumed portion of the task (see the example in Figure 10.11).

4. Release the mouse button to finish the split.

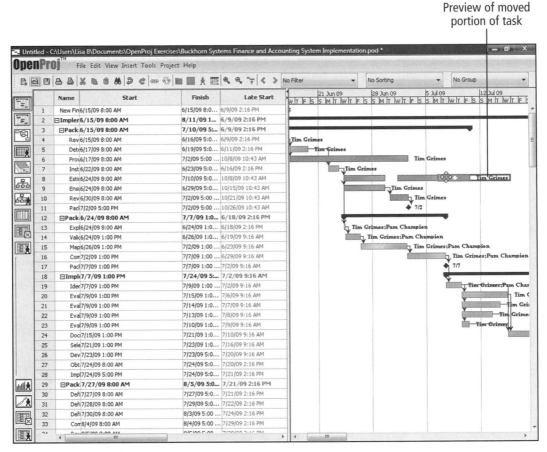

Figure 10.11 Splitting a task inserts a non working period within it.

To remove the split from a task, point to the left end of the split (right) portion of the Gantt bar and drag back to the left until it bumps back into the left portion of the bar as shown in Figure 10.12. When you release the mouse button, OpenProj removes the split.

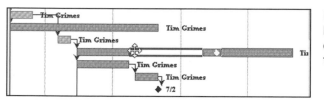

Figure 10.12
Drag the right portion
of the bar to the left
to remove the split.

Chapter Review

In this chapter, you learned techniques for going over the project plan with a fine-toothed comb to identify and correct problems before the work begins. The chapter started by showing you how to find overall statistics about your project that you can revisit as work evolves. You learned what the critical path is and how to use it for planning purposes. You saw how to view and eliminate negative slack, which indicates that a task has a scheduling conflict. You learned how to edit task durations and split a task, and how to find and fix resource overallocations.

Review Questions

Write your answers to the following questions on a sheet of paper.

1. True or False: You can use various views and features in OpenProj to perform a review of your project plan.
2. Access project statistics via the _____ dialog box.
3. A task is _____ when delaying it will delay the finish of the project as a whole.
4. Taking steps to make the _____ shorter will have the greatest positive impact on the project schedule.
5. A critical task has _____ or _____ slack.
6. Display the _____ field set to view the amount of slack for a task.
7. A resource with too much work assigned is _____
8. Name at least one view in which you can see more detail about resource overallocations.
9. Name at least one way to fix a resource overallocation.
10. A _____ inserts a non working period within a task.

Projects

To see the solution files created by completing the projects in this chapter, go to www.courseptr.com, click the **Downloads** link in the navigation bar at the top, type **OpenProj** or this book's ISBN-10 number in the search text box, and then click **Search Downloads**.

Project 1

1. Open the file named *Quick Assignments Adjustments* that you worked with in the projects for Chapter 9.

2. Save the file as *Quick Assignments Review*.

Create a folder named *OpenProj Exercises* in your *Documents* or *My Documents* folder and save your exercise practice files there.

3. Right-click the **select all** button and click **Entry** to redisplay the default Entry field set.

4. Click **Project** and then click **Project Information**.

5. Click the **Statistics** tab.

6. Make a note of the current *Duration, Work,* and *Cost* information. Also make a note of the currently scheduled *Finish* date for the project. Click **Close**.

7. Display the *Schedule* field set by right-clicking the **select all** button and then clicking **Schedule**.

8. Scroll the task spreadsheet portion of the view to the right until you can see the fields identifying slack. Notice that there are no slack entries in the *Total Slack* field.

9. Double-click a task sheet cell in task 4, *Proof and Print*.

10. Click the **Advanced** tab, change the **Constraint Date** to a date that's a day or two before the scheduled finish date for the project that you noted in Step 6. The negative slack appears in the *Free Slack* and *Total Slack* fields. Click **Close**.

11. Click the **Undo** button on the toolbar to undo the change.

12. Redisplay the *Entry* field set by right-clicking the **select all** button and then clicking **Entry**.

13. Save your changes to the file and keep it open for the next project.

Project 2

1. Click the link line between task 2, *Writing*, and its predecessor, task 1, opening the Task Dependency dialog box.

2. Enter **-2** in the Lag box and then click **OK**. This enters some lead time so that tasks 1 and 2 now overlap.

3. Choose **View, ResourceUsageDetail** to change to the Resource Usage view. Notice that the **Tim L** resource is now overbooked starting late in the first week of the project.

4. Choose **View, Histogram** to display the bottom view.

5. Click the **Tim L** resource name in the left side of the Histogram view and then scroll the right side of the upper view to the right to see the graph for the overallocations, if needed.

6. Choose **View, Histogram** to close the Histogram.

7. Choose **View, Gantt**.

8. Display the Assign Resources dialog box (**Assign Resources** button), and remove the Tim L assignment from task 1 (click the **Tim L** resource, and click **Remove**). Click the **Lynne C** resource, click the **Assign** button, and click the **Close (X)** button to close the dialog box.

9. Save your changes to the file and then close the file.

Project 3

1. Open the *Site Search with Ratings* file you worked on during the Chapter 9 projects.

2. Save the file as *Site Search Review*.

3. Right-click the **select all** button and click **Entry** to redisplay the default Entry field set.

4. Double-click a task spreadsheet cell for task 3, *Space*. Click the **Predecessors** tab, click the cell that contains **2** in the *Predecessor* ID column, press **Delete**, and then click **Close**. That action removes the link between tasks 2 and 3 so that task 2 is no longer critical. Its Gantt bar changes from red to blue.

5. Choose **View, ResourceUsageDetail**. Review the assignment hours, and notice that two resources are overallocated (Jane Black and the Realtor).

6. Choose **View, Histogram** to display the bottom view.

7. View the overallocations for the Jane Black and Smith Todd resources by selecting them at the left.

8. Choose **View, Histogram** to close the bottom view.

9. Choose **View**, **Gantt** to change to the Gantt view.

10. Click the **Assign Resources** button and remove the Smith Todd resource from tasks 2 through 5. Click the **Close (X)** button to close the dialog box.

11. Save your changes to the file and close the file.

CHAPTER 11

SETTING THE BASELINE AND TRACKING WORK

This Chapter Teaches You How To:

- Understand, save, and clear the baseline
- Understand interim plans and when to use them
- Mark percentage of work complete on a task
- Update and reschedule work
- View overall statistics and progress
- View costs
- Apply another cost from a cost field set
- Work with overtime
- Override a cost
- Cut the project duration

At this point, your project has arrived at a major transition point: moving from the planning phase to executing and controlling the project. OpenProj offers some great tools to assist you with tracking work, analyzing progress, and managing costs as the work on the project moves forward. This chapter shows you how to save a version of the starting plan for later comparison. You will learn about a number of tools and techniques for tracking work and tasks completed and making plan adjustments as circumstances evolve. You'll also see how to review overall project progress and review how specific tasks compare against the original schedule. And, because projects don't get finished for free, you'll see how to adjust cost information for specific assignments, including looking at ways to save costs or work with overtime work.

Working with the Baseline

When you look back on your work on a project during the closing phase of project management, you'll want to be able to answer key questions like "What went wrong," "What went right," and "Where did we improve on the schedule (or not)?" You'll be better able to answer those questions when you have a detailed record of how the work on the project flowed and how the actual outcomes compared with your original plan.

In OpenProj, you can put yourself in a better position to execute, control, and later evaluate and close a project if you save a **baseline** version of the plan before the work (execution) begins. Saving a baseline saves data about your original plans. Then, as you begin to track progress on the project, you can get a data-based comparison against the original plan.

The **baseline** saves starting data about the project for later comparisons. The saved baseline data includes planned task start and finish dates and cost information.

The Baseline and Tracking

As you have been building your project plan, OpenProj has been calculating task start and finish dates based on the durations and links you specified, as well as adding up cost information based primarily on the resource rates and assignments. That date and cost information, with the dates being charted in the default Gantt view, is the **current** schedule and cost information.

Saving the baseline copies the original plan information from fields such as the task *Start*, *Finish*, and *Cost (total cost)* fields into corresponding baseline fields: *Baseline Start*, *Baseline Finish*, and *Baseline Cost* fields, respectively, for the three fields listed. The saved data becomes the plan's baseline data. The baseline also preserves some other values, such as duration and work values for tasks, timing and cost data about assignments, and timephased values for work and cost. Baseline dates and values do not change as the project evolves over time, whereas current dates and values might change based on the tracking information and other changes you enter.

After you start tracking work performed on the project plan, OpenProj starts recording **actual** data. For example, once you mark any amount of work as completed on a task, the task now has an *Actual Start date* field entry.

By comparing actual data (or current data, where no actual data yet exists) to baseline data, OpenProj can calculate **variance** amounts. A variance indicates the quantity or percentage by which an actual (or current) value falls short of or exceeds the baseline value.

The plan's evolving values comprise the *current* data. When you mark any work as complete, OpenProj records *actual* data. OpenProj compares saved *baseline* data to the actual data (or current data, where no actual data yet exists) to calculate *variances* that indicate early or under budget results or late or over budget results.

The section later in this chapter called "Viewing Project Progress" explains various ways that you can see baseline, actual, and variance data in OpenProj.

Saving the Baseline

When you've finished revising and fine-tuning the plan and have received the necessary approvals and buy-in from stakeholders and team members, saving the baseline marks the transition from the planning phase to executing and controlling the project.

When you save the baseline, you have the option of saving the baseline for all the tasks in the project plan or saving the baseline for only selected tasks. You might save a baseline for selected tasks, for example, if you've only completed and gotten approvals for a portion of the project plan, but you can't wait for approvals on later work before kicking off the project.

After you save the initial baseline, OpenProj also enables you to save up to 10 additional baselines for comparison. Each additional baseline also stores start, finish, duration, work, cost, and timephased information. Typically, you would only save additional baselines for a very lengthy project. For example, for a year-long project, you might save an additional baseline at the end of each quarter. Each additional baseline is numbered, and the fields of information for that baseline have the corresponding number. For example, when you save Baseline 1 (the first additional baseline), the fields of data for that baseline include, among others, *Baseline 1 Duration* and *Baseline 1 Cost*.

When you've saved multiple baselines, you have to insert the specific baseline's fields into the current field set to see the additional baseline information.

Follow these steps to save a baseline:

1. If you want to save the baseline for selected tasks only, drag over the task row numbers. You also can Ctrl+click row numbers to select non-adjacent tasks.
2. Click **Tools**, point to the **Tracking** choice, and click **Save Baseline**. The Save Baseline dialog box opens (see Figure 11.1).

Figure 11.1
Save the baseline for
tracking purposes
using this dialog box.

3. If you need to save an additional baseline after saving the initial baseline, open the drop-down list below the Set Baseline option and click on the numbered baseline (Baseline 1 though Baseline 10) to set.

4. If you selected tasks in Step 1 and want to save the baseline only for those tasks, click the **Selected Tasks** option button under For.

5. Click **OK**. OpenProj saves the baseline information.

 Make sure you save the initial baseline before you track any work in the project plan. Otherwise, to get clean baseline values when work is already ahead of or behind schedule, you will need to remove the tracking changes you already made.

Taking a Look at the Baseline Task Schedule Data

By default, the task spreadsheet portion of the Gantt view doesn't show the fields for the saved baseline data (nor do the other often used task-oriented views such as the Tracking Gantt view). To see the key *Baseline Start* and *Baseline Finish* field data that was saved when you created the initial baseline, you need to display the *Variance* field set.

To view the *Variance* field set, right-click the **select all** button (the gray box where the row and column headers intersect) and then click **Variance**. As shown in Figure 11.2, after saving the baseline the newly saved values appear in the *Baseline Start* and *Baseline Finish* fields.

If you examine Figure 11.2 carefully, you can see for yourself that saving the baseline was essentially a simple copy operation. The *Start* field date for each task was copied to the *Baseline Start* field, and the *Finish* field data for each task was copied to the *Baseline Finish* field.

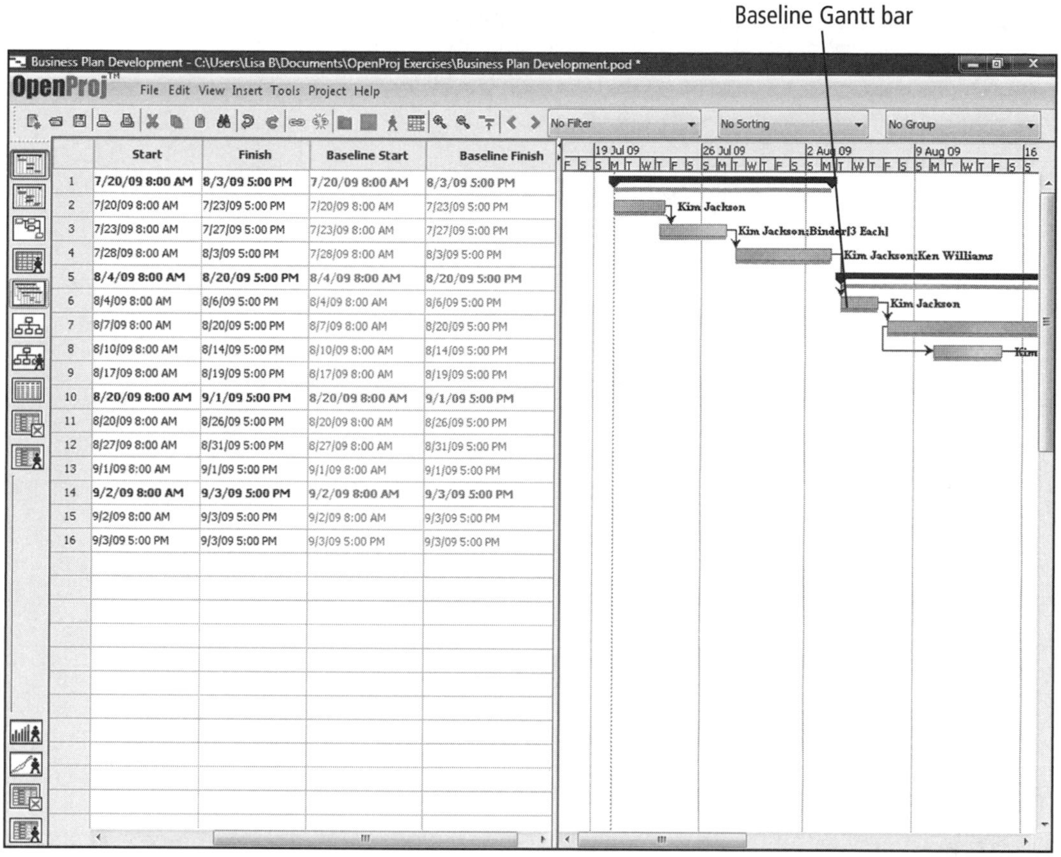

Baseline Gantt bar

Figure 11.2 The *Variance* field set shows the saved baseline data.

Also note in Figure 11.2 that when you save the baseline, a thin gray bar charting the baseline information appears below each Gantt bar in the Gantt view. As you track actual information and any current dates are recalculated, the main Gantt bars will move according to the recalculated schedule but the baseline bars will remain in place to illustrate the original schedule. You can hide and redisplay the baseline bars as needed. To toggle the bars on and off, right-click the graph portion of the view, point to **Bar Styles**, and click **Baseline** (Figure 11.3).

When you finish viewing the baseline data, you can redisplay the default *Entry* field set for the task view that you're using. Right-click the **select all** button and then click **Entry**.

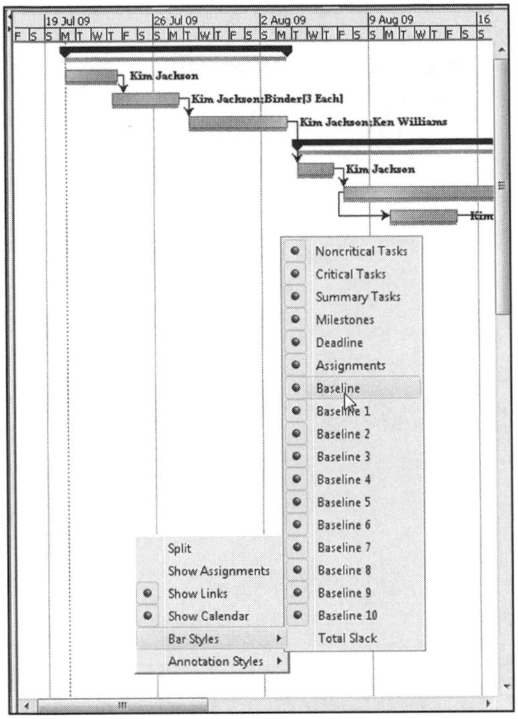

Figure 11.3
Use this command to display and hide baseline Gantt bars.

When and How to Clear the Baseline

In certain situations, saving an additional baseline will not be your best choice for capturing the data that you need to measure project progress accurately. For example, if relatively early during project execution the scope and deliverables undergo a major change, you may need to significantly retool the project and capture a new baseline. If you saved the baseline before you got signoff on the project and the work can't start, you may need to push out the project and start with a baseline that matches the new schedule. Or, if the project started but was subsequently placed on hold due to a change in resource and budget priorities in the organization, the original baseline won't be valid for the project when the work resumes.

In the situations just described, changes in the plan mean that the original baseline is no longer relevant. When you're measuring project progress, you want to measure against the right starting line. If you think of your project as a race, having an outdated baseline is like moving the starting line 10 meters behind the real starting line. The data will look like you're running a slow race even when you're kicking butt and taking names.

In other instances, you might want to create a new project plan by using the Save As command to copy any older plan to a new file. If that older plan contained baseline information, you will need to clear the baseline in the copied file.

To make sure OpenProj can calculate accurate variance data for a dramatically changed or delayed project, you can clear the baseline and then resave it. As when saving the baseline, you can clear the baseline for selected tasks only. So, for example, if the first part of the project is complete and only the latter part is delayed, you can clear and reset the baseline for those latter tasks only.

Use these steps to clear a baseline:

1. If you want to clear the baseline for selected tasks only, drag over the task row numbers. You also can Ctrl+click row numbers to select non-adjacent tasks.

2. Click **Tools**, point to the **Tracking** choice, and click **Clear Baseline**. The Clear Baseline dialog box opens (see Figure 11.4).

Figure 11.4
Clearing an outdated baseline and resaving the baseline provides a more valid basis for progress calculations.

3. If you need to clear a baseline other than the initial baseline, open the **Baseline** drop-down list and click on the numbered baseline (*Baseline 1* though *Baseline 10*) to clear.

4. If you selected tasks in Step 1 and want to clear the baseline only for those tasks, click the **Selected Tasks** option button below.

5. Click **OK**. OpenProj clears the baseline information. You can then make adjustments to the plan as needed and set a new baseline.

You also can ensure your project plan has the most appropriate data by updating (resaving) the baseline rather than clearing the baseline and saving a new baseline. Or, to preserve the existing baseline data but also capture new data in a new baseline, choose another (higher numbered) baseline from the **Baseline** drop-down list in the Save Baseline dialog box. You might use this approach when you don't need to make significant changes to the project plan but just want to capture new baseline data. To update the baseline, use the same steps as described earlier under "Saving the Baseline."

Tracking Completed Work

As work moves forward on your project, you need to track the results of completed effort, usually on a task-by-task basis. OpenProj provides you with a number of methods for tracking completed work. You can choose the method that works best for you based on how often you gather information and the level of tracking detail that you'd like to use.

Maintaining a Routine for Gathering and Entering Data

When using OpenProj as a standalone product, you as project manager must make sure that the most current task work information is gathered and that the plan is updated to reflect it. If you think that this type of data entry sounds about as fun as updating a client database, well, I don't necessarily disagree. However, just as a customer database would, over time, become less accurate as information becomes less current, so will your project plan not reflect the actual project status without an investment of time to enter tracking updates.

You should consider these factors when determining how to keep the plan as up-to-date as possible in terms of tracking completed work:

- **Update frequency.** Determine how often the updated tracking information should be entered in the project. The schedule you set will be primarily based on your needs in terms of controlling project execution. For a relatively brief project, weekly updates might give you the information you need to maintain project momentum. For a longer project, you might need less frequent updates. Stakeholder requirements also might drive update frequency. If your stakeholders require weekly progress reports, you'll need to schedule the update period in advance of the necessary reporting and at the corresponding interval.

- **Method for gathering data.** Unlike the enterprise-based project management solutions, in which resources can enter information about their own progress, with a standalone program like OpenProj, you'll need to gather the data yourself. Decide whether the best method for doing so will be regular e-mail requests, phone calls, status meetings, or conference calls.

- **Who will handle the updates.** Depending on the nature of your organization, you may have another resource available to take on the manual (data input) portion of updating the project plan file to reflect tracked work. It might be possible to make arrangements to have an administrative assistant or temp provide help with that part of the process. For example, a group of electrical utility engineers and the administrative assistant for their group attended a class I taught. They had already agreed that each engineer would be responsible for updating his project file, while the administrative assistant would be responsible for generating printed materials for reporting as well as reporting information from multiple projects.

■ **What will be gathered.** Make sure that there's clear understanding about the level of detail that will be gathered about each task. If you want to just track completion percentages, you need less information than if you want to track completion percentages, actual dates, and even further details about the work completed. Both the reporting resources and anyone who's helping you track the work need to be on the same page about what will be tracked.

You can track work in a number of OpenProj views, but most people do so in either the Gantt or Tracking Gantt views, in order to see schedule changes in both text and graphic formats.

Marking Completion Percentages

The most straightforward way to track completed work is to specify a completion percentage. If the resource(s) assigned to the task tells you about 25% of the work has been completed, you can mark the task as 25% complete. OpenProj will calculate that 25% of the task's duration has passed, and that 25% of the hours of work for the task (based on its duration and the resource assignments) have also been completed. As shown in Figure 11.5, a progress bar appears in the center of the Gantt bar for the partially completed task to illustrate the completion percentage.

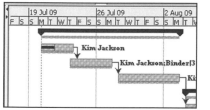

Figure 11.5
A black completion bar graphically illustrates completion percentage in Gantt view.

You can use one of two methods to mark a task completion percentage. For the first method, you specify the completion percentage in the Task Information dialog box. Double-click the task, click the **General** tab if needed, type the completion percentage in the **Percent Complete** text box as shown in Figure 11.6, and then click **OK**. This method has an obvious drawback: You have to work with one task at a time.

When you assign a completion percentage to a task, OpenProj calculates the corresponding amount of Actual Work, in hours, for each assigned resource.

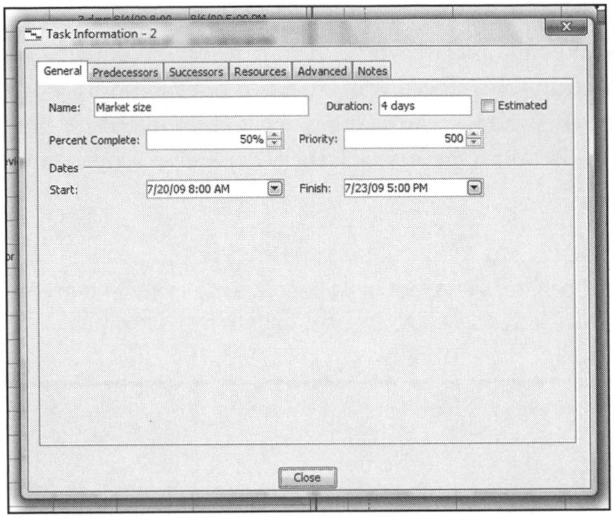

Figure 11.6
Enter a task's completion percentage in the Percent Complete text box.

When you specify completion percentages in a cell or text box, you can select and replace the existing entry or use the spinner arrow buttons that appear.

To skip the need to open the Task Information dialog box to enter completion percentages, you can use the Tracking Gantt view. The Tracking Gantt view by default uses the Tracking field set, which includes fields such as *Actual Start*, *Actual Finish*, and *Percent Complete*. To display the Tracking Gantt view, choose **View**, **Tracking Gantt** or click the **Tracking Gantt** view button at left. Then you can enter completion percentages in the *Percent Complete* field, as shown in Figure 11.7.

If you scroll the task spreadsheet to the right in Tracking Gantt view, the default field set also includes *Remaining Duration* and *Remaining Work* fields, which give you a read of how much longer and how much more effort it will take to complete each task. Remaining values are calculated using the current and actual data.

In the Gantt view, a check mark indicator appears in the *Indicators* field column for any task that you've marked as 100% complete.

These tasks were selected and
marked as 50% complete

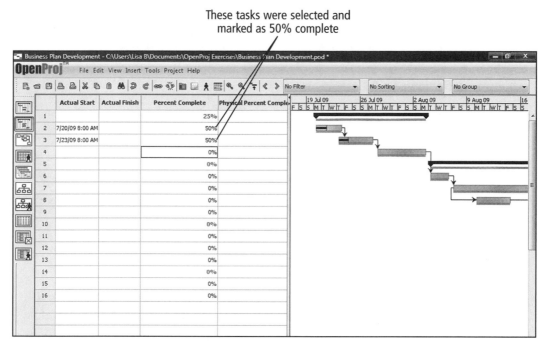

Figure 11.7 Use the Tracking Gantt view to mark completion percentages, even for multiple selected tasks.

Working with Actual Start and Finish Dates

Any time you mark a task as more than 0% complete, that task begins to have actual data along with its baseline and current data. If you've marked some work on a task but haven't yet marked it as 100% complete, the task has an actual start date, among other actuals (some actual work and actual cost data). Marking a task as 100% complete means that it has both an actual start date and actual finish date.

When you enter a completion percentage for a task using either the Task Information dialog box or the Tracking Gantt view, OpenProj assumes that the task started and finished on schedule, unless you specify otherwise by editing the actual start and/or actual finish information. You can specify that actual information by using the Update Tasks dialog box, as in the following steps:

1. Select the task to work with in the task spreadsheet portion of the view.
2. Click **Tools**, point to **Tracking**, and then click **Update Tasks**. The Update Task dialog box appears.
3. Enter or edit a completion percentage for the task in the **Percent Complete** text box.

4. If the completion percentage you specified is less than 100% and the task started on a different date than the *Start* date shown in the *Current* section of the dialog box, specify the real start date in the *Actual* section of the dialog box by typing in the date or using the drop-down calendar for the *Actual Start* text box. See the example in Figure 11.8.

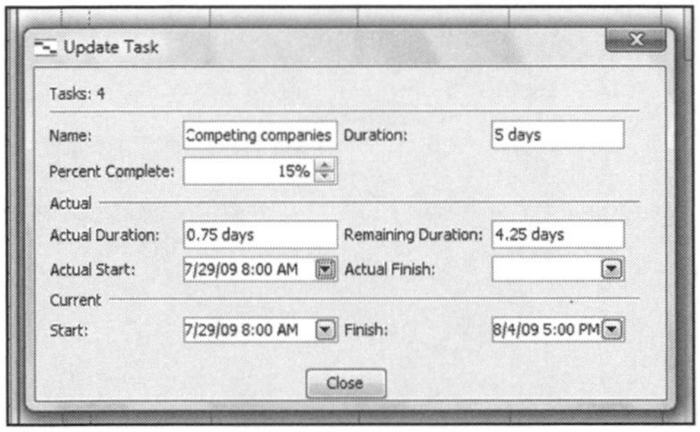

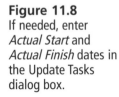

Figure 11.8
If needed, enter *Actual Start* and *Actual Finish* dates in the Update Tasks dialog box.

5. If you've marked a task as 100% complete, you can specify either or both *Actual Start* and *Actual Finish* dates in the *Actual* section to reflect the task's real schedule.

6. Click **Close** to close the Update Task dialog box and apply the completion percentage and task schedule changes.

If the actual start or finish information you entered in the Update Task dialog box affects the schedule for any linked tasks, OpenProj immediately recalculates the project schedule. If you leave baseline bars displayed in the Gantt view, as described earlier in the chapter, you'll be able to see how the actual schedule changes affect the plan when compared with the baseline.

Updating Work Completed by a Particular Date

If you've planned well and no surprises have yet disrupted the schedule, all your resources will give you feedback that their tasks are on schedule. In such a case, you can skip the added work of updating tasks on a one-by-one basis and instead update the tasks all at once. This method marks work as complete on all project tasks up to a date that you specify. So, if tasks 1 through 5 are scheduled to be partially complete as of a particular date, OpenProj can mark them as complete up to that date for you, calculating the proper completion percentages as needed.

Follow these steps to update work to a given date:

1. Click **Tools**, point to **Tracking**, and then click **Update Project**. The Update Project dialog box appears.

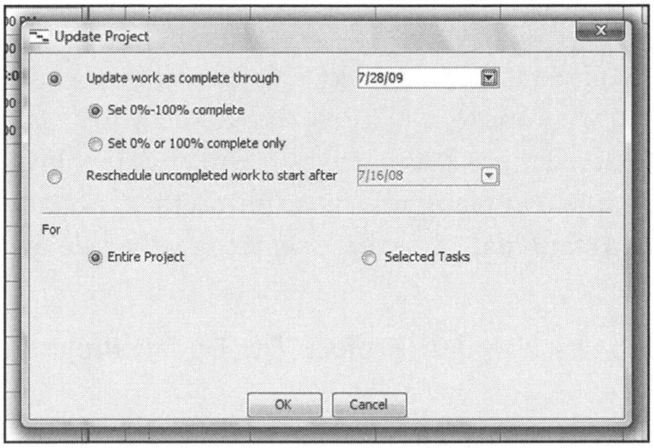

Figure 11.9
You can update tasks through the date specified in the upper-right text box of the Update Project dialog box.

2. Enter the date through which to update the tasks in the **Update Work As Complete Through** text box (see Figure 11.9), or use its drop-down calendar to specify the date.

3. Under **Update Work As Complete Through**, click an option button to specify how OpenProj should update tasks:

   ■ **Set 0% - 100% Complete.** OpenProj marks any task that's completed before the date you specified in Step 2 as 100% complete. For any task that starts before the specified date but doesn't finish until after the date, OpenProj calculates a completion percentage and marks the task as complete to that date.

   ■ **Set 0% or 100% Complete Only.** OpenProj marks any task scheduled to complete before the date specified in Step 2 as 100% complete. For any task scheduled to start before the date but finish afterward, OpenProj leaves the completion percentage set to 0%. In other words, this choice marks a task as 100% complete or does not change the completion percentage at all.

4. (Optional) If you selected any tasks before Step 1, you could click the **Selected Tasks** option button to have OpenProj update only those tasks. You can do this if you have a lengthy, complicated project and only want to update a section at a time.

5. Click **OK**. OpenProj calculates and marks task completion percentages through the specified date.

You also can use the Update Project dialog box to update a project's task to a future date, if you know that the project will be on track at that time. For example, if you have to give a status report on Friday but want to prepare your materials in advance on a Wednesday, you can specify the coming Friday's date as the Update Work As Complete Through date, finish the update, and then print the necessary reporting materials.

Rescheduling an Uncompleted Task

The Update Project dialog box also enables you to reschedule uncompleted work on a task to begin on a date that you set. If the task is 0% complete, OpenProj moves the whole task so that it starts on the status date. If you've marked the task as partially complete, OpenProj leaves the part of the task that's actually complete in place, inserts a split in the task, and schedules the work to resume on the specified status date. Use these steps to reschedule the uncompleted work on a task:

1. Click **Tools**, point to **Tracking**, and then click **Update Project**. The Update Project dialog box appears.

2. Click the **Reschedule Uncompleted Work to Start After** option button to select it.

3. Enter the date through which to update the tasks in the accompanying text box, or use its drop-down calendar to specify the date.

4. Click **OK**. As shown in Figure 11.10, OpenProj reschedules the work on the task to resume on the specified date.

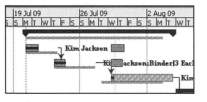

Figure 11.10
You also can use the Update Project dialog box in conjunction with a status date to reschedule uncompleted work.

If you need to reschedule all the work on a task, make sure you reset the task's completion percentage to zero (0%).

OpenProj doesn't limit you to using the Update Project dialog box to reschedule task work. You can, of course, make specific adjustments to task durations, link types, constraints, and so on as execution continues. In fact, remaining watchful of evolving circumstances and staying flexible and creative in addressing new realities are crucial requirements for project execution and control. You retain the power to make the necessary scheduling changes. OpenProj will show you the impact of those scheduling changes versus the saved baseline for the project in the Gantt view and the Tracking Gantt view, shown later in the chapter.

Tracking a Single Resource's Work on a Task

Different projects and environments require managing to different levels of detail. In many instances, tracking task completion percentages suffices because the project manager doesn't need to be concerned with the hours of work completed by each particular resource.

Task and project completion and the successful achievement of deliverables carry the most weight in those situations.

However, you many find yourself in an environment or an instance where you do need to document a reading of a specific resource's performance, especially when one resource assigned to a task isn't delivering when others are. For example, if the resource comes from another department that's been unreliable in the past, you may need to have evidence to support your case if you need to ask for a different or additional resource. Or, if you're dealing with a costly outside vendor and large payments are tied to task completions, you need to track that vendor's completion despite what other assigned resources have contributed.

In OpenProj, you can adjust the Gantt view so that you can see assignments and enter actual hours of work for a resource's assignment on a particular task. The changes described in this section don't affect completed work marked for other resources; you're working with only one resource's assignment. As a reminder, you can open the **View** menu and then click **Gantt** or click the **Gantt** view button to change to the Gantt view.

Once you've displayed the Gantt view, right-click the **select all** button in the task spreadsheet portion of the view and click **Tracking**. Then, right-click the graph in the right side of the view and click **Show Assignments** so you can see the assignment rows. Scroll the field set to the right, and edit the entry in the **Actual Work** field as needed (Figure 11.11). (Alternately, you can change the value in the *Percent Complete* field, which is further left in the same Tracking field set.) This specifies how much work that resource has completed on the task, and OpenProj will recalculate the overall task completion percentage accordingly.

When you finish editing assignments in Gantt view, remember to right-click the graph portion of the view at right and click **Show Assignments** again to hide the assignment rows in the view.

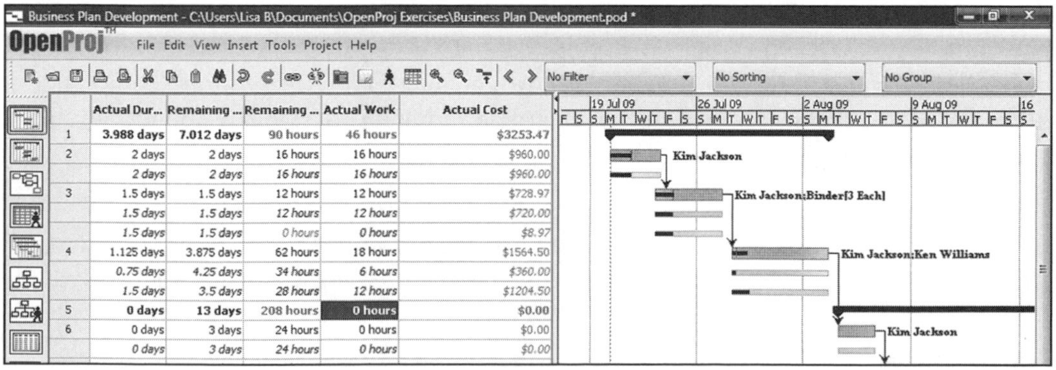

Figure 11.11 Adjust the Gantt view so you can change the completion percentage or actual work value for a single resource's work on a task.

Viewing Project Progress

Tracking work puts you in the position to report to others, including team members and stakeholders, about the progress on your project. OpenProj offers a variety of locations, views, and field sets that show various combinations of tracking information that you might want to share with stakeholders and team members. Take some time to familiarize yourself with the choices presented in this section so that you can choose the information that's most useful and relevant to you in your continuing leadership of the project.

It's a Numbers Game. Or Is It?

OpenProj's ability to calculate and graphically demonstrate progress against a plan may provide you with empirical data you didn't previously have to work as an advocate for your team. But, for a project that's off course, don't be discouraged by the realities uncovered in OpenProj's progress data. Just as OpenProj can't take the place of your human expertise, it also can't account for less tangible indicators of project progress and team accomplishments. For example, if the project is running behind but a brand new team is coming together and turning the corner, OpenProj can't demonstrate that. Or, deliverables and stakeholder satisfaction being provided may exceed the apparent "progress" calculated by OpenProj in terms of tasks completed and work completion percentages. When you're managing your project, make sure that you're keeping mental or written notes about *all* the team's achievements, so you can dole out the kudos and discuss the team's success at appropriate times.

Project Statistics

You learned in Chapter 10 how to view overall project statistics so that you can verify the project's overall finish date, scheduled work, and cost on the Statistics tab of the Project Information dialog box.

Now that you've tracked work in the project, the Statistics tab in the Project Information dialog box provides more information. As shown in Figure 11.12, in addition to the *Current* information, the dialog box includes *Baseline* data and *Actual* data where applicable. It also calculates *Remaining* values for *Duration*, *Work*, and *Cost*.

When you finish viewing the information, click the **Close** button to close the Project Information dialog box. You can redisplay this dialog box and tab as often as needed to get a read on work progress and to check how much of the project budget has been expended.

Gantt View

The default Gantt view doesn't provide any information about project progress beyond the progress bars with the Gantt bars on the chart portion of the view and the check mark

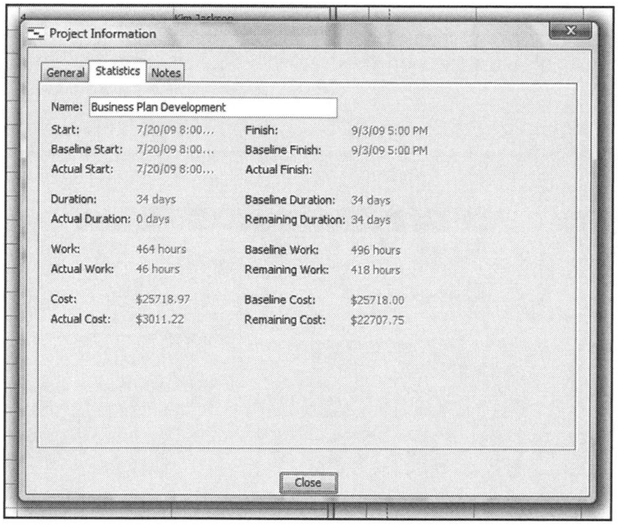

Figure 11.12
As you track work, project statistics evolve and include actual and remaining data.

indicator that appears for any task marked as 100% complete. You can, however, display other field sets in the task spreadsheet portion of the view to evaluate progress information. Choose the field set to view by right-clicking the **select all** button and then clicking the desired field set.

These two field sets display valuable progress information after you begin tracking work in the project plan:

- **Summary field set** (see Figure 11.13). This field set includes the *Cost* and *Work* fields that show the total cost and hours of work scheduled for each task. The *Percent Complete* field shows the marked completion percentage for each task.

- **Tracking field set** (see Figure 11.14). This field set includes fields with actuals for start, finish, duration, cost, and work. You can use the *Physical Percent Complete* field to enter an alternate completion percentage if the *Percent Complete* field doesn't totally reflect the actual work expended. For example, a writing task might take more hours of work earlier and fewer later, when the writer is editing the already-written work.

- **Earned Value Cost Indicators and Earned Value Schedule Indicators field sets.** These two field sets include a number of calculated fields that calculate more complex metrics used by professional project managers to judge project performance. For example, you can check the *BCWP* (budgeted cost of work performed) field to see if the level of work and budget expended are on target. The *CV* field calculates the difference between that field and the *ACWP* (actual cost of work performed) field, basically showing you the variance between the budgeted and actual costs. If the value in the *CV* field for a task is negative, then the task went over budget.

The values for summary tasks are calculated based on the tracking data entered for detail tasks.

		Name	Duration	Start	Finish	Percent Complete	Cost	Work
1		⊟Research	11 days	7/20/09 8:...	8/3/09 5:...	36%	$9783.97	136 hours
2		Market size	4 days	7/20/09 8:0...	7/23/09 5:...	50%	$1920.00	32 hours
3		Competing products	3 days	7/23/09 8:0...	7/27/09 5:...	50%	$1448.97	24 hours
4		Competing companies	5 days	7/28/09 8:0...	8/3/09 5:...	22%	$6415.00	80 hours
5		⊟Content	13 days	8/4/09 8:0...	8/20/09 ...	0%	$9295.00	208 hours
6		Develop outline	3 days	8/4/09 8:00 ...	8/6/09 5:...	0%	$1440.00	24 hours
7		Write narrative	10 days	8/7/09 8:00 ...	8/20/09 5:...	0%	$0.00	80 hours
8		Consultations	5 days	8/10/09 8:0...	8/14/09 5:...	0%	$6415.00	80 hours
9		Revisions	3 days	8/17/09 8:0...	8/19/09 5:...	0%	$1440.00	24 hours
10		⊟Financials	9 days	8/20/09 8:...	9/1/09 5:...	0%	$3600.00	72 hours
11		Develop financials	5 days	8/20/09 8:0...	8/26/09 5:...	0%	$2000.00	40 hours
12		Comprehensive review	3 days	8/27/09 8:0...	8/31/09 5:...	0%	$1200.00	24 hours
13		Corrections	1 day	9/1/09 8:00 ...	9/1/09 5:...	0%	$400.00	8 hours
14		⊟Completion	2 days	9/2/09 8:0...	9/3/09 5:...	0%	$3040.00	48 hours
15		Finalize draft	2 days	9/2/09 8:00 ...	9/3/09 5:...	0%	$3040.00	48 hours
16		Submit to incubator	0 days	9/3/09 5:00 ...	9/3/09 5:...	0%	$0.00	0 hours

Figure 11.13 The *Summary* field set shows the completion percentage (*Percent Complete*) for each task.

		Name	Actual Start	Actual Finish	Percent Co...	Physical Percent Co...	Actual Dur...	Remaining ...	Remaining ...	Actual Work	Actua...
1		⊟Research			36%		3.988 days	7.012 days	90 hours	46 hours	$301
2		Market size	7/20/09 8:0...		50%		2 days	2 days	16 hours	16 hours	$96
3		Competing p	7/23/09 8:0...		50%		1.5 days	1.5 days	12 hours	12 hours	$72
4		Competing c	7/28/09 8:0...		22%		1.125 days	3.875 days	62 hours	18 hours	$132
5		⊟Content			0%		0 days	13 days	208 hours	0 hours	$
6		Develop outl			0%		0 days	3 days	24 hours	0 hours	$
7		Write narrati			0%		0 days	10 days	80 hours	0 hours	$
8		Consultation			0%		0 days	5 days	80 hours	0 hours	$
9		Revisions			0%		0 days	3 days	24 hours	0 hours	$
10		⊟Financials			0%		0 days	9 days	72 hours	0 hours	$
11		Develop fina			0%		0 days	5 days	40 hours	0 hours	$
12		Comprehensi			0%		0 days	3 days	24 hours	0 hours	$
13		Corrections			0%		0 days	1 day	8 hours	0 hours	$
14		⊟Completion			0%		0 days	2 days	48 hours	0 hours	$
15		Finalize draft			0%		0 days	2 days	48 hours	0 hours	$
16		Submit to inc			0%		0 days	0 days	0 hours	0 hours	$

Figure 11.14 The *Tracking* field set provides more actual information.

Tracking Gantt View

The Tracking Gantt view provides the best graphical view of project progress. To display this view, click **View** and then click **Tracking Gantt** or click the **Tracking Gantt view** button in the buttons at the left. As shown in Figure 11.15, the Gantt bars for the Tracking Gantt view also are divided. The top portion of the bar shows the actual (when solid) or current (when shaded) schedule for the task, while the gray bottom portion shows the task's baseline schedule. A current or actual bar that's longer than the baseline bar means that the task took longer than scheduled. A current or actual bar that's shifted to the right of the baseline bar means that the task occurred or is now scheduled to occur later than originally planned; a left shift indicates an earlier schedule.

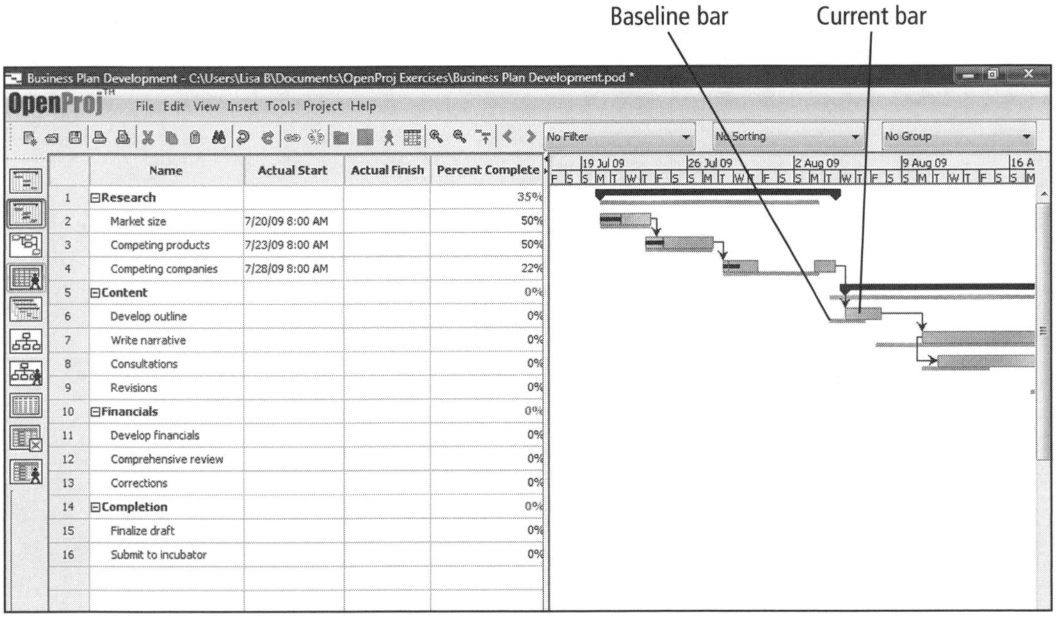

Baseline bar
Current bar
Business Plan Development - C:\Users\Lisa B\Documents\OpenProj Exercises\Business Plan Development.pod *
OpenProj
File Edit View Insert Tools Project Help
No Filter
No Sorting
No Group
Name
Actual Start
Actual Finish
Percent Complete
1 Research 35%
2 Market size 7/20/09 8:00 AM 50%
3 Competing products 7/23/09 8:00 AM 50%
4 Competing companies 7/28/09 8:00 AM 22%
5 Content 0%
6 Develop outline 0%
7 Write narrative 0%
8 Consultations 0%
9 Revisions 0%
10 Financials 0%
11 Develop financials 0%
12 Comprehensive review 0%
13 Corrections 0%
14 Completion 0%
15 Finalize draft 0%
16 Submit to incubator 0%
19 Jul 09
26 Jul 09
2 Aug 09
9 Aug 09

Figure 11.15 The Tracking Gantt view provides a graphical view of progress versus the baseline plan.

Black progress bars illustrate the calculated completion percentages for tasks. The field set at the left enables you to enter tracking information, such as actual data and completion percentages.

GOTTA KNOW

Choose **View, Tracking Gantt** to display a view that charts current or actual task schedules versus the baseline.

Working with Cost Information

Ensuring that resources complete work and the project deliverables arrive on time may absorb the majority of a project manager's attention, but budget management must receive attention, as well, for many projects.

Sometimes new project managers get too ambitious with regard to attempting to track everything in OpenProj the first time around. When you initially begin to use OpenProj to track cost information, you also should track project costs using another trusted method. If that's the case for you, you can export cost information from OpenProj for use in another application; Chapter 13 covers how to export information. Keep in mind that because OpenProj rounds certain values, it doesn't offer the level of precision provided by a company accounting system. OpenProj can be used for overall budgeting and tracking purposes, but not for real accounting.

Viewing Costs in the Cost Field Set

Whether you're working in the Gantt or Tracking Gantt view, you can display the *Cost* field set to view actual costs versus baseline costs, as well as cost variances. OpenProj calculates these values on a task-by-task basis based on the task completion percentages (and therefore hours of work completed) that you track. See Figure 11.16.

To display this field set, right-click the **select all** button and then click **Cost**.

		Name	Fixed Cost	Fixed Cost Accrual	Baseline Cost	Actual Cost	Remaining Cost
1		⊟**Research**	$0.00	End	$9783.97	$3011.22	$6772.75
2		Market size	$0.00	End	$1920.00	$960.00	$960.00
3		Competing products	$0.00	End	$1448.97	$728.97	$720.00
4		Competing companies	$0.00	End	$6415.00	$1322.25	$5092.75
5		⊟**Content**	$0.00	End	$9295.00	$0.00	$9295.00
6		Develop outline	$0.00	End	$1440.00	$0.00	$1440.00
7		Write narrative	$0.00	End	$0.00	$0.00	$0.00
8		Consultations	$0.00	End	$6415.00	$0.00	$6415.00
9		Revisions	$0.00	End	$1440.00	$0.00	$1440.00
10		⊟**Financials**	$0.00	End	$3600.00	$0.00	$3600.00
11		Develop financials	$0.00	End	$2000.00	$0.00	$2000.00
12		Comprehensive review	$0.00	End	$1200.00	$0.00	$1200.00
13		Corrections	$0.00	End	$400.00	$0.00	$400.00
14		⊟**Completion**	$0.00	End	$3040.00	$0.00	$3040.00
15		Finalize draft	$0.00	End	$3040.00	$0.00	$3040.00
16		Submit to incubator	$0.00	End	$0.00	$0.00	$0.00

Figure 11.16 Display the *Cost* field set to compare baseline (budgeted) versus actual costs for completed work.

Cutting Back Costs

When you see that actual costs exceed the amounts you budgeted, you must evaluate whether you need to take action to reduce costs going forward. If you allowed for cost over-runs by being conservative in planning the budget or if the quantity and quality of work being delivered warrants the extra expense, then action might not be required. You can consider a number of different strategies for reducing project costs, and OpenProj can help by recalculating cost information based on changes that you make. Try these techniques when you need to reduce the project's budget:

- **Target expensive tasks.** Identify the more expensive uncompleted tasks (you can look at the *Baseline Cost* field in the *Cost* field set shown in Figure 11.16, for example) and see if you can decrease the scheduled work for them or negotiate a more favorable fee or hourly rate. Then reduce the task duration in Gantt view or change the resource's *Standard Rate* field entry in the Resource view accordingly.

- **Substitute less expensive resources.** As when you were fine-tuning during the planning phase, you can continue to make resource substitutions as part of executing and controlling the project. If you need to remove a more expensive resource and assign a less expensive one, use the same techniques as described in the section "Changing Assignments" in Chapter 10.

- **Ask the outside vendor to substitute a resource with a lower rate.** If you're working with an outside vendor for which you've set up multiple cost field sets because the vendor offers multiple individuals with different skill and experience levels, you can ask the vendor to help you conserve costs by using a less costly individual for some tasks. For example, if you're working with a legal firm, see if more tasks can be handled by an associate rather than a full partner. This technique can save tens of dollars per hour of work. See "Using a Different Cost Rate Table for an Assignment" in Chapter 8 to see how to apply the lower rates to affected assignments once you have the vendor's agreement.

- **Cut deliverables and tasks.** Perhaps the most drastic measure to pursue for a project running way over budget is to revisit overall expectations for the schedule and deliverables. If the stakeholders agree, you may need to eliminate some of the deliverables and tasks from the project plan to set them aside and return to them later as part of a new project with a new budget.

Calculating Overtime, a Workaround

A task may require more work than you originally anticipated. If the schedule is more crucial than the budget, you may want to authorize hours of overtime work for the resource. As of this writing, OpenProj doesn't calculate overtime automatically, nor does it add in costs for overtime.

However, there is a workaround that you can employ to "account for" overtime in the project plan:

1. In the Resources view, review the *Standard Rate* and *Overtime Rate* entries for the resource for whom you want to add overtime. Subtract the *Standard Rate* from the *Overtime Rate* to find the hourly premium for overtime.

2. Edit the number of hours of work completed by the resource on the date for which you want to authorize overtime to reflect the overtime hours. See the earlier section called "Tracking a Single Resource's Work on a Task" to review how to do this.

3. Display the Gantt view and the *Cost* field set. Also be sure to display individual assignments by right-clicking the graph portion of the view and clicking **Assignments**. Multiply the number of hours you added in Step 2 by the premium you calculated in Step 1, and enter that value in the *Fixed Cost* field for the applicable resource assignment.

Accelerating the Finish Date

Of course, if you're asked to increase the project scope or deliverables or accelerate the project finish date, those actions will typically add cost to the finished project plan. It will be up to you to choose the most cost-effective and achievable way to accelerate the project finish, also called crashing the project, again using OpenProj to test the impact of various approaches:

- **Use overtime.** If your organization allows you discretion in asking resources to work overtime, you can authorize overtime work for more assignments. Focus on tasks on the critical path, and make sure that the authorized overtime has a positive impact on the task duration; in other words, it may not be the best choice to add overtime for one resource assigned to a task if you can't do so for other resources, because the task would still have a later finish date.

- **Add more work resources.** Adding more resources into the project plan, particularly to tasks on the critical path, will reduce the schedule. However, this method is likely to add the most cost, as well as increasing the complexity of managing the ongoing project. You'll suddenly have more resources to deal with, and you'll need to integrate the efforts of those resources into the ongoing activities of the project.

- **Cut tasks and deliverables.** As when reducing costs, this remains an alternative for reducing the project schedule when the project is running long. With stakeholder approval, you can eliminate some deliverables and tasks with the intent of returning to them under the auspices of a new project, if the need for that work continues in the organization.

Chapter Review

This chapter ushered you into the execution and control phases of project management and presented some of OpenProj's tools for assisting you with those responsibilities. You learned how to save the baseline before work begins for later tracking purposes, as well as how to clear the baseline or use an interim plan. You learned to use various methods for tracking work, as well as how to specify *Actual Start* and *Actual Finish* dates for a task, automatically update or reschedule work, and how to work with a single resource's progress information. You moved on to learn about some of the ways you can view information about project progress. Finally, you looked at methods for viewing and working with costs; authorizing overtime; and reducing the duration for a project that's running behind.

Review Questions

Write your answers to the following questions on a sheet of paper.

1. Saving the _____ saves initial information about the project plan for later comparison.

2. True or False: You can save more than one baseline.

3. The _____ field set includes a field for marking work as complete on tasks.

4. Use the _____ dialog box to enter *Actual Start* and *Actual Finish* dates for tasks.

5. True or False: OpenProj only reschedules the entire task when you use the Reschedule Work button.

6. The _____ tab of the Project Information dialog box shows baseline and actual data after you save starting information and begin tracking work.

7. Display different _____ in the left portion of the Gantt view to see various fields with calculated tracking information.

8. The _____ view displays two Gantt bars for each task: one for the original schedule and another for the current or actual schedule.

9. Name at least one way to reduce project costs.

10. Use the _____ field set to view and work with costs.

Projects

To see the solutions file created by completing the projects in this chapter, go to www.courseptr.com, click the **Downloads** link in the navigation bar at the top, type **Open-Proj** or this book's ISBN-10 number in the search text box, and then click **Search Downloads**.

Project 1

1. Open the file named *Site Search Review* that you worked with in the projects for Chapter 10.

2. Save the file as *Site Search Track.*

 Create a folder named *OpenProj Exercises* in your *Documents* or *My Documents* folder and save your exercise practice files there.

3. Right-click the **select all** button and click **Variance**.

4. Drag the divider bar between the two sides of the view to the right so that you can see the *Baseline Start* and *Baseline Finish* fields.

5. Click **Tools**, point to **Tracking**, and then click **Save Baseline**.

6. Leave the default settings in the Save Baseline dialog box selected and click **OK**.

7. Observe how the new information appears in the *Baseline Start* and *Baseline Finish* fields.

8. Click **Tools**, point to **Tracking**, and then click **Clear Baseline**.

9. Leave the default settings in the Clear Baseline dialog box selected and click **OK**.

10. Notice that the *Baseline Start* and *Baseline Finish* fields now are blank again.

11. Click **Tools**, point to **Tracking**, and then click **Save Baseline**. Click **OK**. This resaves the baseline.

12. Right-click the **select all** button and click **Entry**.

13. Click **Project** and then click **Project Information**.

14. Click the **Statistics** tab. Notice that the dialog box now shows Baseline information for *Start, Finish, Duration, Work,* and *Cost.*

15. Click **Close** to close the Project Information dialog box.

16. Save your changes to the file and keep it open for the next project.

Project 2

1. Right-click the **select all** button and click **Tracking**.

2. In the Percent Complete field of the task spreadsheet, enter the following completion percentages for the specified tasks:

task 2Infrastructure   100%

task 3, Space   100%

3. Click task 4, *Parking*, in the task spreadsheet portion of the view.

4. Click **Tools**, point to **Tracking**, and then click **Update Tasks**.

5. Enter **33** in the Percent Complete text box. In the Actual section of the dialog box, specify an actual start date of **2/4/10** by typing the date in the Actual Start text box or using the drop-down calendar. Click **Close** to close the dialog box and apply the completion percentage and actual start date.

6. Click **Tools**, point to **Tracking**, and then click **Update Project**.

7. Specify a status date of **2/5/10** by entering the date in the Update Work As Complete Through text box in the upper-right corner or by using the drop-down calendar. Leave the rest of the options as is and then click **OK**.

8. Right-click the Gantt graph portion of the view and then click **Show Assignments**.

9. For the Jane Black assignment under task 5, *Expansion*, change the *Percent Complete* field entry to **100**.

10. Right-click the Gantt graph portion of the view and then click **Show Assignments**. Also right-click the **select all** button and click **Entry**. Notice that the Gantt bar for task 5, *Expansion*, now expands beyond its original schedule.

11. Save your changes to the file and keep it open for the next project.

Project 3

1. Choose **Project, Project Information** and click the **Statistics** tab.

2. Review the information that appears on the Statistics tab. Note that the current Finish date now is two days later than the Baseline Finish. Note also that the current *Duration* is two days longer than the *Baseline Duration*, and the current *Baseline Work* and *Cost* amounts differ from their baseline values.

3. Click **Close** to close the dialog box.

4. Click **View** and then click **Tracking Gantt**.

5. If needed, scroll the chart portion of the view to display the Gantt bars. Notice the scheduling changes that have resulted in the work tracking so far.

6. Choose **View, Gantt**.

7. Right-click the **select all** button and click **Cost**.

8. Click the **Fixed Cost** field for task 6, *Document*, and enter **100**.

9. Scroll the field set to the right to compare those *Baseline Cost* and *Remaining Cost* field entries to see the impact of the change you made in Step 8.

10. Right-click the **select all** button and click **Entry**.

11. Save your changes to the file and close the file.

PART FOUR

REVIEWING AND SHARING RESULTS

CHAPTER 12

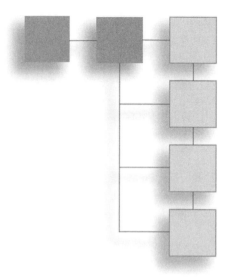

USING AND
PRINTING VIEWS

This Chapter Teaches You How To:

- Review the usefulness of views
- Control information in a sheet by filtering or sorting
- Zoom in or out
- Change formatting for Gantt bars
- Set up a printout and print

Throughout the phases of managing your project—from circulating a hard copy of the preliminary plan to stakeholders for approval to the point when you're closing down the project and archiving the final documentation—you'll need to be able to provide the project information in hard copy when required. In working through the last few chapters, you've seen the many views OpenProj offers and how specialized the information in each view can be. This chapter gives you even more information about working with views, including finding the view you need, adjusting what the view shows, and finally sending what you need to the printer. Don't yawn, folks. You'll appreciate what this chapter has to teach you when crunch time comes.

Finding the View You Need

Because you can't get far in building your project plan without changing views, you've already worked quite a bit with selecting a view from the View menu. The top of the View menu lists ten top views and four bottom views. To change to any of those views, click the **View** menu and then click the view name or click the applicable view button at the left.

Here's a review of each of the top views you'll find in OpenProj:

- **Gantt.** This is the default view in OpenProj, showing the task spreadsheet at the left and the chart portion with Gantt bars at the right. After the baseline has been saved, a thin gray bar with each Gantt bar charts the task baseline schedule.

- **Tracking Gantt.** In Tracking Gantt view, the Gantt bars include a gray bar showing the task baseline schedule. The left spreadsheet portion of the view shows the Tracking field set, with fields for actual information. You learned about this view in Chapter 11.

- **Network.** The Network view displays tasks in a format resembling a flow chart (see Figure 12.1). You can drag to link tasks, or click the link line between tasks to work with link settings.

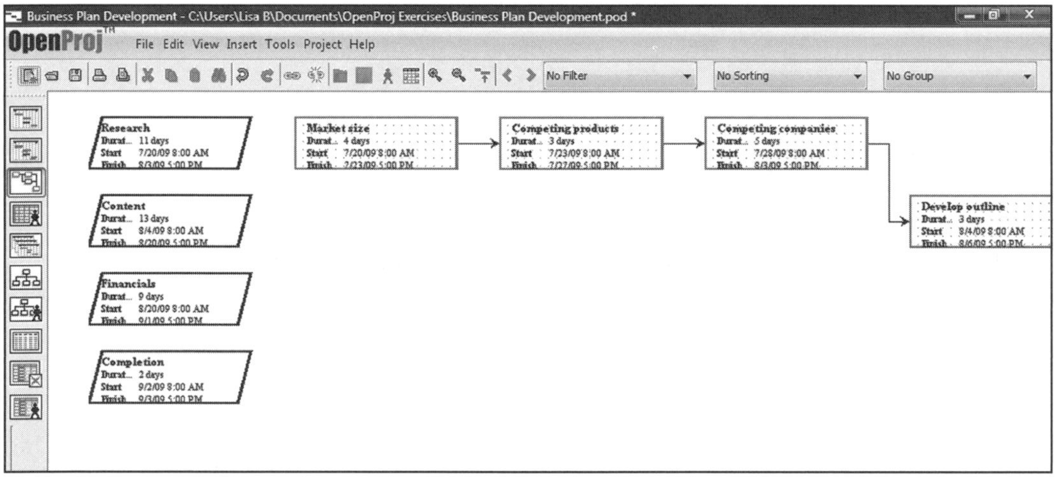

Figure 12.1 The Network view gives an idea of task flow.

- **Resources.** Use the fields in this view to add resources to your project plan file, as described in Chapter 7.

- **Projects.** When you have multiple project plan files open, this view provides overview information about each project, as shown in Figure 12.2.

- **WBS.** This view shows the hierarchical relationships of tasks in the project plan. Subtask boxes flow from summary task boxes, as shown in Figure 12.3.

- **RBS.** If you've used outlining to define the resource hierarchy as described in the section called "Creating the Resource Hierarchy" in Chapter 7, then changing to RBS view displays a graphical resource hierarchy similar to the WBS view shown in Figure 12.3. If you haven't applied the outlining, then the view shows the resources but not the relationships between them.

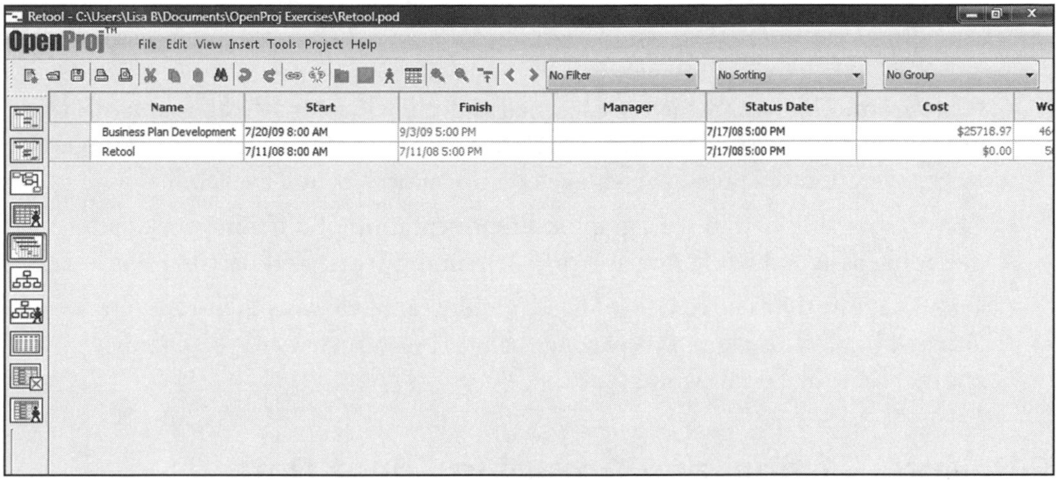

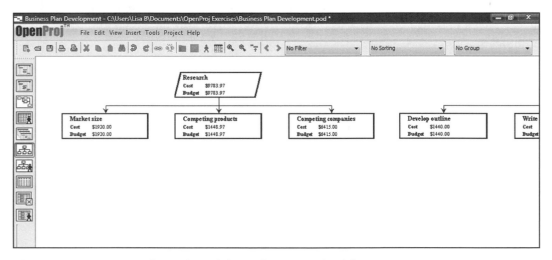

Figure 12.2 Use Projects view to review statistics from open OpenProj files.

Figure 12.3 WBS view shows the task hierarchy in a graphical format.

- **Reports.** The Reports choice on the View menu doesn't really display a view, but displays a print preview where you can choose and print a report. Reports will be covered in more detail in Chapter 13.
- **Task Usage (TaskUsageDetail).** This view groups assignments by task, and you can use the timephased grid at the right to view and enter daily work and cost values.
- **Resource Usage (ResourceUsageDetail).** This view, covered in various earlier chapters, combines a resource sheet on the left that identifies the assignments for each resource with a timephased grid on the right that you can use to enter daily actual costs, daily scheduled work and completed work, and more.

The bottom views appear in a bottom pane and work in conjunction with the selected top view. Here's a review of the bottom views:

- **Histogram.** This view, which you learned about in Chapter 10, can graph information about a resource's daily and cumulative costs, scheduled work and cumulative work, overallocated times, percentage of work allocated, and availability.

- **Charts.** Use this view to see a graphical representation of different work data, including assigned Work, Actual Work, Remaining Work, and Baseline Work.

- **Task Usage and Resource Usage.** These are the same views as their top-view twins. You just have the option of displaying them as bottom views so you can display another view like Gantt view at the top.

Filtering, Sorting, and Grouping Sheet Data

When you're working with a list of information, you might want to view that information in a different order, or eliminate some of the displayed information to see only what you need. That's why you can sort lists of information in various databases and spreadsheet programs.

OpenProj also gives you the ability to sort or filter information in a spreadsheet. If that information is part of a view that shows Gantt bars, those, too, will appear in the sorted or filtered order. Most often, you'll want to sort and filter information in the Resources view, but sometimes sorting or filtering a view like Gantt can help you see the information you need in a project.

Sorting changes the order of the information in a list. In OpenProj, you can sort by a single field only. OpenProj reorders the task rows or resource rows according to the contents in the selected field.

Follow these steps to sort information:

1. Change to the view in which you want to sort information.
2. Click the **Sort** button on the toolbar, which reads **No Sorting** when there's no sort applied.
3. Click the field by which you want to sort in the drop-down list that appears. Open-Proj immediately applies the sort.

To remove any sort, click the **Sort** button again, and then click **No Sorting**. This returns the list of resources or tasks to its original order based on the resource or task IDs.

OpenProj's group feature works similar to applying a sort. Instead of merely rearranging the list of tasks or resources, *grouping* also adds a summary item that you can use to collapse and expand the items in the group. Use the **Group** button at the far right end of the toolbar to apply and remove grouping. Figure 12.5 shows the Gantt view, with tasks grouped by *Resource Names*. To remove the grouping, click the **Group** button again, and then click **No Group**.

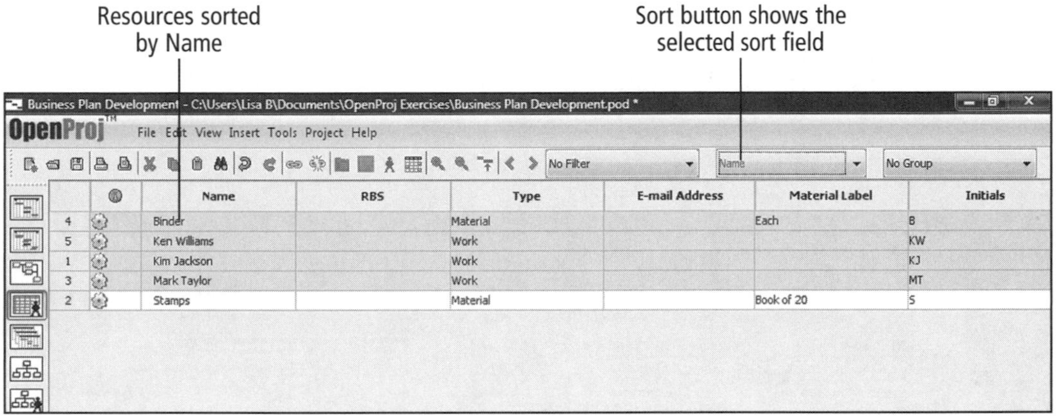

Resources sorted
by Name

Sort button shows the
selected sort field

Figure 12.4 The resources have been sorted by *Name*.

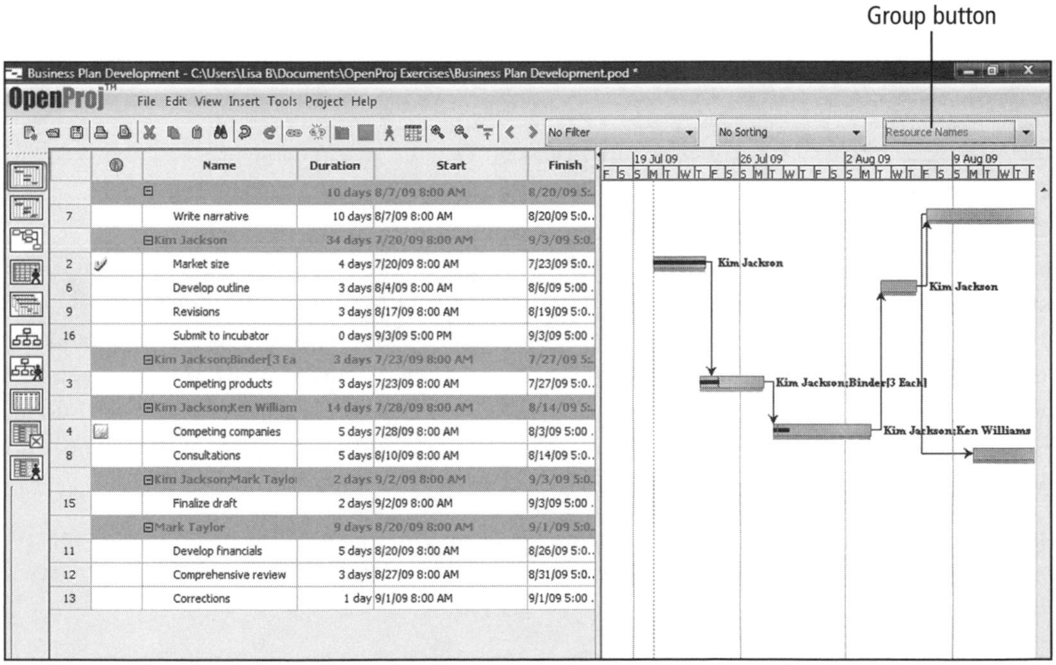

Group button

Figure 12.5 The tasks have been grouped by *Resource Names*.

Just as a field set controls the columns that appear onscreen, *filtering* controls which rows appear onscreen. When you filter the list of tasks or resources in a sheet, you tell OpenProj to display only those rows that match the specified criteria. Think of it this way: Filtering helps you to "look for" the information you want by eliminating the information you don't want from view. So, if you want to see a list of tasks that are in progress so you can follow up with the resources assigned to those tasks, you can filter the Gantt view to show only in-progress tasks, as shown in Figure 12.6.

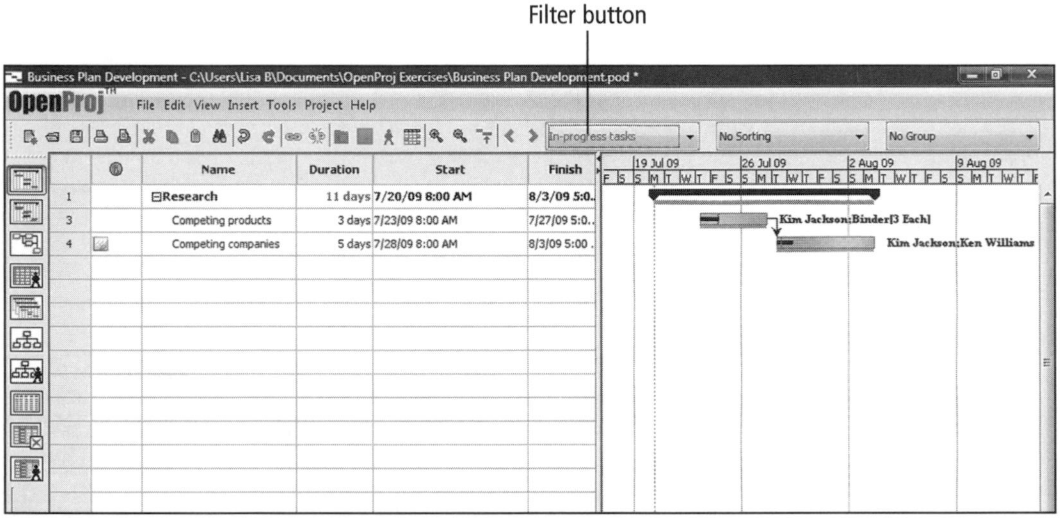

Filter button

Figure 12.6 Only in-progress tasks appear with this filter applied.

OpenProj includes a number of filters that limit the list of tasks or resources to match one or more criteria. Click the **Filter** button (which reads **No Filter** when filtering is off) and then click the desired filter in the menu of available filters. The filters that appear vary depending on whether you're viewing a task- or resource-oriented view. For example, when viewing tasks the filters include Completed Tasks, Incomplete Tasks, and Late/Overbudget Tasks. When viewing resources, the available filters include In Progress Assignments and Work Resources.

If you select certain filters, like the Date Range filter, OpenProj will prompt you to specify additional filter criterion, such as a resource name or dates for task filtering. To remove a filter, click the **Filter** button again and click **No Filter**.

Sorting changes the order of tasks or resources in a sheet. *Filtering* hides tasks or resources that don't match specified field criteria. *Grouping* rearranges tasks or resources into summary-like sets that you can expand and collapse.

Zooming In and Out

Many users struggle to get the chart portion of the Gantt view to provide information at the appropriate scale. In a short project with a lot of tasks that are a few hours long, the default setup for the Gantt makes the bars look so small that they're almost meaningless. On the other hand, if you're viewing a long-term project with many long tasks, you might wish to compress more information into view on the chart. You can use the two methods presented here to wrangle the graph portion on the right side of the view into the scale you need. (Or to zoom other views, for that matter.)

You can zoom a view to resize it. In a view like Gantt view that has a time axis, zooming adjusts the time increments shown on the lower of the two bands on the time axis.

The commands for adjusting the zoom are found on the View menu. Use the **Zoom In** choice to enlarge the charted information, which also shows smaller increments on the lower portion of the time axis. For example, in Figure 12.7, zooming in on the Gantt view scaled the lower portion of the time axis to 2-hour increments. .

Use the **Zoom Out** command on the View menu to take a higher-level view and view more information onscreen at any time. Starting from the original view size, you can zoom in or out twice, so once you zoom all the way in or out, the applicable Zoom In or Zoom Out command will become disabled and you'll only be able to zoom in the opposite direction.

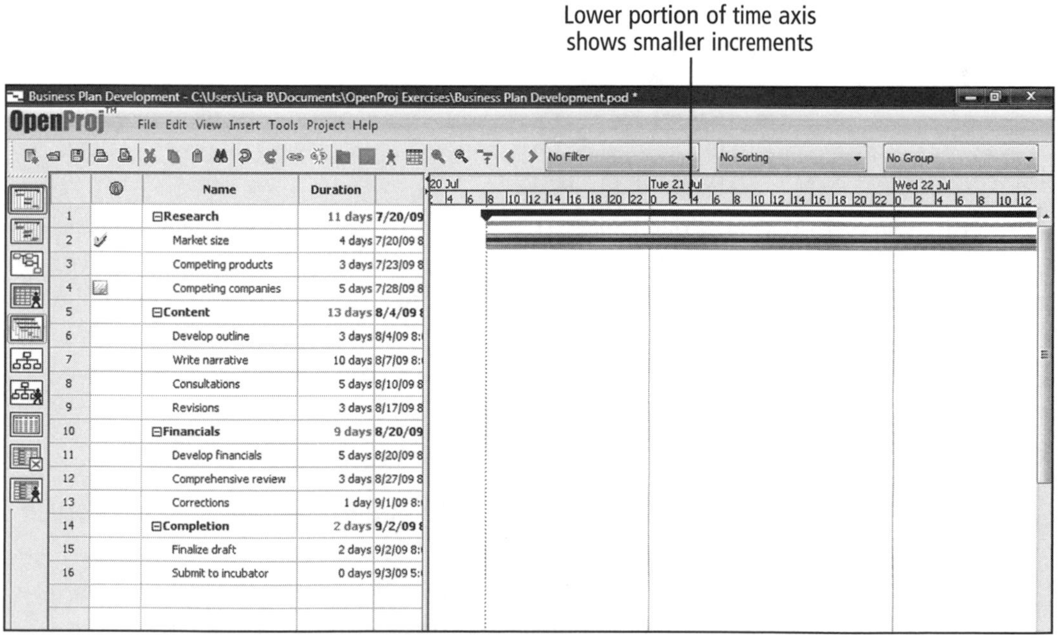

Figure 12.7 Zooming enables you to display more or less information in the view.

When printing the project, it prints with the same zoom that's currently displayed onscreen.

Formatting Chart Elements

When you right-click a Gantt graph at the right side of the view, a context menu appears with commands that lead to the options for formatting that particular chart. As you've already seen in a prior chapter, right-clicking and then clicking **Show Assignments** toggles assignment rows on and off in Gantt view.

The context menu offers several other choices for toggling portions of the chart on and off, as follows:

- **Show Links.** Click this command to toggle the link lines between tasks on and off.
- **Show Calendar.** Click this command to hide or redisplay the vertical lines that mark the work weeks on the calendar.
- **Bar Styles.** Point to this command to see a submenu (Figure 12.8) in which you can click various bar styles to hide and redisplay them. For example, clicking **Milestones** hides the diamond markers (bars) for milestone tasks.
- **Annotation Styles.** Point to this command and then click either **Normal Tasks** or **Milestones** to hide or redisplay the label text that appears beside the specified type of bar.

Creating a Custom Field Set

If you often want to display a particular set of fields in a task or resource sheet, you can create a custom field set to present those fields. A custom field set can include any combination of default fields that come in OpenProj and custom fields that you add. While you can add a large number of fields, as a practical matter, you want to limit the fields to the number that can display onscreen at one time, which may only be three or four if you plan to use the field set in combination with a chart in a view.

Follow these steps to create a custom field set for task information:

1. Start in the default Entry field set. To hide any unwanted field, right-click the field column header and click **Hide Column**.
2. To insert a field, right-click the column header for the field to the right of where you want the new field to appear, and click **Insert Column.** Choose the field to insert from the **Field** drop-down list of the Insert Column dialog box, and then click **OK**.

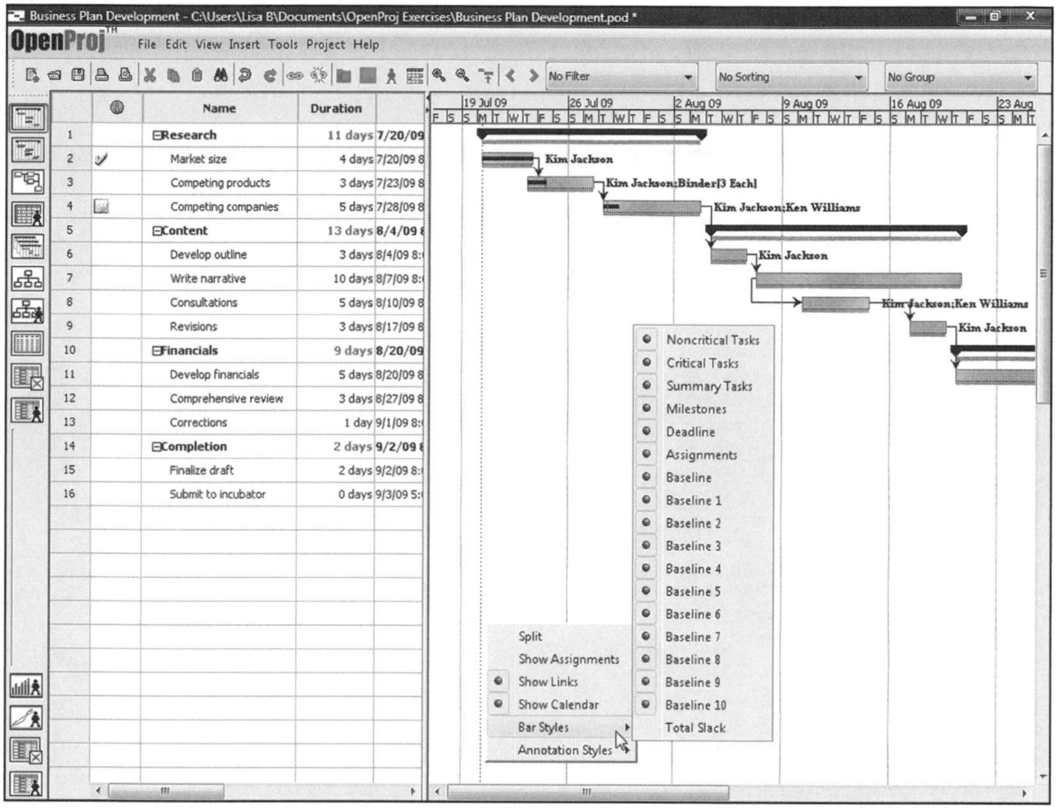

Figure 12.8 The context menu and its submenus enable you to show and hide various graph elements.

3. If you inserted one of the placeholder fields that is there for you to customize, such as Text2, you can change the field name. To rename the placeholder field, right-click the field column header and click **Rename**. Type the new name for the field in the **New Name** text box of the Rename dialog box (Figure 12.9), and click **OK**.

 Fields you add to a default field set may not necessarily redisplay by default when you reopen the file. Saving a custom field set should eliminate this problem. If it doesn't, the renamed custom field should still be in the file; you'll just need to insert it back into the field set.

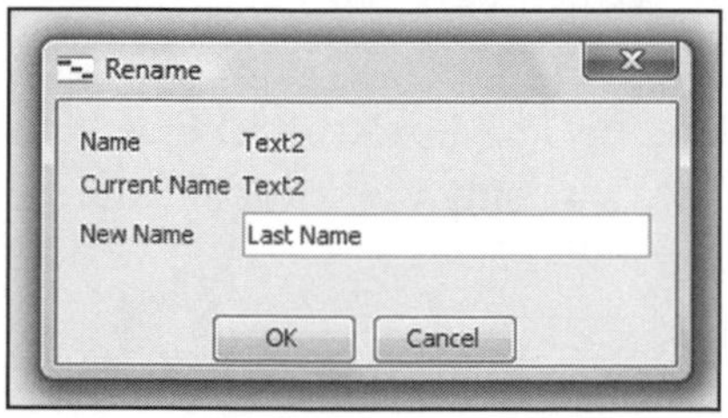

Figure 12.9
You can rename a placeholder field.

4. Drag fields by the column headings to move them into the desired positions, as shown in Figure 12.10. Note that this works best when you have room onscreen to work, rather than having the full screen filled with fields.

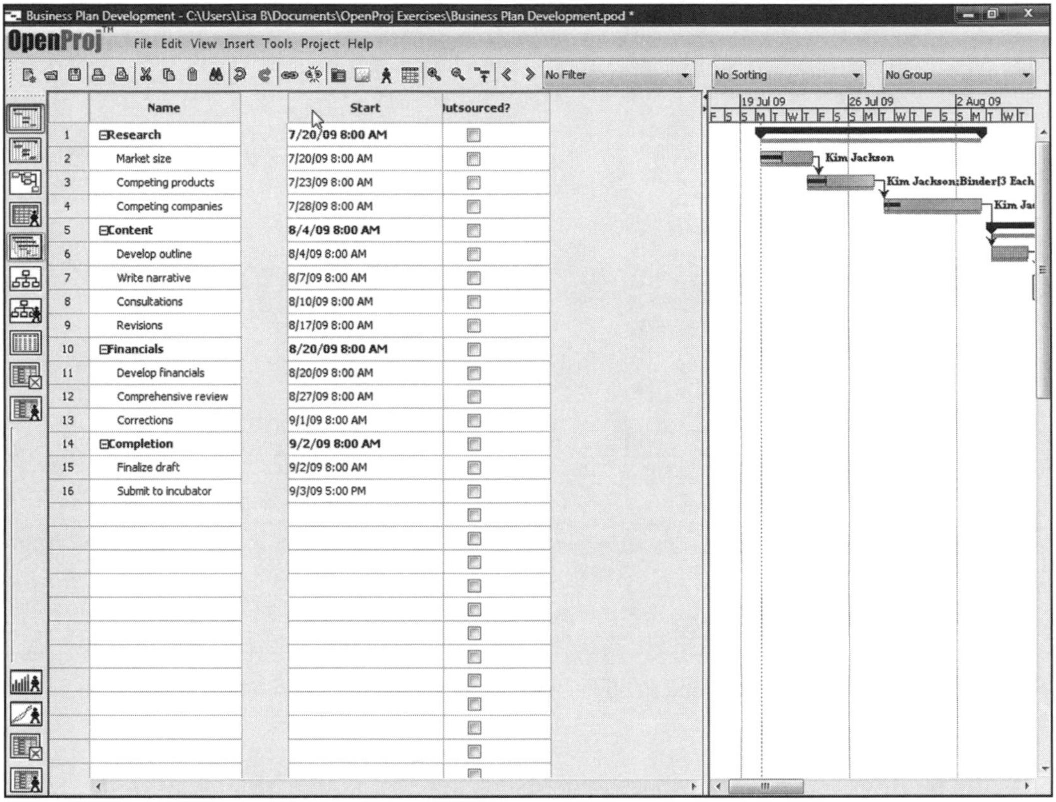

Figure 12.10 Drag a field by its column heading to move it into a new position.

The *Outsourced?* field shown in Figure 12.10 is a Flag placeholder field that's been renamed. Flag fields offer a check box so you can indicate whether a condition is true or not.

5. Right-click the **select all** button, and click the **Entry (Click to rename)** choice as shown in Figure 12.11.

6. Edit the entry in the **New Name** text box of the Rename Task Spreadsheet dialog box, and click **OK**. You then can select your new field set using the select all context menu.

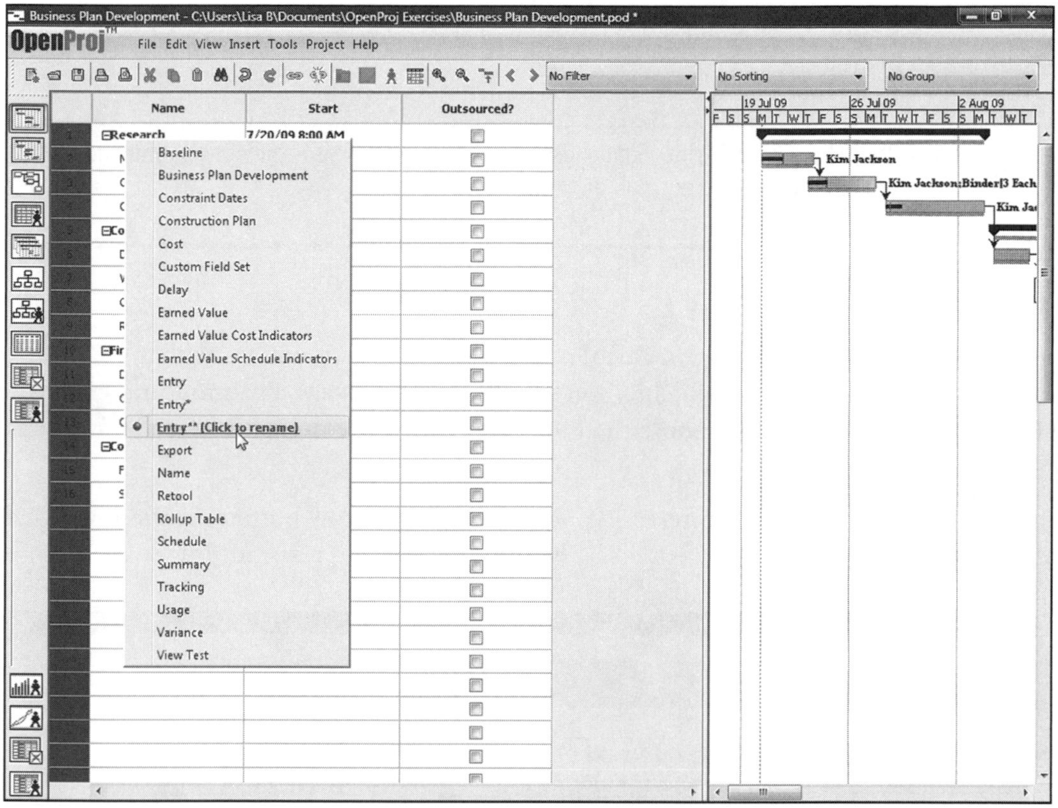

Figure 12.11 After customizing the Entry table, rename it.

As of this writing, sometimes saving a custom field set does not work, even if you're careful to save your changes to the file. And sometimes, if you rename the field set and close and reopen the file, the project file *Title* (in the Project Information dialog box) is assigned to the custom field set. This functionality may be corrected in future OpenProj builds. Also, if you have multiple files open in OpenProj, you will see field sets from both files in the select all context menu. So, when working with fields and field sets, it's a good practice to work with one file at a time and to close and reopen OpenProj between files.

Choosing Print Settings and Printing

The traditional method of sharing information, via a printout, continues to be a common means of informing others about project planning and execution. With OpenProj, you may find yourself printing even more than with other applications because many of the project stakeholders and team members may not have the OpenProj program with which to open OpenProj files. Printing in OpenProj is a little different than printing in some other applications, so this section presents an overview of the process.

Always keep in mind that in OpenProj, the first step to printing is to choose the view that you want to print.

The Print Preview and Print commands on the File menu present the options you need to prepare and make a project plan printout.

Previewing the Printout

Because the nature of the views in OpenProj does lead to some printouts with mostly blank pages and other unexpected glitches, you should always preview a printout in OpenProj. To open the Print Preview, choose the **File, Print Preview** command, or click the **Print Preview** button on the toolbar.

In the Print Preview (see Figure 12.12), you can use the arrow buttons in the upper-left corner to move between various pages. The three magnifying glass buttons enable you to

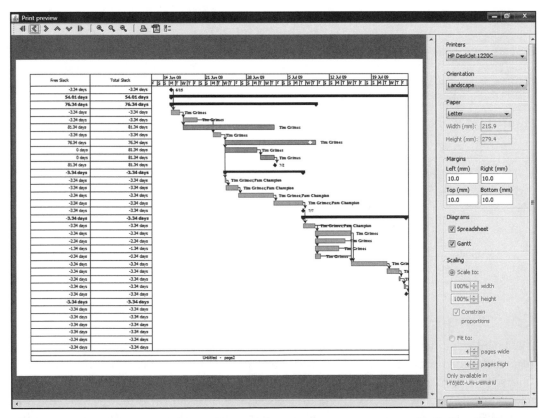

Figure 12.12 Previewing a printout gives you the opportunity to save paper by finding glitches before you print.

zoom the print preview. Clicking the left button zooms in, clicking the center button returns to the default zoom, and clicking the right button zooms out.

The pane at the right shows page setup choices, which you'll learn about next. Otherwise, click the **Print** button to go to the Print dialog box and send a printout to the printer, or click the window **Close (X)** button to close the Print Preview.

Working with Page Setup Choices

Checking the page setup before you print helps you avoid printed boo-boos in any application. The page setup choices appear in a pane at the right side of the Print Preview (see Figure 12.13).

The page setup choices include:

- **Printers.** Choose the printer you want to use for your printout from this drop-down list.
- **Orientation.** Choose whether you want the printout to be in wide (Landscape) or tall (Portrait).
- **Paper.** Choose the paper size to use for your printout from this drop-down list.

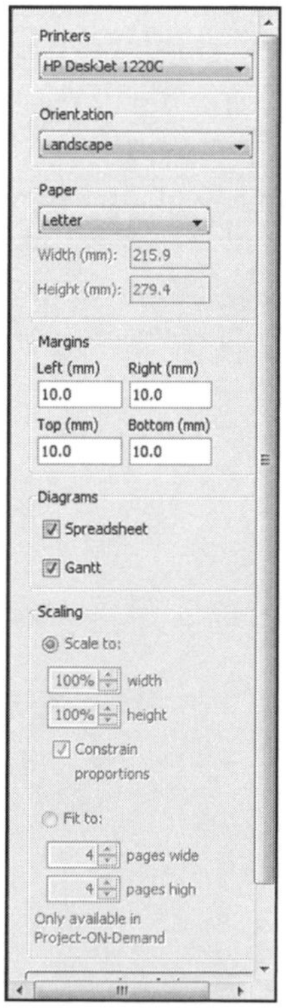

Figure 12.13
Control printout appearance using choices available at the right side of Print Preview.

- **Margins.** Enter the size you want for the margin on each edge of the page in the applicable text boxes. Because OpenProj is used internationally, enter margin sizes in mm (millimeters).

- **Diagrams.** Use these check boxes to specify whether the printout should include the **Spreadsheet** (left side), **Gantt** graph (right side), or both.

 The other settings in the pane are grayed out because they are only part of OpenProj's enterprise big sister, Project-ON-Demand.

- **Make Default.** After you've chosen your other page setup settings, you can scroll down in the pane and click the **Make Default** button to choose those settings as the default for printouts.

Sending the Job to the Printer

Other print settings, such as specifying how many copies to print, are found in the Print dialog box. To open the Print dialog box, click the **Print** button on the toolbar or in Print Preview; or click **File** and then click **Print**; or press **Ctrl+P**.

In the Print dialog box, you can change to another printer using the **Name** drop-down list. Click the **Properties** button if you want to open a dialog box with settings specific to your printer. To print only selected pages in the project plan, use the **Page(s) From** and **To** settings in the Print Range section. You also can specify the **Number of Copies** to print. Click **OK** when you finish making your choices to send the printout to the printer (see Figure 12.14).

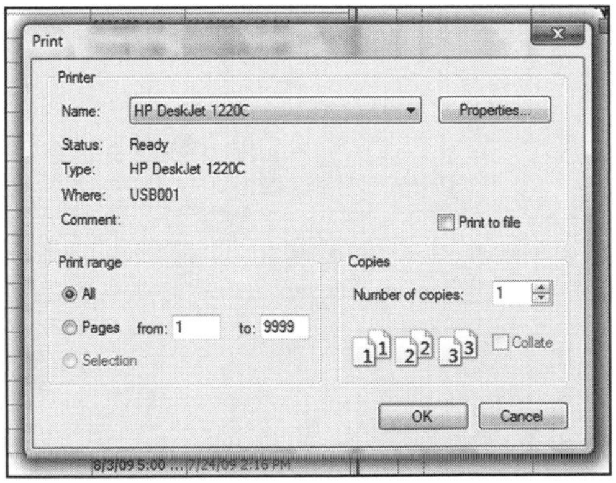

Figure 12.14
Nail down a few last print choices here and then click **Print**.

Chapter Review

This chapter presented information you need to know about using views in OpenProj. The chapter kicked off with a review of the available views. From there, you learned to sort, group, and filter data in a sheet, how to zoom the view, and how to format chart elements. You also learned how to set up custom field sets. Finally, you learned the essential settings for making printed output in OpenProj. In the next chapter, you'll learn about another key way to communicate about project status—reports.

Review Questions

Write your answers to the following questions on a sheet of paper.

1. Open the _____ menu to access all of OpenProj's available views.

2. _____ the view to change how the timescale appears.

3. To change the order of tasks or resources, _____ the sheet.

4. To hide tasks or resources that do not match a specified criterion, _____ the sheet.

5. OpenProj offers a number of _____ fields that you can rename and customize.

6. A custom _____ defines a set of fields to appear in a spreadsheet.

7. True or False: You can drag a field to a new location.

8. Click the _____ command on the File menu to see how a document printout will look.

9. Find the Page Setup choices here.

10. Click the _____ command on the File menu to start the process for creating a hard copy output of the project plan.

Projects

To see the solutions file created by completing the projects in this chapter, go to www.courseptr.com, click the **Downloads** link in the navigation bar at the top, type **Open-Proj** or this book's ISBN-10 number in the search text box, and then click **Search Downloads**.

Project 1

1. Open the file named *Site Search Track* that you worked with in the projects for Chapter 11.

2. Save the file as *Site Search Views*.

 Create a folder named *OpenProj Exercises* in your *Documents* or *My Documents* folder and save your exercise practice files there.

3. Click the **Network** top view button.

4. Scroll through the view to review its appearance.

5. Click **View** and then click **Resources**.

6. Click the **Sort** button, and then click **Group**.

7. Scroll to the right to see the impact of the sort.

8. To return the list of resources to its original order, click the **Sort** button, and click **No Sorting**.

9. Click the **Histogram** bottom view button.

10. Click the **Gantt** top view button.

11. Click the **Histogram** bottom view button again.

12. Choose **View, Zoom In**.

13. Choose **View, Zoom Out**. Leave the file open for the next project.

Project 2

1. Right-click the **select all** button and click **Entry** to redisplay the default entry table if needed.

2. Delete each of the following columns by right-clicking the column heading and clicking **Hide Column**:

   Start
   Finish
   Predecessors
   Resource Names

3. Right-click the *Duration* column heading and click **Insert Column**.

4. Open the **Field** drop-down list in the Insert Column dialog box, click **Actual Work**, and click **OK**.

5. Drag the *Actual Work* field to the right of the *Duration* field. (Drag by the column heading.)

 Remember that custom field sets may not save correctly in current OpenProj versions, so if you close and reopen the file for this project, you may not see the field set changes you made above.

6. Save your changes to the file and keep it open for the next project.

Project 3

1. Click **File** and then click **Print Preview**.
2. Select the desired printer from the **Printers** drop-down list in the page setup dialog box at the right.
3. Choose **Portrait** from the Orientation drop-down list.
4. Use the arrow buttons to scroll through the various pages in the preview.
5. Click the **Print** button.
6. Enter **2** in the **Number of Copies** text box, and then click **OK** to print the custom view of your project.
7. Click the Print Preview window **Close (X)** button to close Print Preview.
8. Save your changes to the file and close the file.

CHAPTER 13

REPORTING PROJECT INFORMATION

This Chapter Teaches You How To:

- Know what reports you can use
- Open and print a report
- Change report settings
- Export data to another format

Team members and stakeholders have different information needs, as do you, the project manager. For this reason, OpenProj enables you to provide information in a number of different ways. In addition to printing views, which you learned about in the last chapter, you also can print and distribute different types of reports. This chapter introduces you to OpenProj reporting. You'll learn how to select and display a report, print a report, change report settings, and take a crack at exporting project information so that it can be used in another program.

Reviewing Available Reports

Reports present different types of information, generally organized in a list or tabular format. Reports provide a fast, attractive, and sometimes easier to understand alternative to a printed view. For example, Figure 13.1 shows the Resource Information report, which presents fields with resource information.

OpenProj offers four reports, listed in Table 13.1.

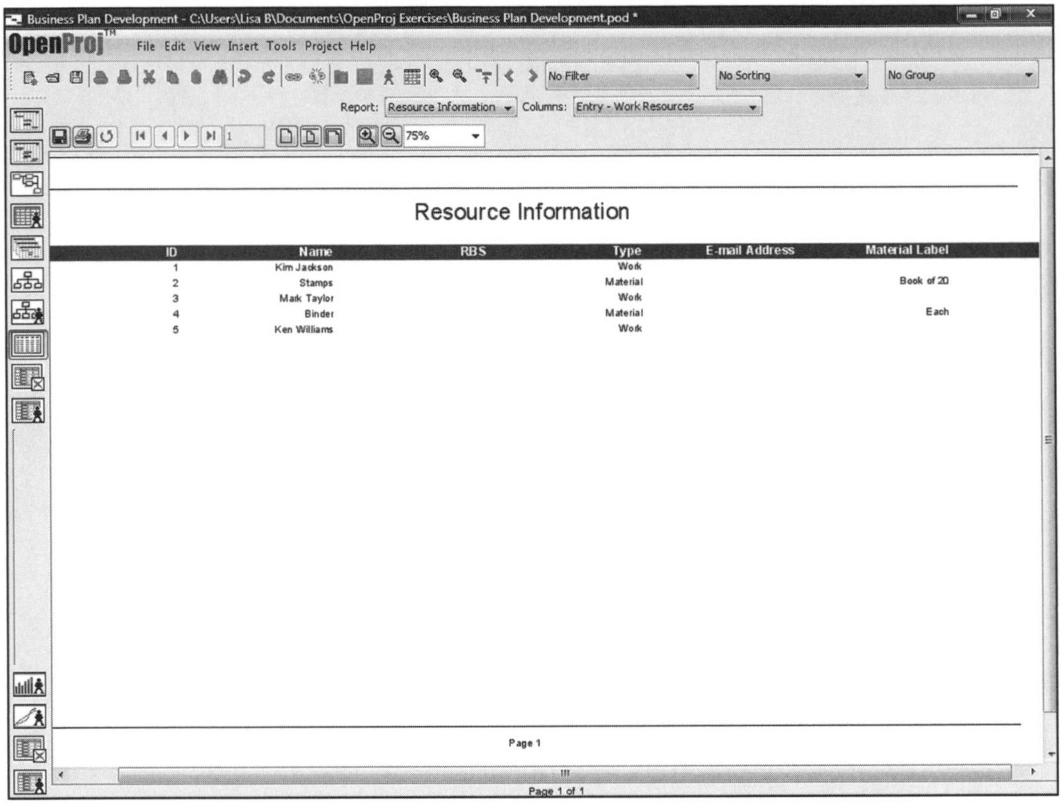

Figure 13.1 Reports provide an attractive alternative to view printouts.

Table 13.1 Standard Reports in OpenProj

Name	Description
Project Details	Presents the same information shown in the Statistics tab of the Project Information dialog box, as well as additional information about task and resource status
Resource Information	Provides fields of resource information, offering the choice of five field sets by default: Earned Value, Earned Value Cost Indicators, Earned Value Schedule Indicators, Entry – Work Resources, and Name
Task Information	Provides fields of task information, offering the choice of 16 field sets by default; if a custom field set has been added, it also will be available for use in the report
Who Does What	Provides a list of assignments by resource

The names and descriptions in Table 13.1 should give you a decent idea of when to use a particular report. For example, if a project is running behind, you might print the Task Information Report with the Variance field set to focus your attention there. Or, if you're looking for which resources may need some assistance to stay on track, the Who Does What report could be useful.

What the Heck Is Earned Value?

Earned value is a technical form of analysis used to determine how the project's progress and costs compare with the baseline. You don't have to worry about making any of the calculations—OpenProj makes them for you. But behind the scenes OpenProj calculates values like the BCWP (budgeted cost of work performed), ACWP (actual cost of work performed), and BCWS (budgeted cost of work scheduled). OpenProj also calls the *BCWP* field the *Earned Value* field in the Earned Value report.

OpenProj uses these values and others to calculate indexes and variances of schedule and cost performance. The Earned Value report includes the *SV* (earned value schedule variance) and *CV* (earned value cost variance) fields, which give an indication of progress and cost versus the plan. For the *SV* and *CV* fields, positive (greater than 0) values mean the project is ahead of schedule or under budget and negative (less than 0) values mean the project is behind schedule or over budget.

Viewing and Printing a Report

The regular reports in OpenProj appear as a print preview. You display the desired report onscreen, change any page setup and print settings as needed, and send the report to the printer. You can't change the fields it contains and you can't save the data it displays on a particular date.

The report print preview does offer a Save button that gives the option of choosing a file format into which to save information from a report. As of this writing, that feature doesn't appear to be fully implemented in OpenProj, but given the Files of Type choices in the Save dialog box, the developers appear to have a plan to include the ability to save in PDF, RTF, Excel, XML, and other formats. As of this writing, not all the save formats are working correctly.

Once you've displayed a report, the process for selecting page setup and print settings works similar to the process described for views in Chapter 12, so I won't rehash those details here, and you can refer to the previous chapter, if needed. Follow these steps when you're ready to get that report on paper:

1. Click the **View** menu and then click **Reports**, or click the **Reports** button in the top view buttons at the left. The report print preview appears.

A *report* presents selected project data in a nice format for printing. Choose **View, Reports** to display the report print preview. Select a report type from the Report drop-down list, and then choose a Columns setting if needed.

2. If you want to view a report other than the Project Details report, click the **Report** drop-down list button, and then the report you want to display (Figure 13.2).

3. If the Columns drop-down list appears, click it and then click the desired field set as shown in Figure 13.3.

The report appears onscreen as a print preview, like the example shown in Figure 13.4.

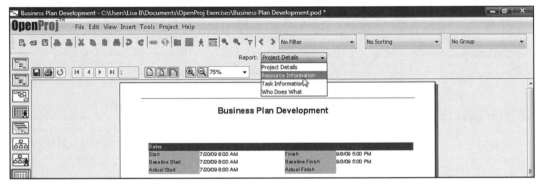

Figure 13.2 Choose a report from the drop-down list.

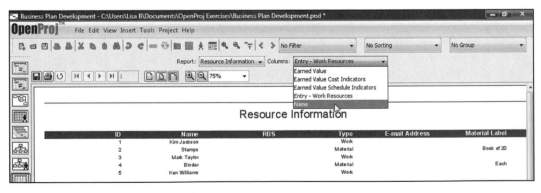

Figure 13.3 Specify the field set for the report.

Navigation
buttons

Magnifying glass
buttons

Printout
dimensions

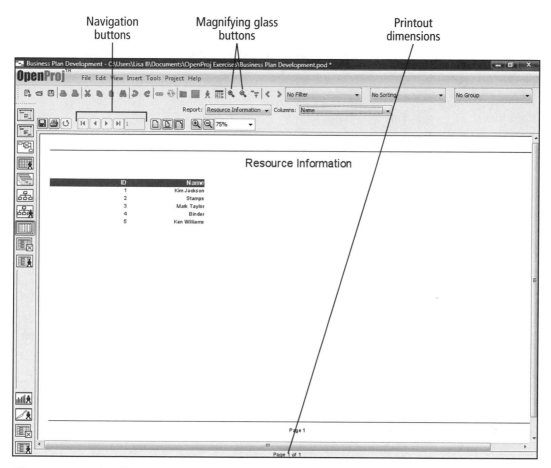

Figure 13.4 Like all reports, this Resource Information report appears as a print preview.

4. If the report includes multiple pages, you can use the navigation buttons to move through the pages in the report to review it for potential changes.

5. You can use the magnifying glass buttons or the page size buttons to the left of them to change the zoom for the report so you can check the report information.

6. When the report is ready to print, click the **Print** button. Make any desired changes in the Print dialog box (Figure 13.5), such as specifying the number of copies to print, and then click **OK**.

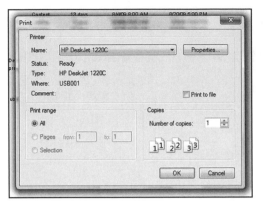

Figure 13.5
Choose print settings here, just as when printing a view.

Exporting to Project 2003 XML Format

Exporting converts information from an OpenProj file and saves it in an XML format usable by other programs that can work with XML data (including Microsoft Project 2003).

Project 2007 can import Project 2003 files seamlessly, so if you need to use your OpenProj data in Project 2007, export it in the Project 2003 format, as no Project 2007 export option is available.

Exporting data from a project plan file works much like saving a file. The overall steps are the same no matter what type of file you want to export your data to:

1. Make any needed changes and save the project plan file you want to export.
2. Click **File** and then click **Save As**. The Save dialog box appears.
3. Click the **Files of Type** drop-down list and then click **Microsoft Project 2003 XML (*.xml)**.
4. Edit the **File Name** and save location, if desired. (It's a good idea to remove the .pod file name extension that remains by default in the File Name text box.)
5. Click **Save**. OpenProj saves the file.

If you double-click the XML file in a folder window in the Windows operating system, the file automatically opens in Notepad. You also can open XML files in Microsoft Excel and some other applications.

Chapter Review

In this chapter, you took on reporting in OpenProj, a vital area to understand when you need to review project information for execution and control purposes, as well as when you need to communicate with team members and stakeholders. You learned what reports OpenProj offers, how to display and print a report, and how to export the project file information as an XML file. This finishes your expedition through OpenProj.

Review Questions

Write your answers to the following questions on a sheet of paper.

1. OpenProj includes this number of built-in regular reports.
2. Use the _____ menu to access reports.
3. True or False: A report you create appears in its own separate window.
4. Use the _____ button to choose the report type.
5. True or False: You can change the fields contained in some reports.
6. Some of the buttons for zooming a report look like this.
7. True or False: Exporting report data requires that you complete a wizard.

Projects

 To see the solutions file created by completing the project in this chapter, go to www.courseptr.com, click the **Downloads** link in the navigation bar at the top, type **Open-Proj** or this book's ISBN-10 number in the search text box, and then click **Search Downloads**.

Project 1

1. Open the file named *Site Search Views* that you worked with in the Projects for Chapter 12.
2. Save the file as *Site Search Reports*.

 Create a folder named *OpenProj Exercises* in your *Documents* or *My Documents* folder and save your exercise practice files there.

3. Make sure your printer is turned on.
4. Click **View** and then click **Reports**.

5. Use the method of your choice to zoom in on the Project Details report that appears, and then zoom back out.

6. Use the **Print** button to print one copy of the report.

7. Click the **Report** drop-down list button, and then click **Who Does What**.

8. Click the right navigation arrow button (**right arrow**) twice to view the two other pages of the report.

9. Click the left navigation arrow button (**left arrow**) twice to return to the first page of the report.

10. Click the **Columns** drop-down button, and then click **Tasks Assigned**.

11. Use the **Print** button to print one copy of the report.

12. Click **File** and then click **Save As**.

13. Open the **Files of Type** drop-down list in the Save dialog box, and click **Microsoft Project 2003 XML (*.xml)**. Delete the **.pod** from the file name in the **File Name** text box, and then click **Save**.

14. Save and close the file, and close OpenProj.

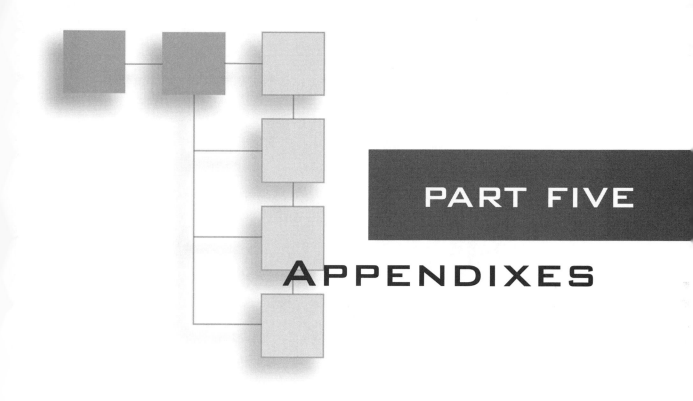

PART FIVE

APPENDIXES

APPENDIX A

OPENPROJ INSTALLATION NOTES

OpenProj is an open source application, and like most open source applications, you can't walk into the local computer store and buy it. If your company uses the StarOffice suite, in certain locations (such as Europe), OpenProj will be included with StarOffice and may already be installed on your desktop. Other distribution deals may be in the works right now. However, most of us will have to seek out OpenProj if we want it.

Getting OpenProj

The latest version of OpenProj is available as a free download for Windows, Linux, and Mac on the Projity website. Go to www.projity.com, navigate to the download area, and download the installer file(s) for your operating system. It's a relatively small download (about 6.5M for the Windows installer), so you can manage it even with a slow dialup Internet connection. You can then run the installer to install OpenProj. For Windows and Mac operating systems, this generally involves double-clicking the installer file. In Linux, you will have to open a terminal and run the installer file.

OpenProj requires the Java Runtime Environment 1.5 or later. If you haven't updated your Java installation recently, you may want to go to www.java.com to download and install the latest version prior to installing OpenProj. Java 1.5 is preinstalled on systems with Mac OS X 10.4. On a Linux system, it depends on the distribution. Some distributions don't install Java by default but include it as an add-on.

Starting Up the First Time

The process for starting up OpenProj will vary depending on the operating system you're using. For example, the Windows installer by default places a startup icon on the desktop that you can use to start the program.

One thing that's the same on all versions is that on the first startup, you will need to accept the Projity OpenProj License. Click the **I Accept** button. In the Projity OpenProj Customer Information dialog box that appears, enter your e-mail address in the **E-mail address** text box, and click **OK**.

OpenProj also displays a quaint Tip of the Day dialog box on startup. You can use the **Back** and **Next** buttons to view tips, and click **Close** to close the dialog box when you finish. If you prefer not to see further tips, click the **Show tips on startup** check box to clear the check before clicking **Close**. To turn tips back on, choose **Help, Tip of the Day** and recheck the check box.

APPENDIX B

CHAPTER REVIEW
SOLUTIONS

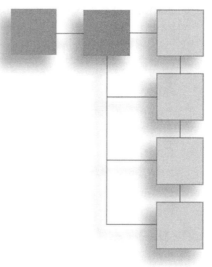

Chapter 1: The Project Management Process and OpenProj

Review Questions

1. **What's the difference between a To Do list and a project plan?**

   A To Do list provides a list of activities that may not be related to a single purpose or outcome. The items on the To Do list might not have specific starting or ending dates. A project plan lists related activities that, when completed, will yield specified goals and deliverables. The project plan and the activities within it all have specific starting and ending dates/times.

2. **What are the overall steps in managing a project?**

   Initiating, Planning, Executing, Controlling, Closing

3. **What is a task?**

   A task is an activity with a specific starting point and ending point.

4. **What is a resource?**

   A resource is a person, piece of equipment, or quantity of consumable material used to complete one or more tasks.

5. **What is an assignment?**

   An assignment occurs when you apply a resource to a task, indicating that the resource is responsible for or will be used in completing the task.

6. **Name one phase or part of the project management process that OpenProj can help with.**

(Any of the following four answers are acceptable.)

Planning. OpenProj helps a project manager build a more detailed and accurate project plan.

Executing. OpenProj provides tools for tracking work and communicating progress.

Controlling. Track and reschedule work as needed with tools in OpenProj. Review views and reports to help identify when corrective actions may be needed.

Closing. Refer to previous project plans to review lessons learned.

Chapter 2: Learning OpenProj Basics

Review Questions

1. **Name one way each to start and exit OpenProj in Windows.**

For starting OpenProj, any of the following are acceptable:

- Click **Start**, click **All Programs**, click **OpenProj**, and then click **OpenProj**.
- Click **Start** and then click **OpenProj** if it appears on the left side of the Start menu.
- Click **Start**, type **OpenProj**, and then click **OpenProj**.

For exiting OpenProj, any of the following are acceptable:

- Click **File** and then click **Exit**.
- Click the OpenProj window **Close** (X) button.
- Press **Alt+F4**.

2. **The _____ appears below the menu bar and offers buttons you can click to perform actions in OpenProj rather than having to choose menu commands.**

Toolbar

3. **To find the name of a tool, do this:**

Move the mouse over the button (tool) until the tool name appears.

4. **The _____ appears at the top of each column in a spreadsheet view.**

Field Name, Column Name, or Title. Partial credit can be given for Column Heading.

5. When you add a task, its _____ appears in the row header cell to the left of the task name.

   Task ID Number or ID Number

6. The default view in OpenProj is called the _____ view.

   Gantt

7. Access one of the ten top views on the _____ menu.

   View

8. When you click a task name, click the _____ button on the toolbar to scroll its Gantt bar into view on the graph at the right.

   Scroll To Task

9. What is a field set in OpenProj?

   The specific collection of fields that appears in a spreadsheet view.

10. Because OpenProj is open source, its online help was created as a collaborative _____.

   Wiki

Chapter 3: Jump Start: Create and Manage a Project

Review Questions

1. True or False: The calendars that come with OpenProj have holidays marked.

   False

2. The information you specify to define overall project parameters include the _____ and the _____.

   project start date

   project calendar or base calendar

3. To define each task, enter its _____ and _____.

   Task Name

   Duration

4. To enable OpenProj to calculate task schedules, _____ the tasks.

   link

5. Change to the _____ view to enter resources.

   Resource Sheet

6. What is a material resource?

   A resource that is consumed in quantity when completing a task.

7. **What is effort-driven scheduling?**

The task scheduling method that OpenProj uses by default, where OpenProj will recalculate the task duration, making it shorter, if you add more resources to a task to which you've already assigned one or more resources.

8. **Use the _____ dialog box to add resources to tasks.**

Assign Resources

9. **Save the _____ so that you can track work against the original schedule.**

baseline

10. **For each task, the Tracking Gantt view shows:**

d. Both a and b

Chapter 4: Creating a Project Plan File and Calendar

Review Questions

1. **Why do you store each project plan in a separate file?**

Every project has a specific starting and ending point, with specific tasks, goals, and deliverables. Storing each project in a separate file ensures that you can review the data about a single project without having to consider information from other projects.

2. **Do I have to start every new project from scratch?**

No, you can use an existing file that supplies basic information, such as the custom calendar, list of tasks and estimated durations, and list of resources.

3. **My employer doesn't follow an 8 a.m. to 5 p.m. schedule. How do I match my project schedule to the real work schedule?**

You can create and apply a custom calendar using the **Tools, Change Working Time** command. Also be sure to adjust the settings in the Duration Settings dialog box to match your calendar by clicking the **Options** button in the Change Working Time dialog box.

4. **Why do I enter a project start date?**

Because the assumption is that you are planning your projects in advance of the actual work. Use the Project Information dialog box (**Project, Project Information**) to set the project's start date and calendar.

5. True or False: Duration Settings options must match the custom calendar applied.

True. If you don't change the Duration Settings options to match the calendar, OpenProj might not schedule the correct hours of work per day.

Chapter 5: Adding and Organizing Tasks

Review Questions

1. Where do you enter the list of tasks?

In the task spreadsheet, usually in the default Gantt view.

2. What two pieces of information should you enter to create each new task?

The *Name* and *Duration* field entries.

3. Why should you not type dates for a task?

Because OpenProj will add constraints that may prevent it from rescheduling the task when needed.

4. What's the duration you enter to have OpenProj mark a task as a milestone, and when would you use a milestone?

0 (zero). Use a milestone task to mark an event that doesn't have associated work.

5. What is the task ID number for the task named *Competing products* in Figure 5.7?

3

6. Click the _____ to select the entire task.

Task ID number or task row number

7. In an outline, _____ tasks summarize the data for the _____ under them.

Summary, Tasks, or Subtasks

8. Use the _____ button on the toolbar to demote tasks to the next lower outline level.

Indent (right arrow)

9. _____ subtasks hides their task names and Gantt bars.

Collapsing

10. What tab in the Task Information dialog box shows the WBS code?

Advanced

Chapter 6: Scheduling the Project by Linking Tasks

Review Questions

1. **Why do you skip typing in Start and Finish dates for tasks?**

   Because you want OpenProj to retain the ability to reschedule tasks as needed.

2. **How do you instead build the task schedules?**

   After entering task durations, link the tasks. OpenProj uses the durations you enter and the dependencies (links) between tasks to calculate start and finish dates for tasks.

3. **The _____ task drives the schedule of its _____ task.**

   predecessor

   successor

4. **Name the default task type and its abbreviation.**

   finish-to-start, FS

5. **How do you link two tasks using the toolbar?**

   Select the tasks by dragging over the task ID numbers or Ctrl+clicking on them, and then click the **Link** button.

6. **How do you display the Task Information dialog box?**

   Double-click a cell in the task's row on the task spreadsheet.

7. **What tab in the Task Information dialog box do you use to change the link type?**

   Predecessors

8. **How do you open the Task Dependency dialog box?**

   Click the link line between tasks.

9. **Enter lead time as a _____ value and lag time as a _____ value.**

   negative

   positive

10. **Enter lead or lag time in the _____ text box in the Task Dependency dialog box.**

    Lag

Chapter 7: Listing the Resources You Need

Review Questions

1. **What menu and command do you choose to change to Resources view?**

   View, Resources

2. **Name the two main types of resources.**

   Work and Material

3. **A _____ resource represents a consumed quantity.**

   Material

4. **Make an entry in the _____ field of Resources view if the resource charges a fee every time you use or assign it.**

   Cost Per Use

5. **The entry in the _____ field of Resources view indicates whether the resource will be working full time or part time on the project, or whether multiple persons will be used for each assignment.**

   Max. Units

6. **How do you replace a resource throughout the project plan?**

   Click in the *Name* field for the resource to replace in Resources view, type a new resource name, and press Enter.

7. **How do you display the Resource Information dialog box?**

   Double-click a resource in Resources view

8. **What tab in the Resource Information dialog box do you use to specify a rate increase or set up cost tables?**

   Costs tab

9. **True or False: OpenProj always follows the project's base calendar, no matter when a resource actually works.**

   False. If you make changes to a resource's calendar, then the resource's calendar will override the project base calendar if needed any time you assign the resource to a task.

10. **When a resource can only work on your project during a fixed time period, specify that resource's _____ in the Resource Information dialog box.**

    Availability

Chapter 8: Assigning Resources to Tasks

Review Questions

1. **What button on the toolbar do you use to open the Assign Resources dialog box?**

   The Assign Resources button

2. **Briefly describe how to make an assignment for a work resource once the Assign Resource dialog box is open.**

   Click the task in the task spreadsheet portion of the Gantt view, click the resource in the Assign Resources dialog box, and then click **Assign**.

3. **Briefly describe how to make an assignment for a material resource once the Assign Resource dialog box is open.**

   Click the task in the task spreadsheet portion of the Gantt view, click the resource in the Assign Resources dialog box, enter the quantity of the resource to consume in the Units column, and then click **Assign**.

4. **To take off a resource assigned to a selected task, use the _____ button in the Assign Resources dialog box.**

   Remove

5. **To replace a resource throughout the entire project, type a new Resource Name in the _____ view.**

   Resources

6. **True or False: An assignment with a 50% units setting is a full-time assignment.**

   False. That is a part-time assignment.

7. **If a resource such as an outside vendor or another department will be supplying two people full time for an assignment, what should the units setting for that assignment be?**

   200%

8. **The _____ and _____ views list project assignments.**

   Resource Usage and Task Usage

9. **If a resource charges different rates and you need to specify which rate to use, choose another _____ in the Assignment Information dialog box.**

   Cost Rate Table

10. **The default task type is _____ with _____ turned on.**

    Fixed Units, effort-driven schedule

Chapter 9: Enhancing Task and Resource Information

Review Questions

1. Type in extra information on the _____ tab of the Task Information or Resource Information dialog box.

    Notes

2. True or False: Notes print by default.

    False. Notes do not print by default.

3. Do this to see what an indicator means.

    Move the mouse pointer over an indicator and a pop-up box or tip appears to tell you what the indicator is alerting you about. Or, for a note indicator, the pop-up shows you the note's contents.

4. When a task follows a different schedule than the overall project, assign a _____ to the task.

    Calendar. You can apply another task calendar on the Advanced tab of the Task Information dialog box. The task's assigned calendar will then override the project base calendar.

5. A(n) _____ reduces OpenProj's flexibility in rescheduling a task.

    Acceptable answers include:

    - constraint assigned to a task
    - assigned task calendar
    - assigned resource's calendar.

6. If you add a _____ to a task, a yellow diamond on the task's Gantt bar appears and an indicator appears when the task runs late.

    deadline

7. Do this to display another field set.

    Right-click the **select all** button (gray box where row and column headers intersect), and click the desired field set in the context menu.

8. Unlike other costs associated with resources, you enter a _____ for a task.

    Fixed cost. OpenProj then adds the fixed cost to any resource-related costs to arrive at the total cost for the task.

9. **Do this to a column header to begin the process for hiding or inserting a field.**

   Right-click it and then click **Hide Column** or **Insert Column**.

10. **True or False: OpenProj offers placeholder fields that you can use for custom information.**

    True. OpenProj offers a variety of cost, text, number, and other fields that are available to hold your custom data.

Chapter 10: Reviewing and Adjusting the Plan

Review Questions

1. **True or False: You can use various views and features in OpenProj to perform a review of your project plan.**

   True: You should perform a thorough check of your plan to identify schedule problems and resource overallocations, and to ensure that the plan is thorough and realistic, before implementing it.

2. **Access project statistics via the _____ dialog box.**

   Project Information

3. **A task is _____ when delaying it will delay the finish of the project as a whole.**

   Critical

4. **Taking steps to make the _____ shorter will have the greatest positive impact on the project schedule.**

   Critical Path

5. **A critical task has _____ or _____ slack.**

   zero or negative

6. **Display the _____ field set to view the amount of slack for a task.**

   Schedule

7. **A resource with too much work assigned is _____.**

   Overallocated or overbooked

8. **Name at least one view in which you can see more detail about resource overallocations.**

   Resource Usage or Histogram

9. **Name at least one way to fix a resource overallocation.**

   Acceptable answers include:

   - Remove the resource from the task and assign another resource
   - Make manual changes to the resource's assignments in Resource Usage or Task Usage view
   - Split the task

10. **A _____ inserts a non working period within a task.**

    Split

Chapter 11: Setting the Baseline and Tracking Work

Review Questions

1. **Saving the _____ saves initial information about the project plan for later comparison.**

   Baseline

2. **True or False: You can save more than one baseline.**

   True. You can save the initial baseline, plus 10 more. You also can save up to 10 interim plans.

3. **The _____ field set includes a field for marking work as complete on tasks.**

   Tracking

4. **Use the _____ dialog box to enter Actual Start and Finish dates for tasks.**

   Update Task

5. **True or False: OpenProj only reschedules the entire task when you use the Reschedule Work button.**

   False: If the task has some percentage of work marked as complete, that actual work will not be rescheduled. OpenProj will only reschedule the uncompleted portion of the task.

6. **The _____ tab of the Project Information dialog box shows baseline and actual data after you save starting information and begin tracking work.**

   Statistics

7. Display different _____ in the left portion of the Gantt view to see various fields with calculated tracking information.

    field sets

8. The _____ view displays two Gantt bars for each task: one for the original schedule and another for the current or actual schedule.

    Tracking Gantt

9. Name at least one way to reduce project costs.

    Acceptable answers include:

    ▪ Identify the most expensive tasks and see if you can reduce the work (and therefore costs).

    ▪ Substitute less expensive resources.

    ▪ Ask the outside vendor to substitute a resource with a lower rate.

    ▪ Cut deliverables and tasks.

10. Use the _____ field set to view and work with costs.

    Entry

Chapter 12: Using and Printing Views

Review Questions

1. Open the _____ menu to access all of OpenProj's available views.

    Views

2. _____ the view to change how the time axis appears.

    Zoom

3. To change the order of tasks or resources, _____ the sheet.

    Sort

4. To hide non-matching tasks or resources, _____ the sheet.

    Filter

5. OpenProj offers a number of _____ fields that you can rename and customize.

    Placeholder or numbered

6. A custom _____ defines a set of fields to appear in a sheet.

    field set

7. **True or False: You can drag a field to a new location.**

   True. You can drag a field by its column header to the left or right to reposition it in the field set.

8. **Click the _____ command on the File menu to see how a document printout will look.**

   Print Preview

9. **Find the Page Setup choices here.**

   Print Preview

10. **Click the _____ command on the File menu to start the process for creating a hard copy output of the project plan.**

    Print

Chapter 13: Reporting Project Information

Review Questions

1. **OpenProj includes this number of built-in regular reports.**

   4

2. **Use the _____ menu to access reports.**

   View

3. **True or False: A report you create appears in its own separate window.**

   False. A report you create appears as a print preview rather than its own window.

4. **Use the _____ button to choose the report type.**

   Report

5. **True or False: You can change the fields contained in some reports.**

   True. You can use the columns drop-down list to change the field set for the Resource Information, Task Information, and Who Does What reports.

6. **Some of the buttons for zooming a report look like this.**

   A magnifying glass.

7. **True or False: Exporting report data requires that you complete a wizard.**

   False. Exporting saves information directly to an XML file.

INDEX